THE
ENTHUSIAST

"In *The Enthusiast*, Jon Sweeney takes the world's most popular lawn ornament and makes him a real, live human being with a complicated friend who almost destroyed St. Francis's entire life's work. Sweeney shows us that even saints (and their well-meaning friends) are never that simple, and he's refreshingly comfortable with the contradictions and tension at the heart of history, friendship, and humanity."

Jessica Mesman Griffith
Coauthor of *Love and Salt*

"In *The Enthusiast*, Jon Sweeney uses his sharp historical insight to shed light on the widely known but little understood friendship of St. Francis and Elias of Cortona. This book is an immense and important contribution to our understanding of the great saint."

Richard Rohr, O.F.M.
Center for Action and Contemplation
Albuquerque, New Mexico

"Among the hundreds of biographies of St. Francis of Assisi, *The Enthusiast* stands out as a truly great read. By telling the story of Elias of Cortona—who, in his zeal to honor his friend, nearly destroyed the Franciscan legacy—Sweeney shows his gift for meticulous historical research and an eye for satisfying human drama."

Paula Huston
National Endowment of the Arts fellow and author of *Simplifying the Soul*

"Drawing on historical accounts, early Franciscan narratives, and his own imagination, Jon Sweeney creatively tells the story of Francis of Assisi anew, introducing along the way a key figure in the medieval drama too often overlooked: Brother Elias. Remembered as part-villain and part-hero, Elias's role in Franciscan history needs to be brought to light, and Sweeney does his part to introduce the early friar to a new generation."

Rev. Daniel P. Horan, O.F.M.
Author of *The Franciscan Heart of Thomas Merton*

"Jon Sweeney takes away the calcified, garden-statue image of St. Francis and returns to us something much more valuable. In *The Enthusiast*, we meet the human saint surrounded by the men and women who accompanied him in life and death. We meet a Francis who is flawed, strange, and disruptive but unmistakably holy."

Kaya Oakes
Author of *Radical Reinvention*

THE UNTOLD STORY OF ELIAS OF CORTONA

THE
ENTHUSIAST

How the Best Friend of Francis of Assisi
Almost Destroyed What He Started

JON M. SWEENEY

AVE MARIA PRESS AVE Notre Dame, Indiana

© 2016 by Jon M. Sweeney

All rights reserved. No part of this book may be used or reproduced in any manner whatsoever, except in the case of reprints in the context of reviews, without written permission from Ave Maria Press®, Inc., P.O. Box 428, Notre Dame, IN 46556, 1-800-282-1865.

Founded in 1865, Ave Maria Press is a ministry of the United States Province of Holy Cross.

www.avemariapress.com

Paperback: ISBN-13 978-1-59471-601-0

E-book: ISBN-13 978-1-59471-602-7

Cover image © Peter Baritt/Peter Baritt

Cover and text design by Brian C. Conley.

Printed and bound in the United States of America.

Library of Congress Cataloging-in-Publication Data
Names: Sweeney, Jon M., 1967- author.
Title: The enthusiast : how the best friend of Francis of Assisi almost destroyed what he started : the untold story of Elias of Cortona / Jon M. Sweeney.
Description: Notre Dame, Indiana : Ave Maria Press, 2016. | Includes bibliographical references and index.
Identifiers: LCCN 2015040662| ISBN 9781594716010 | ISBN 1594716013
Subjects: LCSH: Elia, da Cortona, frate, -1253. | Francis, of Assisi, Saint, 1182-1226--Friends and associates.
Classification: LCC BX4705.E4 S94 2016 | DDC 271/.302--dc23
LC record available at http://lccn.loc.gov/2015040662

To the memory of Paul Sabatier

It is spiritual work to seek behind the legend for the history.

—**Paul Sabatier**
Vie de S. François d'Assise

CONTENTS

PROLOGUE

We already know Francis of Assisi. Don't we?

During the hippie era, we got a definite view of St. Francis fed to us by pop culture. Franco Zeffirelli's 1972 film *Brother Sun, Sister Moon*; Nikos Kazantzakis's novel *Saint Francis* (1962); and the *Brother of the Universe* comic (1980) drew us a picture of a romantic, serenading, saccharine sort of pacifist. This image filtered into television documentaries, off-Broadway plays, and hundreds of other books and influenced how we view the world's most popular saint.

But while that portrait of Francis made sense in the milieu of the 1970s and '80s, I believe it isn't very helpful for the current generation. It's for this group of people, who no longer embrace the hippie ideal, that I wrote *The Enthusiast*—a biography of Francis for the twenty-first century. Yet, even for those who already know him, it tells a story that has been hidden until now.

There is no late-chapter surprise: Elias of Cortona is "The Enthusiast." One of Francis's closest friends in their spiritual brotherhood—a friend since childhood—Elias is one of the first to join Francis, to believe in him and his religious vision, to embrace the Gospel-loving, poverty witness that Francis is living. Many think Francis is crazy, but from the early days, Elias is his friend, follower, and confidant.

The two men grow up together in the final decade of twelfth-century Assisi. Before thousands of others are attracted to Francis like pigs to slop, they lead a spiritual movement to rebuild churches, care for the sick, free the complacent, and dance and sing as "God's troubadours" to the delight of people who have grown tired of a sometimes tumultuous, often irrelevant Church. The movement grows quickly. But at the height of the spiritual renaissance they've sparked—Francis as its saint, Elias, its ecclesiastical head—something goes terribly wrong. Elias becomes "the devil" in the eyes of many, a traitor to the ideals.

For all his prescience in other aspects of life, Francis is blinded by affection for his friend. And by the time he dies prematurely, the situation has grown worse. Ousted from leadership, Elias relentlessly insists on building a lavish basilica to honor Francis's memory and is supported in this work by the pope. One night, distrustful of everyone around him, he secretly buries Francis's body in a stone sarcophagus deep in the crypt of the new church. Francis's bones are not seen again for six hundred years. Eventually, Elias leaves the order altogether and aligns himself with the emperor, who is at war with the pope.

Oscar Wilde once said, "Every great man nowadays has his disciples, and it is usually Judas who writes the biography." Was Elias Francis's Judas? I don't believe their story is that simple. I do believe that one cannot understand who Francis was without understanding what happened between Francis and Elias and what Elias did with what Francis started. For those reasons, this biography takes a different approach from all the others. *The Enthusiast* tells the story of Francis's life through the lens of the relationship that most consoled him but that also most challenged, disturbed, and upset him. Above all, this biography of Francis reveals the complexities of the relationship between the two men and shows how it changed their world, along the way drawing a full picture of how idealism can be undone by the enthusiasm of one devoted follower.

I have been captivated by Elias of Cortona (also known as Elias of Assisi) for almost as long as Francis of Assisi has held my attention. Paul Sabatier's biography of Francis (first published in French in 1894; English, 1906) introduced me to the life of the *Poverello*, or "Little Poor Man," as Francis liked to call himself, and Elias plays no small part in it. Soon after reading Sabatier's account as a teenager, I turned to the *New Catholic Encyclopedia*, volume 5, *Ead to Foy*, page 273; I must have read the 317-word entry on Elias and gazed at the characteristically dark picture of him dozens of times.

Decades later, when I began research for this book, I went back to volume 5 and was captivated by the credit for that picture: it states that the image of Elias was reproduced from an obscure portrait "based upon his image in a painting of the Crucifixion in the upper basilica of St. Francis at Assisi." It hasn't been possible for hundreds of years to scrutinize the painting in question, made upon an icon crucifix by Giunta Pisano, a contemporary of Elias's. The painting was lost long ago, but we know from other sources that Pisano created it in 1236 on commission from Elias and that the inscription he wrote on it almost cheekily read, "Brother Elias had me made, Giunta Pisano painted me, in the year of our Lord 1236. Jesus Christ have mercy on the prayers of pious Elias."

That work of art came from a painter whose style bent toward the Gothic, suffering Christ, which we see in three extant signed icon crucifixes created by Pisano. In contrast to such a deathly looking Savior, the early-twelfth-century icon of the crucified Christ that spoke to Francis in the church of San Damiano imagined a different Christ—one with an open face, smiling, offering himself.[1] It is that image, not the Gothic man of suffering, that continues to "speak" to spiritual seekers of the real Francis.

Another painting, one on the wall of the Lower Church at the basilica in Assisi, deserves our attention. Historians believe that, while not necessarily the oldest image we have of Francis, it is probably the most accurate and realistic. This painting, likely by Cimabue, reveals a short, swarthy, simple man, not a handsome knight. He's showing the marks of stigmata on his hands, but what you see is more of a humble friend than a saint. Art historians pondering that portrait have wondered if there was once another portrait matching it on the other side of the wall, beside the Madonna and Christ Child. *The Enthusiast* goes a long way toward imagining a portrait of one of Francis's closest friends hanging there—what the man looked like and then why his likeness would eventually have been erased from the wall.

In *When Saint Francis Saved the Church* (2014), I attempted to convey the spiritual genius of the man. In *The Enthusiast*, I tell of his struggle.

There is a naiveté to the popular images of Francis. Zeffirelli and Kazantzakis have taught us the myth of the wandering nature poet, lover of song and women, communicator with wildlife. They didn't create this soft Francis out of thin air: the legends were well established before them. These powerful images are probably even part of our collective unconscious when it comes to holy people. The Brothers Grimm knew the meme when in 1812 they had Cinderella communicating with pigeons; that's how they heard the story from old Germans, who had passed it down for centuries. The saint who talks to critters is a romantic motif that connects a human figure with deep spiritual undercurrents.

There's no question that Francis held a special relationship with the created world. He was gentle in ways that we hardly understand. But those were not his defining qualities. Even John Keats had to go from "Smiling upon the flowers and the trees" to "find[ing] the agonies, the strife / Of human hearts."[2] So did Francis, and then some.

In *Young Man Luther* psychologist Erik Erikson wrote, "Human nature can best be studied in the state of conflict,"[3] suggesting that we may have the opportunity to know Francis best by focusing on difficult periods in his life. The early biographers didn't linger on Francis's sadness, his feelings of having been betrayed, and for political reasons they also did not linger over the reasons for those emotions or his abdication. But we should, and we will. The romantic narrative of generations ago also obscures the secondary characters in the story; they come across as caricatures rather than real people. Pope Innocent III, for example, usually appears older and less nuanced than he really was, and Clare usually looks and sounds like Cinderella.

I've invented dialogue in order to tell this true story. Conversations such as the ones you will read here took place, but we have few records of what precisely the characters said to each other. Their words occasionally come from my imagination, or are slightly adapted from the sources. This is because, although I stick assiduously to the written record, I also write as one who might have witnessed the humble events: the conversion of Francis and his friends as they took their gospel ways to the world. I try to tell this story as one who witnessed and has just come running back from it—similar to how the stories of the fall of Troy or Rome were once told. "For history, after all, is valuable only in so far as it lives."[4]

I also presume to imagine the desires of the characters in this account. One of the great historians of the last century, Herbert Butterfield, wrote: "The primary assumption of all attempts to understand the [people] of the past must be the belief that we can in some degree enter into minds that are unlike our own. If this belief were unfounded it would seem that [people] must be for ever locked away from one another, and all generations must be regarded as a world and a law unto themselves."[5] I agree.

Most Italian proper names for people have been anglicized, particularly *Francis*, most of the time, while most of those for places are left in the original. There are exceptions. Francis's father, for instance, is sometimes *Pietro* in keeping with tradition (not to anglicize his name) but also in order to distinguish him from *Peter* Catani, the third friar. Most often, though, Francis's father is *Bernardone*, which is what Francis called him after their break.

Now, to the story, which leads off with the crisis the friars felt at the death of their friend and founder, before going back to the beginning. As Thomas Carlyle once said, "Narrative is *linear*, Action is *solid*."[6]

DRAMATIS PERSONAE

Angelo Tancredi—the first knight to join Francis and one of the original twelve friars. Educated, handsome, well-spoken, the same age as Francis. At the end of Francis's life, we see him asking Angelo to sing of death, taking up lines from his just-composed "Canticle of the Creatures." First appearance: chapter 2.

Anthony of Padua—the most important of the second generation of Franciscans; a brilliant scholar, enamored with ideas. Fourteen years younger than Francis and Elias. A priest and monk before he became a Franciscan; after his death in 1231 he quickly became the second Franciscan saint. Boyish, gentle as a teacher, but without much emotional intelligence. First appearance: chapter 25.

Bernard of Quintavalle—the first person to join Francis in poverty. A well-educated, respected man of means and influence in the Assisi community, he was ten years Francis's senior. Loyal, judging, but kind. A balding man with a slightly furrowed brow. First appearance: chapter 11.

Caesar of Speyer—received into the Franciscan Order by Elias in 1217 while preaching in the Holy Land as a crusader. In Francis's final years, Caesar listened to Francis, who dictated his final version of the Rule to him. By 1239, Caesar, a leader of the "Spirituals," in opposition to Elias, was jailed by him and there clubbed to death. Small and wiry. First appearance: chapter 22.

Clare of Assisi—a woman of wisdom and strength. Left privilege behind at eighteen to become the first woman to follow Francis. Founder of the Second Order, the Poor Clares, but at first she was just another "brother." Died on August 11, 1253. Piercing eyes, resolute. First appearance: chapter 2.

Frederick II of Hohenstaufen, Holy Roman Emperor—believed himself a direct descendant of ancient Roman emperors. Born in the Marches region of Italy, was baptized in Assisi when Francis was thirteen. Crowned by Pope Honorius III in 1220 and excommunicated by Pope Gregory IX seven years later. When Elias felt the Church had turned against him, he felt there was no one to whom he could turn but Frederick. Brilliant, handsome, arrogant, ultimately repentant. First appearance: chapter 4.

Giles of Assisi—the third friar to join Francis and an exact contemporary, growing up in and around Assisi with Francis and Elias. Disdained learning even more than Francis and is known for his travels in the Marches, to Santiago de Compostela in Spain, and to the Holy Land as a friar missionary. He lived into his seventies. Confident, bold, a man of intense physical strength. First appearance: chapter 5.

Pope Innocent III—began life as Lothar of Segni. His father was the Count of Segni; his uncle, Pope Clement III. Studied theology in Paris and canon law in Bologna before being elected pope at the young age of thirty-eight. Became one of the most powerful popes of the later Middle Ages. Mostly tolerant of reform movements, yet virulently responsive to dissent. First appearance: chapter 7.

Leo—became Francis's closest friend during the saint's final years. Replaced Elias as Francis's confessor and travel companion, to the consternation of Elias. Some of the most popular stories of Francis's life are from the writings of Leo, who published them anonymously after Francis's death. Died an old man in 1271. Inquisitive and active. First appearance: chapter 2.

Pietro Bernardone—Francis's father, who haunts the story of his son's first twenty-five years. A conservative, demanding man, a merchant with ambition. St. Bonaventure says that Bernardone reared Francis "in vanity amid the vain." First appearance: chapter 5.

Rufino—a cousin of Clare's, probably a decade younger than Francis, named for the third-century martyr/patron saint of Assisi. One of Francis's closest friends at the end of his life—for instance, he accompanied him to Mount La Verna in the fall of 1224 and was the first one to know that an angel had miraculously touched Francis there. Noble and trustworthy. First appearance: chapter 2.

Thomas of Celano—a scholarly man from the remote Abruzzi, home to hermits and poets. Introvert by temperament but willing to take personal risks to evangelize Franciscanism. Joined the order in 1215 and was sent to Germany in 1221, where he became vicar of that province. Entrusted with writing the first biography of Francis after the saint's death. His sunny countenance was a reflection of his good nature. First appearance: chapter 1.

Cardinal Ugolino—eleven years older than Francis and Elias; appointed by Pope Honorius III in 1220 to oversee Francis's movement. Became Pope Gregory IX just after Francis's death, elected because of his friendship with the soon-to-be saint. A man of true religious sincerity who became a power broker in the Church. First appearance: chapter 2.

CHRONOLOGY OF EVENTS

1181   Francis is born in central Assisi while his father, Pietro, is away on a business trip. Elias is born in Castel Britti, an Assisian suburb.

1198   Rioting breaks out in Assisi between those who support imperial rule and those who want independence: between the nobility and the merchant class.

1202   Francis taken prisoner in Perugia after the Battle of Collestrada.

1203   Francis remains in a Perugian jail until Pietro ransoms him.

1204   Frequent illness lays Francis low.

1205   Again healthy and dreaming of knighthood, Francis joins Walter of Brienne's small army. After an emotional crisis, he deserts. Makes pilgrimage to Rome. Begs at St. Peter's. Returns to Assisi. Faces a leper without fleeing. Hears God speak in the ruined church of San Damiano.

1206   The most intense year of Francis's conversion. In winter, Francis faces his father at the bishop's palace, before most of Assisi's citizens. Renounces father's wealth. Leaves for a Benedictine monastery outside Assisi. Upon returning, takes up his first temporary residence—at San Damiano, repairing the church.

1207   Continues to repair dilapidated churches, including the one he called Portiuncula, a small church in the Spoleto valley. Takes on the neomonastic clothes of a penitent.

1208   Bernard of Quintavalle joins him as the first brother. On April 16, Francis discovers God's directive for his apostolate, together with Bernard and Peter Catani, by taking to heart three gospel passages: Matthew 19:21, Luke 9:1–3, and Luke 9:23. A week later and Giles is with them, as well, and Francis and Giles soon journey to the March of Ancona on their first preaching mission.

1209   The brothers' number reaches twelve. In July, Pope Innocent III launches the bloody Albigensian Crusade in the Pyrenees.

1210   The brothers take up residence at Rivo Torto in Assisi, then travel to Rome to see Innocent III; he receives them and offers tacit approval of their way of life. They return to Assisi and move to Portiuncula.

1212   Francis's first, aborted attempt to travel to Muslim-occupied land (in Syria). The first woman—Clare of Assisi—joins as a "brother" on Palm Sunday evening, March 28. Her sister Agnes soon joins her, and Francis sets both up at San Damiano as the founding Poor Ladies of San Damiano.

1213   Francis takes his first trip to Mount La Verna. He also travels to Spain, wanting again to make it to Muslim lands (this time, Morocco) but has to turn back due to illness.

1215   Francis likely attends the Fourth Lateran Council in Rome in November. Probably meets St. Dominic there.

1216   Pope Innocent III dies. Pope Honorius III elected.

1217–   Francis sends friars on missions to North Africa, Germany,
1219   Spain, France, Hungary, and Syria (Elias). Francis travels to crusader-occupied Acre (Christian-held kingdom in the Holy Land), then on to Damietta in Egypt, where he meets Sultan Malik al-Kamil in May 1219.

1220   Friars are martyred in January in Morocco. On September 29, Francis appoints a vicar general for the order: Peter Catani.

Cardinal Ugolino is appointed protector of the Franciscans by Honorius III.

1221   Peter Catani dies in March, and Elias is appointed to replace him at the Pentecost chapter meeting. Francis preaches throughout Italy.

1223   Anthony of Padua's influence in the order grows. More friars are drawn to his theological work. In the autumn, Francis goes on retreat near Rieti with Leo and Caesar of Speyer to draft the last Rule, which came to be known as the *Regula bullata*. On Christmas Day, Francis is in Greccio putting on the first live nativity. He begins to deal with encroaching blindness.

1224   Elias sends friars to England for the first time. Francis experiences the stigmata on Mount La Verna between the Exaltation of the Holy Cross and the Feast of St. Michael the Archangel.

1225   Francis again preaches throughout Italy, returning to the Marches, where he first preached. He stays at San Damiano, near Clare. Composes the first vernacular Italian poem, "Canticle of the Creatures." His eyes are treated. He is almost blind.

1226   Francis writes his "Testament" in late spring. Returns to Assisi and stays put, knowing that he has little time to live. He dies late on October 3.

1227   Honorius III dies on March 18. Cardinal Ugolino is elected pope the following day, taking the name Gregory IX. John Parenti is elected the first minister general of the order at the first general chapter meeting following Francis's death. This effectively removes Elias from leadership.

1228   On April 29, Gregory IX issues a decree announcing his intention to build a special church in Assisi to honor Francis. July 16 sees Francis formally canonized.

1229   Thomas of Celano completes his *First Life* (the *Vita Prima*) of Francis in February; it is approved.

1230   On May 23, Elias secretly hides the body of Francis in the rock beneath the basilica he's building in Assisi. In June, the friars punish him for this: he fails to win election as minister general at general chapter.

1231   Pope Gregory IX institutes the Papal Inquisition, recruiting inquisitors almost exclusively from the Franciscan and Dominican orders.

1232   The basilica in Assisi is mostly complete. Elias is elected minister general. He rules, often tyrannically, for seven years.

1238   Elias jails Caesar of Speyer, who is beaten to death in prison.

1239   Gregory IX, Elias's old confidant and friend, deposes him.

1240   Elias is excommunicated and seen at the side of the equally excommunicated Emperor Frederick II, who is openly at war with the Holy See.

1241   Pope Gregory IX dies on August 21.

1243   Innocent IV becomes pope.

1247   Brother John of Parma elected minister general. He sends friars to visit Elias in Cortona, asking him to confess and submit to his authority. Elias refuses.

1250   Frederick II, Elias's protector, dies.

1253   After Clare intercedes on his behalf, Elias is allowed to make a full deathbed confession and is received back into the Church but not into the Franciscan Order. He then dies on April 22 in Cortona. One month later, Innocent IV dedicates the Basilica of San Francesco in Assisi.

PART ONE

Poetry is History, could we tell it right.
—Thomas Carlyle
in a letter to Ralph Waldo Emerson, 1834

CHAPTER 1

DEATH OF A SAINT

October 3, 1226

It was Saturday evening and the Umbrian sun was setting on the little pink town.

"We have to hide his body or we risk losing it forever!"

Brother Elias was barking at three of his fellow friars, and Francis wasn't even dead yet. Their shadows thrown long on the walls of Portiuncula, the little chapel in the Spoleto valley given to them in 1210 by the Benedictine monastery of Mount Subasio, these were the few Franciscans Elias believed he could trust to understand the urgency at hand. Portiuncula lay unprotected, surrounded by woods, close to the highway, a long way in the dead of night from the protective walls of the city.

Elias was a small, spare man who still possessed the black hair of his youth. Beard showed on his chin after only a day without shaving. For fifteen years, he'd been an erudite, quick-witted, brilliant administrator and a skilled entrepreneur. The graciousness in all personal matters for which he had been universally recognized as a younger man had given way to a certain form of native dynamism.

A moon was already visible in the sky just over the shoulder of Mount Subasio. Francis of Assisi lay unconscious on a straw mat in the dimly lit chapel where his religious reform movement had been born sixteen years earlier.

Elias reached over to a side table for a wooden box containing thin tapers. Lighting one, he held its light up to the butt of a second in order to melt drops of wax into each of three candlesticks. Then he placed the first and second candles into their sticks, lit a third, and fixed it as well. Light quickly filled the dark room.

By this time, the moon was a few inches higher in the sky. It was going to be a clear night, and Elias worried about who might snatch the body of his saint. If a burglar would kick down a door to grab an iron pot or a new rug—which he might sell for pennies to a passing trader the following day—what might someone do with the body of the Poverello?

Francis had never wanted possessions of any kind. "We'd then have to protect them," he once explained to the bishop of Assisi. But now, Francis was himself the possession worth protecting. The world had never seen someone like him, and people were already trading patches of his clothing like jewels.

An hour after Elias's outburst, Francis took his last breath. Thomas of Celano would write three years later: "Larks are birds that love the daylight and flee the darkness of twilight. But on the night that St. Francis flew to Christ, they came to the roof of the house, even though twilight had fallen, flying around it for a long time making a great clamor. They were either expressing joy or sadness with their singing; we don't know for sure which." City officials, Thomas goes on to say, also diligently guarding Portiuncula that night, were astonished at the behavior of the birds. "They were the ones who called others to come and witness to it."

CHAPTER 2

THE FOLLOWING MORNING

October 4, 1226

After leading his brothers in reciting three *Pater Nosters*, Elias made the Sign of the Cross over the body and ran out into the night. He told no one where he was going. It was none of their business.

. . . *Et ne nos inducas in tentationem, sed libera nos a malo.* ". . . And lead us not into temptation, but deliver us from evil." *Amen.* The words floated in the air like swallows.

Angelo and Rufino took turns reading the penitential psalms aloud, but quietly, to each other. Psalm 6, then 32, 38, 51, 102, 130, and 143. Then they started again. Brother Leo (the only friend of Francis who ever bothered to preserve a note from him; he, in fact, saved two, and they are the only two autographs of Francis we possess) sat closest to the body, singing the *Agnus Dei*.

These were Francis's best friends, a handful among his first friars, who rarely left his side for two years leading up to his death. They'd been his nearly constant companions since September 1224, when they accompanied Francis to Mount La Verna, "that rugged rock 'twixt Tiber and Arno," according to Dante, writing ninety years later. There, they bore witness to and became keepers of Francis's dearest secret. It was upon La Verna that something mysterious happened to his body, a spiritual piercing by God, a physical identification of Francis with Christ, and Francis's friends kept this mystery to themselves.

Angelo, Rufino, and Leo stayed awake throughout the night after their friend died. They prayed, sang, and told stories. Before dawn, they laughed. And with the first sound of magpies pecking in the sunflowers, they hugged each other, weeping like children. Thank God Elias had run out.

Within minutes of leaving Portiuncula, Elias reached the town of Assisi; he began making arrangements and attempting desperately to get word of Francis's death to Cardinal Ugolino, the papally appointed "protector" of the Franciscan Order in Rome. Elias relied heavily on Ugolino and was his one true ally. Born in 1170 in the Papal States, the son of a count and a cousin of Pope Innocent III, Ugolino studied theology and canon law in Paris before being made a cardinal-deacon at twenty-eight by his cousin. Eight years, later he was appointed cardinal bishop of Ostia, a diocese within Rome itself (one of seven so-called suburbicarian dioceses). Knowing such an insider was helpful, to say the least. In this instance, Elias knew that he and the cardinal already agreed on what must be done.

Only one week earlier, four different men—younger friars hand-picked by Elias—had stood outside the stable doors of a local blacksmith in nearby Foligno.

"What are we doing here?" one asked, looking around at the others. The question went unanswered.

"One . . . two . . . *three!*" Elias called out a moment later, and at once, the four hoisted a massive sarcophagus to their shoulders. Taking three steps toward the double carriage before them, they lowered it slowly onto the back of it. The double team trotted a step forward for balance, and one horse let out a whinny.

Guido, the youngest of the friars gathered there, paused a moment, bending at the waist to kiss the handle he'd just set down. Elias yelled "Come!" in Guido's direction, and Guido jumped up to join the others. They all walked like Roman soldiers beside the carriage for the two-hour journey back to Portiuncula, where Francis lay dying.

That same moment, back at Portiuncula, Francis was asking his brothers to help him lie down on the bare ground.

"Take off my clothes," he begged. "I want to feel the ground on my skin."

The friars did as he asked, but looking at each other, some wondered, *Is he mad with fever?* Angelo, Rufino, and Leo did not wonder—they knew.

———— ❧ ————

A week later, these three helped carry Francis's body into town in the morning after watching over it for the night. Elias had returned from whatever he was doing, instructing the friars that they were to take Francis to the church of San Giorgio.

"He will be safe there until we know better what to do," Elias said.

Angelo, Rufino, Leo, Elias, and a few others gently lifted Francis onto a cot they had fashioned out of branches and began carrying him down the road to Assisi. They knew that Francis had wanted to embrace death like a sister and experience it as a natural part of life that leads to something else. Giotto would immortalize this embrace as a gesture between the friar and a figure of death in his famous fresco *St. Francis and Death*, on the wall beside what later became the doorway from Magdalen Chapel to the north transept in the Lower Church of San Francesco. But back on October 3, 1226, people were lining the road from the valley into the city. They'd heard the news during the night that Francis was nearing the end. They were holding candles, singing hymns, and waving branches in a scene reminiscent of the way a few residents of Jerusalem welcomed Jesus to their city before Passover.

A path cleared on the winding way down to the convent at San Damiano. Even greedy, grieving peasants had some manners. At San Damiano, the friars stopped to see Clare. They set down the body of their founder and removed the grille that usually separated the men from the women. For two hours, Clare and the other women took turns talking to Francis, blessing him, touching his head, weeping, and praying for him. Some prayed quietly to him, as if he'd already been made a saint.

Clare's grief was probably increased by worry over what was happening to the movement that she and Francis had founded. Elias and Cardinal Ugolino were slowly and deliberately steering things away from the original Rule. Cardinal Ugolino's power in the Church was increasing. *He may even become pope one day*, Clare thought to herself.

The friars left San Damiano with the body en route to the church of San Giorgio (today a chapel within the Basilica of Santa Chiara), where Elias had already arranged for the holy remains to lie in state. Some knew that this was where Francis had first preached the Good News just after he exchanged the leather belt and look of a hermit for the robe of a simple friar, complete with a rough cord and sandals. People jostled each other for a chance to touch the cot, even the body. Occasionally Elias slapped their hands away with a juniper stick he'd picked up on the road. He kept looking nervously over his shoulder, fearing that someone from Rome might come forward, demanding to take the body of this obvious saint to the Lateran or Old St. Peter's. He wouldn't allow that to happen. Francis was to the Umbrian hill towns what Jesus was to the shores of the Sea of Galilee.

By the time the procession reached the city, bitter tears were replaced with joy and gladness, according to Thomas of Celano's account. From Francis's place of burial in San Giorgio, Celano went on to say, "he enlightens the world."[1]

Before he died, Francis asked Elias to pass something along to all of the friars.

"Bless them all on my behalf," he said, "and tell them that they have nothing to fear and have done nothing wrong."[2]

Then, their grave walk over by dusk, Elias retired to his room. There, he began to compose a letter. His emotion poured out in a way that would surprise the brothers who knew him best. "Before I say anything, I sigh, and for good reason," he emoted. "My groans are gushing forth. The comforter is far from us, and he who once carried us like lambs has fled to some far off country." He included other beautiful turns of phrase, such as "His presence was a light, and not only for those of us who were near, but to those who were far from us both in calling and in life."[3] But also in that singular letter, Elias told the world a secret that Angelo, Rufino, Leo—and Francis himself—never wanted anyone to know.

CHAPTER 3

THREE-AND-A-HALF YEARS LATER

May 22, 1230

Upon the rock that perches Assisi above the plain below, at the southwestern corner of town, is a promontory named by Roman city planners the *Collis Inferni*, the "Hill of Hell." It was a place where criminals were executed, their bodies tossed over the side, left to rot in the sun and rain out of view. Children were told by their mothers never to go near that miserable place hanging above the valley.

The Romans modeled the Hill of Hell after Gehenna on the outskirts of the Old City of Jerusalem. "It is better for you to lose one of your members than for your whole body to be thrown into hell," Jesus preached in the first century (Mt 5:29). Except that the word translated "hell" is, in the original, *Gehenna*, a place name that was familiar to first century residents of Jerusalem. So, there are ancient foundations for the idea that the unrepentant and the heretic could not, according to medieval laws, be buried in holy ground. That is why places such as the Hill of Hell existed in medieval towns: the bodies of those who died outside the Church had to be buried somewhere.

Ironically, there was no corresponding law against burying a good Christian in such an unclean place.

Only five months after Francis's death, Cardinal Ugolino was elected to the chair of St. Peter. Taking the name Pope Gregory IX, he built his papacy from the beginning upon his reputation as friend of the greatest saint since the apostles. Some said that Francis had turned to Ugolino for fatherly guidance for his order, to protect it and its ideals from those who would steer it down ungodly paths. Others saw things differently—that Ugolino, together with Elias and others, seized this control and were themselves party to steering the friars away from the ideals of their founder.

Less than eighteen months after Francis's body was laid in its wooden tomb at San Giorgio, Elias acquired the Hill of Hell in a series of land grants from prominent Assisian citizens. On April 29, 1228, Pope Gregory IX issued a papal bull announcing that plans were underway to build a great church, there, transforming the land to the glory of God.[1]

Both Gregory and Elias remembered conversations with Francis about sin, the body, and death. Perhaps they believed that burial on the Hill of Hell was in keeping with Francis's desire to be regarded as the lowliest of all. Medieval people often pondered how they might appear before the Judgment Seat of Christ after death. The belief was that a dead person, body and soul, would go to judgment to face the question of eternal destiny, and it was important to make the right impression. Even the sixteenth-century German emperor Maximilian I, who was no saint, left instructions that, in death, his head should be shaved, his teeth smashed in, and his body burned. Despite what the earthly record might show, Maximilian wanted to at least seem physically penitent when he appeared before God.[2]

"We will make Assisi the new Jerusalem," Elias was saying to all who would listen. He was devoted to the places he and Francis had shared, especially their beloved Assisi. It was more beautiful than Compostela, closer than Jerusalem to the center of the Holy Roman Empire, devoid of Rome's stench and menace, and deserved—Elias believed, because of Francis—to become the world's pilgrimage destination.

With pilgrims come coins—stitched into their belts or folded into their shoes. Pilgrims possessed gold and silver and quietly carried it to where it might do them the most good. Assisians needed their gold, now more than ever. Even Solomon had to beg and hoard in order to build a temple. A couple of lines from Shakespeare capture the sentiment of what was cusping: "Th' abuse of greatness is when it disjoins / Remorse from power."[3]

———— ❧ ————

Pope Gregory arrived in Assisi on July 16, 1228, intent on putting Elias's plans into action. In a papal bull three months earlier, he'd announced that the Inferno hill was to be renamed Paradise and offered forty days of indulgence to anyone who helped fund the construction.[4] During an elaborate ceremony at San Giorgio, he pronounced Francis a saint of heaven, which was a surprise to no one. A few months earlier, Celano had written in his *First Life* of Francis: "New miracles are constantly happening at Francis's tomb. The blind have recovered sight, the deaf their hearing, the lame their ability to walk, the mute their voices, even those with gout start to jumping; and lepers become clean. His dead body heals those who are alive."[5] San Giorgio was a busy marketplace of miracles for nearly two years; the evidence for the pope's declaration was overwhelming.

Two days later, on July 18, the pope laid the foundation stone on a vast platform where this new paradise was under construction; while Francis's body still lay in a wooden tomb upon the floor in the crypt of San Giorgio, Elias was named the architect of the new basilica. It was as if the vision of Ezekiel of a valley of dry bones was becoming a reality, taking place in Umbria. "I will make his name great on earth, as it is now in heaven," vowed Elias.

A new church building of the magnitude of the Basilica of San Francesco was not undertaken lightly. From the start, Elias and Gregory envisioned this place as a new tabernacle of Moses, a divine space where God would dwell with his people. It would quite literally be a gateway to heaven, having as its foundation the bones of the saint whom they knew so well. Within two years, the Lower Church was completed, and six years later, the Upper Church was under construction, to be adorned several decades later with frescoes by Giotto and other great artists depicting soon-to-be iconic scenes from the life of Francis and his brothers. Gold-leaf paintings even adorn the ceilings—all to honor a man who didn't even want his brothers to own their own breviaries.

"Why should I defend them?" Elias said to anyone who challenged his decisions. "It was our Lord himself who praised the man who builds a house upon a firm foundation, secured deep in the rock below! When the rains come—and they will come—that house will be safe."

The basilica became one of the greatest architectural and artistic achievements of the Middle Ages, even though the Franciscans who oversaw its design and construction assured themselves that their church stood apart from the ostentation of French Gothic, then in vogue. (Their building left off façade towers and kept the windows on the façade only circular.) There is no denying the tremendous talent that Elias possessed for architecture and organization. Apses and transepts were his gift; they are magnificent. The speed and efficiency of the construction were remarkable. The only accurate comparison and medieval precedent for Elias—a monastic religious leader who was also architect of a great church—is Abbot Suger at Saint-Denis outside Paris, a century earlier.

In April 1230, Gregory IX would honor Elias by declaring through another papal bull that the new basilica was the mother church for all Franciscans, a title that had previously been used by the Poverello for his beloved tiny chapel, the "Little Portion," *Portiuncula*. This disgusted a handful of Francis's closest friends.

Three years' worth of pilgrims had flowed to San Giorgio from all parts of Christendom, but Elias believed that resting place was only a temporary solution. God's protective arm had kept danger from visiting his friend's remains, but there also was a question of paying proper respect. Elias was determined to secure Francis's honor and legacy for all time. Rotten Perugians threatened Assisi at every turn and surely wouldn't hesitate to take the hill town's most blessed hero.

The body of the greatest saint since St. John the Evangelist was to be transferred in its coffin to the crypt of the Lower Church before a gathered assembly that included cardinal legates sent by Pope Gregory IX, members of the papal curia, friars, bishops, invited guests, and townspeople. A ceremony was planned for May 25, 1230.

Bonaventure, in the penultimate paragraph of his "official" *Life of Saint Francis*, writes that on that day as "the holy treasure . . . was being removed" to its new resting place, God "deigned to work many miracles, so that by the fragrance of the healing power of Francis's body the hearts of the faithful would be drawn closer to Christ."[6] But as most of the thousands of friars who were gathered (the Pentecost general chapter meeting was set to begin the following day) would never realize, Francis's body was not there. Elias had secretly buried it two days earlier.

Or so he said. The exact location of the body of Francis would remain a mystery for six hundred years.

On May 23, 1230, Elias pounded in the rock below the altar in the Lower Church, finishing preparations that had already been extensive and detailed. He worked hard at Francis's final resting place: a stone sarcophagus, wrapped by a cage of iron bars, in a cavern hewn from the mountainside. In the dead of night, Elias was the last person to seal up that rocky tomb. Reaching into his cassock pocket, he took out a handful of coins. Holding them up, just enough to catch the flickering light of a candle, he paused a moment to consider the silver. The Franciscan

Rule forbade a friar from even handling money. But Elias gently placed the coins beside the dead hand of his friend. Whether this was a strange gesture of repentance, a prescient recognition that someone in the future would someday need to authenticate the body of Francis, or a gift of misunderstanding, we'll never know for sure.[7]

"I am sorry, Holy Father," I imagine he said. "Forgive me now for what I must do."

Two days later, a purple-draped, oxen-drawn wagon carried the sturdy wooden coffin that had witnessed many miracles at San Giorgio to the Lower Church of San Francesco. The crowd tried to touch what they believed contained the holy relics of their holy brother and favorite son all along the way. Walking solemnly behind that carriage was an orderly gathering of friars and bishops and cardinals. Trumpets blew. Less than a handful of those present knew it was all for show.

Pilgrims' guides and pamphlets would for centuries indicate only that the tomb of St. Francis was located "under the high altar" of the Lower Church; not unlike St. Peter's bones, which have for two thousand years been considered the very foundation of his basilica in Rome.

Certain Franciscans and popes would know the precise location of the body in subsequent centuries. This knowledge was passed down, like all the most intimate secrets of the Church, in private conversations from one dying minister general, cardinal protector, or pope to the next. The rest of the world was left to believe that in burial, just as in life, Francis was like Christ. As Bartholomew of Pisa put it, late in the fourteenth century, "As Christ's tomb was sealed and watched by guards, so St. Francis's tomb has been sealed, to prevent his body ever being visible to anyone."[8]

CHAPTER 4

THE FOUNDER AND THE ENTHUSIAST

The big picture

Francis and Elias had a long and complicated relationship.

The most common interpretation of what happened on May 23, 1230, in Assisi is that Elias acted with selfish or sinister intent. The accusation that he hid Francis's body in the tomb would come to be seen in the wider context of a general degrading of his reputation that took place over the next twenty years. But events are never that simple. Francis himself never accepted that understanding of his close friend, even though things began to turn sour long before his death.

The first person to specifically accuse Elias of this deception was another Franciscan, Thomas of Eccleston. But strangely, Thomas waited until 1258, more than a generation after the events took place. Elias's ignominy had been firmly established by that time. There was plenty of later evidence for demonizing him.

For example, at the general chapter meeting immediately following Francis's pretend burial, Elias was carried into the gathered assembly on the shoulders of a handful of friars chanting for him to be reelected minister general. The arrogance of Elias at that moment was astounding. Many brothers believed that Elias's self-promotion was morally wrong and reflected a spirit that ran counter to what anyone would expect from a Franciscan.

Another friar, John Parenti, had been elected minister general in 1227, and it was John who was reelected at that general chapter meeting in May 1230. No matter, Elias rationalized, for he needed time to construct his shrine for Francis. Once he put the finishing touches on the Lower Church, he would more properly maneuver himself into a position of leadership.[1]

Gregory IX was aware of what Elias was doing but couldn't be in Assisi that day. He was in Rome attempting to negotiate a truce with Emperor Frederick II. But Elias must have had at least tacit approval for hiding Francis's body in the Lower Church; this explains why Gregory didn't name Elias in the furious bull he issued to Assisian officials three weeks later. Gregory was incensed because he was not consulted about the exact time for smuggling Francis's bones. Gregory had arranged for one of his cardinal legates to be present at Elias's side when the holy cadaver was laid in its final resting place. In other words, Elias wasn't supposed to do it early, and not alone. That last-minute betrayal is what led Gregory to fire off the papal bull even though he couldn't reveal all the conniving behind the scenes.

Gregory threatened to excommunicate the city officials unless they explained what happened. He imagined that someone—those officials or perhaps one of the two bishops to whom he directed the bull—replaced him as Elias's confidant. He didn't realize just then that it was all Elias, with a few obedient, nameless friars.

Elias's motivations for secreting the body seemed to him to be pure. He was protecting Francis, as he had done many times in the past. Elias had secured a firmer footing for the order during Francis's lifetime, helped his ailing friend find medical care, guided a blind Francis clear of possible physical danger, and designed a basilica to honor his legacy. Elias also knew, in a way not yet comprehended by Pope Gregory, how Assisi might remain the geographical and spiritual locus of the Franciscan movement. Elias's fear of body snatchers even extended to the pope himself, who might have had designs on some small bit or piece of the holy corpus, to be laid to rest in the Eternal City for the benefit of pilgrims, locked safely in a jewel-crusted reliquary.

But instead of interpreting the secret transition of Francis in light of what happened in the weeks, months, and years after it happened, we should try and understand what happened subsequently. We have to first go back to the beginning.

―――――――⁂―――――――

There was also plenty of evidence for lionizing Elias. Three years after Francis's death, in his *First Life* of Francis, completed and approved in February 1229, Thomas of Celano recorded that Elias was "the one whom Francis chose to be as a mother to himself, and also as a father to the other brothers." Francis taught that a friar was never to be alone but always serving others or in the company of a spiritual brother. At the time he wrote the *First Life*, Celano knew nothing about what was to come in Elias's ignominious future.

Francis appointed Elias as minister to the all-important province of the Holy Land and later visited him there just after abdicating his leadership of the order. Elias was one of the privileged few to have seen up close and firsthand what happened to Francis's body upon Mount La Verna two years before Francis's death. And when Celano described Francis's deathbed scene, he wrote: "There was a brother there whom Francis loved with the greatest affection."[2] Some have suggested that this beloved brother was Leo, but most experts agree it was Elias.

There was no question of Elias's devotion to Francis. He was Francis's friend, confidant, and source of strength. The only one able to insist that Francis take medicine to alleviate pain, Elias interceded when others failed. Even a decade after Francis's death, Elias still possessed ardent defenders. Clare of Assisi, for instance—an unimpeachable witness and another of Francis's closest confidants—praises Elias in one of her letters to Agnes of Prague written in 1236, just before the troubles with Elias were about to reach their highest pitch. Agnes is concerned about compromises to the ideals of Franciscan poverty being allowed by Pope Gregory IX. Clare encourages Agnes to "follow the advice of our venerable father, our Brother Elias, minister general"; she writes, "Prefer his advice to the advice of others and consider it more precious to you than any gift."[3] Behind the iron grille that kept her separated from the world, Clare was probably unaware of all that Elias was doing. Her advice to Agnes was based on Elias's reputation rather than his current standing.[4]

But Celano never once mentions Elias by name in his *Second Life* of Francis completed in 1246. When Celano has Francis teaching the qualities of a good friar to his brothers, his words sound as if they are pointed directly at condemning the sorts of things Elias had been recently accused of doing. His Francis speaks of "wicked men who carry poison on their tongues" and "a double-tongued man who is the scandal of religion."[5] The history of Francis's adult life and his friendship with Elias was being rewritten.

In 1232, we see Elias succeeding John Parenti, elected to the post of minister general. Elias's work of protecting the body of Francis and building Assisi into a place of pilgrimage is largely over, but the growth of the order becomes his preoccupation. Over the next seven years, Elias expands the role of the friars in the world, welcoming the ownership of property, the cultivation of learning, and the construction of splendid churches and monuments.

In 1239, about three years after Clare wrote that letter to Agnes, Elias is deposed by the pope in response to the overwhelming demand of his spiritual brothers. They find him arrogant and lusting for power. Fellow friar and historian Salimbene of Adam tells us that Elias has turned against his own after the founder's death. Writing at the end of his life, in 1285, Salimbene clearly felt betrayed by Elias, for he also remembered the "good" brother who had received him as a postulant in 1238 while minister general, graciously sheltering him from his angry father, who wanted to thwart the conversion.[6]

Like everyone else, Elias was a combination of good and bad.

When he is finally deposed in 1239, Elias responds with rebellion, joining with the excommunicated Holy Roman Emperor Frederick II, who is at war with the pope. Worst of all, Elias lends credence to Frederick II's cynical claims to divine authority. In a rapid, startling turn, he changes from confidant to a saint to vicar of a despot, the Church's number one enemy.

He takes some of the Franciscan friars with him in his fight, and the reputation of the order is forever damaged. Salimbene recounts, "I myself have heard a hundred times" the singing of a little ditty by the Umbrian peasants, whenever a friar was passing by:

"Frater Elias is gone astray

And hath taken the evil way."

At the sound of this song, the good brothers were cut to the heart.

But that is not how it all began when Francis and Elias were boys growing up together in Assisi.

PART TWO

There have been few more brilliant victories in history than those of St. Francis, and few more pathetic failures.

—G. G. Coulton
From St. Francis to Dante[1]

CHAPTER 5

WHEN WE FIRST MET

1181–1195, Umbria

Assisi remains a magical place in the twenty-first century because it is actually possible to imagine how it looked in 1181, the year of Francis of Assisi's birth. With the exception of the Basilicas of San Francesco and Santa Chiara hanging on to the west and east edges of the Umbrian hill town, much of Assisi remains as it was eight hundred years ago.

The pinkish beauty of Mount Subasio looms over Assisi, perched upon its western flank, now as it did then. So do cypress trees and their shade, home for magpies and ravens, as well as the soft lines of the groves of olive trees, many as ancient as the stories we have from this beautiful land of sunrises and sunsets.

A typical boy in twelfth-century Assisi was familiar with the Roman temple to Minerva, the imperial fortress, and the Piazza del Mercato—for shopping, gossip, and trade—as well as the niches on the fortified wall that surrounded the city of three to four thousand inhabitants. But Francis spent most of his days in the green lushness of beech forests and upland pastures, walking the serious but gentle hills of the upper Tiber valley, spying real mountains in the distance.[1] Farmland and olive groves abounded around Assisi; the plains were even more full of cultivated land, as its soil rich was from ancient lakes. A man might live his entire life in the Province of Umbria and never feel the need to climb the Apennines to the southeast.

It is no accident that Francis's personality, as evidenced in the stories told of him and glimpsed in his bucolic poem the "Canticle of the Creatures," resembles that of Virgil (born in 70 BC in the Po River valley) more than that of Dante (born in 1265 in Florence) in the attention to sense perception, desire to look outside himself for truth and meaning, and connections—sacred as well as divine—felt between humankind and the creatures of the natural world. The scenery of Francis's childhood is the countryside of Virgil's *Eclogues* more than the metaphoric and metaphysical panorama of *The Divine Comedy*. It was not only the man but also Francis the boy who "glowed with great love toward even little worms."[2]

He was born in Assisi in the springtime while his father was away on business. One wonders if Pietro even knew of the child before his wife, Pica, had him baptized with the name Giovanni, or "John." The baptism took place either on Easter's Holy Saturday or on the eve of Pentecost, fifty days later, these being the two great events of the church each year.[3] Notice that Bernardone did not plan to be in town for these predictable holy days on the calendar. When he did return a few weeks later, delighted with his recent success in selling his silks among the French, he immediately began calling the boy *Francesco*, or "Francis."

We know of only one older sibling, Angelo, who took his mother's last name; this was in contrast to Francis, who would always refer to himself using the patronymic. This difference suggests that Angelo was born to Pica from a first marriage, which must have ended with the death of her first husband. It also suggests that Francis grew up as the only young child in the home, spoiled by mother and father, who put great hope in him.[4]

The family had a busy home that was typically unconcerned with both church and school. Francis was meant to help around the house and in his father's business, which he was doing by the time he was fourteen. Otherwise, he had time to wander.

The *Eclogues* were part of his meager education, but most of all, the world of the ancient Roman poet of the countryside and small towns educated Francis's sensibilities. Quiet days spent mashing acorns, eating quince and pear, sauntering along roads and beside rivers, admiring summer hemlocks and fennel, drinking water from melting snows under a February sun, and lamenting lousy harvests or the hungry wolf who got a neighbor's goat filled a boy's imagination. Rich rustic and bucolic details—farmers with oxen and plows, hills and hay, bulls after cows, shepherds and their sheep, swineherds, early morning light, the sun and moon, and singing to girls from the beech trees—all these taught Francis, like Virgil, to almost see Pan.[5]

But despite these generous opportunities, we know very little about Francis's early years. The philosopher Hegel said that periods of happiness are like empty pages in the history books, so we can hope that Francis's silence on that period of his life indicates a happy childhood. He didn't even write about his baptism, which was never a touchstone for understanding his own conversion. Perhaps this is because he was baptized as an infant into an ecclesial community with which he had no meaningful involvement until well into adulthood. Theologically speaking, baptism is a second birth, a seal to God and to the Church. But in the communes of Italy in the twelfth century, it was also, for many, simply a gesture of becoming a citizen.

We know even less about the childhood of Elias. Salimbene of Adam, a Franciscan born in 1221 in Parma, captured a few details in his chronicles, but they aren't always accurate. "Elias was of humble parentage—his father was from Castel de' Britti in the bishopric of Bologna and his mother from Assisi—and before he entered the [Franciscan] Order he used to earn his living by sewing cushions and teaching the children of Assisi to read their psalter," Salimbene wrote, probably confusing Castel Britti, the suburb of Assisi, with some other place.[6]

We know that the boys were born within a few months of each other and grew up in and around Assisi. The land was rich with memories and associations of past greatness. They heard the stories of Italy's noble past: the brothers Remus and Romulus suckling with a she-wolf before one of them founded the city he named for himself; St. Peter's upside-down crucifixion where his basilica stands in Rome; and, to the south, the eruption of Mount Vesuvius that long ago laid waste to Pompeii and Herculaneum.

We don't know for certain that Francis and Elias knew each other as children or that they knew others among the earliest Franciscans (such as Giles, who was born in Assisi also at the time). But a close childhood familiarity between Francis and Elias would go a long way toward explaining the strange intimacies and complications in their relationship later as men. Ease and pleasure would have filled their youth before the anxiety of adulthood pressed into their lives.

Status preoccupied young Francis and Elias, as it did everyone in that age. To have a title was paramount. Short of that, money, coins in the pocket, was everything. Without money, you were stuck with whatever life had given you from the start.

Anything more than some rudimentary schooling was out of the question. Medicine was a privilege; entertainment, fleeting but available; justice, whimsical. Religion was, however, absolutely predictable, as the festivals, feasts, and fasts were observed with perfect regularity, and confessions, as well as Mass attendance, demanded annually. Everyone knew precisely what was expected of them before God.

Still, there were small entertainments. Goliard poets sang and played their Latin songs from Paris to Naples. They were rebels, mostly—student scholars, former monks, secular priests—who clearly hadn't found whatever they were looking for in the academy or cloister or church, so they sang in praise of drink and lechery instead. They didn't convince anyone, but they pleased many. Literature, too, entertained, and it was often erotic. The late twelfth century, the earliest pre-Renaissance throughout Western Europe, saw philosophers and poets rediscovering the classics of their Roman past such as Ovid and his *Art of Love*, which was about seduction and sex—nothing that a Christian was supposed to know of love.

———— ✿ ————

It would have been typical for a man born in Umbria never to travel outside the province from birth until death. Most Assisians never even bothered to visit Perugia, fifteen miles to the west, just across the Tiber River, particularly because relations between the two cities were tense. During a small civil war of 1197–1198, many of the well-bred nobles of Assisi were exiled to Perugia by the working classes in town. Francis and Elias were teenagers at the time.

This violent conflict was a movement of workers in rebellion against imperial rule, in which pro-papal and anti-imperial (later termed *Guelf*) supporters openly fought against the presence and pressure of German lords in their city. Francis was at the ripe age of seventeen. Surely, he and Elias were there when hundreds of youths and adults destroyed the *Rocca Maggiore* ("Major Rock"), the fortress-like castle looming above Assisi designed to protect the people, which was given to the German count Conrad of Urslingen by the Holy Roman Emperor Frederick Barbarossa. A viceroy was stationed there to represent the interests of the emperor. But instead of being a symbol of strength or a place to shelter the town in case of invasion, the Rocca's towers and turrets became a sign of imperial power. Rioters left its walls and ramparts in ruins, which is how Francis would know it for the rest of his life.

Although allied with this popular uprising, Francis's own family was well off. As their money was new and therefore not as respectable, they were always conscious of the fact that they were not a part of the Assisian nobility.

It has become common to assume that Francis's father was vain and coarse while his mother was humble and quiet. However, in the opening paragraph of his *First Life* of Francis, Thomas of Celano told us that "his parents [plural] reared him to arrogance . . . with the vanity of the age," adding that for a long time Francis was "imitating their worthless life and character." In other words, woman, be not spared. Life at home was clearly ordered by those things a religious person would deem unworthy of the *imago Dei*.

We actually know little about Pica, except to speculate that she was French and devout, in contrast to Pietro, who may have met her on one of his journeys to France. We also assume that Francis's love of music comes from listening to her singing in her native Provençal dialect. The stories of Francis suggest that he sang and wrote songs in Italian and French both before and after his conversion. Music remained one of the few constants in his life, a connection from his childhood to his mature life as a friar.

Growing up in the Bernardone home had its privileges. By thirteenth-century standards, Francis led a rich life of privilege and significance, frequently traveling beyond Italy as a child, speaking both his native Italian and some of his mother's native tongue, and although he wasn't traditionally educated, before forty we see him visiting not just France but Spain, Morocco, and parts of the Levant, meeting people of faith, influence, and power.

Bernardone was an entrepreneur in the nascent commercial revolution at the turn of the thirteenth century. He was an early, frequent, and eager traveler to and from other commercial and trading regions in Western Europe, particularly Champagne, where clothiers often exchanged and purchased wares and raw materials. An ambitious man, he probably also traveled across the Swiss Alps with his wares. Bernardone and other merchants like him stood outside of all three of the primary categories for living in a Mediterranean medieval community: those who prayed, those who worked, and those who fought. This made him a stranger even when he was at home.[7] He must have also been a man who knew how to protect himself because the highways and mountain passes were the most dangerous places for any man in the late Middle Ages.

He traded, accumulated capital, sought new markets for his products, borrowed, and sold on credit. His wife was usually looking for her husband to return, enjoying the riches when trade was good or prices went up. It may have been her dowry that purchased his business in the first place.[8]

Young Francis watched all this. Using money in commercial transactions—helping to build the new monetized economy—was rather new in the last quarter of the twelfth century. The birth of capitalism and the emergence of a bourgeois class can both be traced back to this time. Long before Jesus preached against it in the gospels and threw it to the floor in the Temple, the Greek philosopher Aristotle wrote of money's "unnaturalness," calling it "a dead thing that managed to reproduce itself."[9]

Even though the money economy was new, we have accounts of religious reformers before Francis who disdained it, wanting money separated from what religion aimed to accomplish. In northern France a century before Francis's birth, the monk Bernard of Tiron said to a follower after they had been begging together, "Either you cease to be my companion or you cease carrying those coins."[10] Closer to home, Ubaldo, the great bishop of Gubbio, canonized by Pope Celestine III in March 1192 when Francis and Elias were about eleven years old, gave his family riches to the poor and for the founding of monasteries. Legendary for acts of piety, he'd also been strong enough to keep Frederick Barbarossa from sacking his beloved Gubbio.

So it is no wonder that the command of Jesus to the rich young man in Matthew's gospel ("If you wish to be perfect, go, sell your possessions, and give the money to the poor") would become revelatory to Pietro's boy. For his part, Bernardone surely wanted nothing more than to pass along what he was accumulating to his only son. There was nothing a father would have been more intent upon doing than protecting and providing for the next generation.

CHAPTER 6

WHAT EVERY CHRISTIAN KNOWS

Ca. 1200, western Christendom

"Brother Francis, I beg your permission to own my own breviary," a young novice asked one afternoon at Portiuncula, soon after their religious order was approved by the pope.

"No, no," Francis responded, turning away from him.

Then, three days later: "Please, Francis!" the lad pleaded again.

"No, no!" Francis said again. "Why not? Because then you will sit like a bishop in your chair. You will say to one of your brothers, 'Will you bring me my breviary?'" Francis pronounced the words with theatrical panache, a mocking tone of high-minded seriousness. Then he turned away again from the young novice. He couldn't bear this.

Until a moment later, when he rushed back to where the young man stood. "*This* is your prayer book! *This* is your prayer book!" Francis shouted, poking his finger at the young man's chest.

The novice walked away, dejected and more than a little confused. Moments later, Francis chased and caught up with him, yet again, this time begging for forgiveness.

"Okay," he began. His love was often confused with his principles. "If you must own a prayer book, so be it." That simple novice had no idea what a battle was being waged inside of the man he revered.

This scene illustrates the relationship with books and learning that Francis had his whole life—but he wasn't unlearned. No one involved in religious life was unlearned in the late Middle Ages.

Jacob Burckhardt is part of the problem. He stands like a boulder in the way of anyone who wants to understand the era of Benedict of Nursia, Gregory the Great, Hildegard of Bingen, Francis of Assisi, Dominic of Guzmán, and Catherine of Siena. A nineteenth-century historian and Swiss Protestant, Burckhardt may have discovered the Age of the Renaissance, as is often said, but he did so at the expense of perpetuating one of the Renaissance's great myths: the notion that the centuries leading toward that cultural flowering were "barbaric." It was Burckhardt, for instance, who made notorious the nomenclature *Middle Ages*, popularizing a term created to belittle the millennium between the Fall of Rome and the rebirth of Hellenism one thousand years later. Since Burckhardt's time it has become common, even and especially in school, to first encounter the time of Hildegard, Francis, and Thomas Aquinas as "childish and grotesque."[1] It was anything but.

The myth of the "Dark Ages" persists even among modern scholars of the period. There were undoubtedly dark periods during those centuries, when corruption riddled the Church, emperors selfishly served their own interests, and landowners (always male) were the only ones with freedom and opportunities. But the human spirit has always been what it is: hoping, seeking, intelligent, turning toward what is new, curious, and bright. There was no time in history when human beings suddenly became "enthralled with the concept of reason," as one of our best historians recently wrote about the tenth century.[2] What an absurd thing to suggest, unless one is referring to a prehuman species. The truth is that there were many obstacles in the way of learning before Francis's twelfth century, and these had to be overcome in order for the human spirit to rise into its sweet spot.

Equally absurd is the notion that the Middle Ages was an era when "it was virtually impossible not to believe in God."[3] There is no evidence to tell us that theism was once somehow reflexive in human nature. Rather, what we know of how men and women lived in those centuries (remarkably similarly to how they have always lived: focused on personal gain and pleasure, usually taking in just enough religion to satisfy popular convention and the clergy in authority) suggests that for all practical purposes the atheist was quite present even in the time of Francis's youth. The majority of men and women were subservient to landowners, left without time or resources to discover and learn. Schools did not exist except in monasteries. Unless highborn, boys and girls were destined for predetermined lives of duty and responsibility centering on servitude, sales, or folly. But it is ridiculous to suggest that these limitations caused curiosity, reason, and the desire to know what one doesn't know to cease to exist in the human heart. Such curiosity remained and, in fact, was prompted by a variety of ways of learning.

Francis's religious education was meager by contemporary monastic standards but extensive by any twenty-first century measure. We imagine that we have progressed far beyond medieval people, but in some respects, we are wrong. How many Catholic young adults today would know every word of the Apostles' Creed, the Ten Commandments, the Seven Virtues, the Seven Deadly Sins, the Seven Works of Mercy, as well as the Our Father, Hail Mary, and Sign of the Cross? Perhaps one in a hundred.

Every young person in Europe in the Middle Ages learned these articles of the Apostles' Creed and could repeat them from memory (that—memory—is an aspect of the medieval mind largely unshared today):

1. I believe in God, the Father Almighty, maker of heaven and earth:
2. And in Jesus Christ, his only begotten Son, our Lord:
3. Who was conceived by the Holy Ghost, born of the Virgin Mary:
4. Suffered under Pontius Pilate; was crucified, dead and buried: He descended into hell:
5. The third day he rose again from the dead:
6. He ascended into heaven, and sits at the right hand of God, the Father Almighty:
7. From thence he shall come to judge the quick and the dead:
8. I believe in the Holy Ghost:
9. I believe in the Holy Catholic Church: the Communion of Saints:
10. The forgiveness of sins:
11. The resurrection of the body:
12. And the life everlasting. Amen.

That first line was, of course, understood literally, as this was the pre-Copernican, Ptolemaic, geocentric world in which the center of the universe was Earth, which was God's "footstool," as God himself states in Isaiah 66:1. There was no plurality of worlds according to the medieval mindset. Nor were there "different motions" of Earth, as John Milton would put it, even post-Copernicus, in *Paradise Lost* Book 8. But cosmic space existed fully. It was mysterious—God's very abode. It could be pondered by the mind no more than it could be seen with human eyes. Twelfth-century people knew the universe in basically the same way that the authors of the psalms had known it.

The Apostles' Creed was the beginning of what every Christian knew of the faith. *Credo in Deum Patrem omnipotentem* . . . Francis and Elias would have repeated the Creed so many times that knowing it by heart was simple and natural; it was also obligatory. According to tradition, each of the twelve apostles of

Christ contributed one article to the statement of belief. Illuminations abounded in manuscripts depicting the twelve faces— Andrew, James, John, Peter, Bartholomew, etc.—each attached to one. Four centuries before Francis, one popular preface to the Creed explained it as "a token of the Catholic faith, a sacramental oath of the eternal religion. Therefore prepare your senses suitably with all reverence; listen to the Creed that the Holy Catholic Church has passed down to you today in the mother tongue."[4] No insubstantial catechesis.

The resounding of Church teachings in the heart and mind was Francis and Elias's real schooling. Memory was the prime virtue of understanding. St. Benedict's famous Rule instructed monks to read "in a low voice" while doing their daily spiritual reading, so as to build their memory stores. Throughout antiquity and the Middle Ages, to read invariably meant speaking the words aloud, and spiritual reading was usually directed at schooling the memory. On one occasion much later in his life when he lay ill, Francis was asked by a friar, likely Elias, whether he'd like to hear read aloud a passage from one of the Hebrew prophets. Francis declined, saying, "It is good to read Holy Scripture and seek God's word for us there. For me, though, I've already memorized so much that I have more than enough to meditate upon and turn over in my mind."[5] Today, imagination, creativity, and easy access to facts and data have replaced memory as the primary mark of learning.

The Seven Virtues, and their ability to overcome human tendencies toward the Seven Deadly Sins, were also central to the youthful education of young men such as Francis and Elias. They knew by heart:

Benevolentia (kindness)	*Invidia* (envy)
Caritas (charity)	*Avaritia* (greed)

Castitas (chastity)	*Luxuria* (lust)
Humilitas (humility)	*Superbia* (pride)
Industria (diligence)	*Acedia* (sloth)
Patientia (patience)	*Ira* (wrath)
Temperantia (temperance)	*Gula* (gluttony)

Then there was the importance of participating in the sacraments through the Church—beginning at birth with baptism, continuing through confirmation as a young teenager, followed by reception of the Holy Eucharist, and then two options: matrimony or holy orders. Francis "split the difference," so to speak, when he passed the essential age to decide between that last pair and instead became a friar, which hadn't previously been an accepted alternative.

The Fourth Lateran Council in 1215 would reiterate the importance of the doctrinal statements in the Creed, urging the clergy to teach them often and in detail. The bishops in Rome also made sure that both the faithful and their clergy were reminded of the centrality of the assembly and its sacraments in the spiritual life of a Catholic. Later, these themes became the essence of Francis's 1213 pastoral letter, "My First Recommendation to the Faithful."

———— ☙ ————

Which raises a question: From where did Friar Francis take his authority to preach? Whom did he recognize and acknowledge as his spiritual elders? A monk looks to his abbot in order to know God's direction for his life—but Francis was not a monk. A priest looks to his bishop—but Francis was not a priest. Yet, as we will see in chapter 12, by 1208–1209 he began to preach to the people of Assisi. He did this with the blessing of Bishop Guido of Assisi, who had been assigned to the diocese in 1204. Guido permitted Francis to preach first at San Giorgio and soon thereafter also from other pulpits in town.[6]

But Francis was also taking part in a lively tradition of lay vernacular preaching throughout western Christendom at that time. With vernacular preaching came popular access to theology, just one example of the oral culture of the Middle Ages (something that changed quickly a few hundred years later with the invention of the printing press). Most clergy were wary of lay preaching because the popularity of a lay preacher's exhortations in the language of daily life usually outshone the reception of a local bishop or priest's Latin homilies. But Guido was a self-assured man who knew a heart for God when he met one, and he nurtured it in Francis. Still, the trust that he placed in the young would-be friar was unnerving to many of his colleagues in those first days.

It would never occur to us to think of Francis as arrogant, but he was never theologically trained, so surely he was at least presumptuous to "hear" God when he was alone, without reference to others, and act without asking those experienced in such matters what to do. "The Lord gave me . . . the ability to do penance," he later wrote in his autobiographical "Testament." Then, "The Lord gave me a faith in churches." And then, "God gave me brothers. No one else showed me what I was supposed to do; but the Most High revealed to me that I should live according to the ways of the Gospel."

Francis's presumption, if it was that, also had precedents. Many hermits, penitents, and reformers—some heretical, others saints—had taken a similar approach in the century before him. Norbert of Xanten, who later became a bishop and a saint, was once asked where he got his authority to preach; he responded by pointing to the manner of his life—the charity and poverty that marked his existence. His Gospel living was the source of his authority. Similarly, Stephen of Muret, who would found the Order of Grandmont and also become a saint, once replied to an accuser who wanted to know to which religious order he belonged: "I am of the order of apostles."[7]

Unlike most serious religious people in his day, Francis didn't value education—which means he didn't think of rhetoric, grammar, theology, or any of the late medieval "sciences" as important. And as is well known, he basically forbade his early followers from theological study. Education was not for them, who were to be "little brothers." Nor was the owning of books. Although he inspired many of the great spiritual thinkers who followed him—such as Petrarch, who always carried his pocket-sized *Confessions* of St. Augustine—Francis believed that owning books would mostly make a man proud.

There is no indication that he read or studied like nearly all of his contemporaries in the twelfth- and thirteenth-century world of popular preachers. James of Vitry and Fulk of Neuilly, from the generation before him, were preachers schooled in Paris. Dominic of Guzmán, Francis's elder by eleven years and the founder of the Dominican Order, also called the Order of Preachers, studied theology for four years in northern Spain before his conversion, readying him for a life of poverty and preaching, some would say.

One reason for Francis's ignorance was probably purely accidental: the first universities were born in Paris, a world away from Umbria, and Bologna, still 155 miles north of Assisi. Another reason was temperament. Personality types in the late Middle Ages usually centered around physiological diagnoses, but Francis surely had some type of what we today call attention deficit disorder. He had trouble sitting still. There are numerous stories of him singing in the fields and in the Umbrian plains, on the roads walking between towns and provinces but none whatsoever of him studying. Books didn't hold what Francis needed.

One recalls the words of the late-twentieth-century Polish poet Czeslaw Milosz, who said, "I have read many books, but to place all those volumes on top of one another and stand on them would not add a cubit to my stature. Their learned terms are of little use when I attempt to seize naked experience, which eludes all accepted ideas."[8]

Theological students had their noses in Peter Abelard and Peter Lombard, masters of subtlety and erudition. They were reading Ambrose's commentary on Romans and Augustine's *City of God*. Not the Poverello. His contemporary Dominic's first religious act was to give away his theological books (to feed a starving family in Palencia, Spain), but Francis freed birds in the marketplace. He sang and spoke in ways that are deeply resonant with the ideas in these great works, but that is simply because he, too, lived with the words of holy scripture intimately on his lips.

Perhaps he was even dyslexic; that would explain what seems to have been his feeling of repugnance toward (or was it avoidance of?) newly written words. Francis knew passages of scripture as well as anyone; he repeated them easily and asked his friends to read them aloud to him, but he never once made reference to the burgeoning field of new writing that was exciting his contemporaries, living as they were on the cusp of the era of university education, cathedral schools, and the first great public religious intellectuals. To him, learning was organic and Gospel-centered.

CHAPTER 7

AVOIDING THE DIVINE GRASP

1201–1205, Umbria

If Thomas of Celano, our most reliable source, is to be believed, Francis was debauched as a teenager, even into his young twenties. His parents gave him everything he desired, allowing him to waste away his time and to ignore any responsibilities. Their boy was vain and foolish, a rich kid, an extravagant squanderer of resources and of his own life. They raised him with relatively little reference to the essential Christian values.

Celano is either harsh, brutally honest, or both when he summarizes Francis as a young man: "Almost up to the twenty-fifth year of his age, he squandered and wasted his time miserably. Indeed, he outdid all his contemporaries in vanities and he came to be a promoter of evil and was more abundantly zealous for all kinds of foolishness."[1] This would indicate that he wasn't innocent or just playful, wasting time as teenagers do, but doing wrong deliberately and leading others in similar rebellions.

His father, Pietro, was influenced by the anticlericalism common throughout the growing French middle class of the late twelfth century. To such a mindset, clergy were mostly corrupt, and the monotony of life was best broken with satire and comedy, often at the clergy's expense. For many, religion was simply a set of exercises one was obliged to perform and its sentiments and true pieties were entirely optional. This attitude would explain the poor reputation of Bernardone in the early literature about his son.

However, we don't all turn out like our parents—in fact, many deliberately run counter to what is modeled. This was not Francis, or not at first; he seems to have willingly followed the easy path set for him until at least his twenty-third year. He had an easy joy, an unquestioning way of progressing in the world. "Rome is humming my verses," the poet Martial wrote long ago, "and my verses please me!" Francis was just such a poet. He might have remained like this his entire life, without a care, had he not eventually fallen ill.

He composed and strolled, looked kindly and sang. He did not know the work of his Roman literary fathers such as Martial, but he shared their poetic heart. Southern France and northern Italy were known for cultivating the artistic temperament as well as rebellion of an ecclesiastical and political sort. Individualism was fostered as it wasn't anywhere else in western Christendom. So it was natural, given the subject matter most interesting to him, that while he was young, Francis was discovering Pan still walking in the woods. He was like Ovid without knowing it.

St. Augustine wrote in chapter 10 of the *Confessions*: "People are moved to wonder by mountain peaks, by vast waves of the sea, by broad waterfalls on rivers, by the all-embracing extent of the ocean, by the revolutions of the stars. But in themselves they are uninterested."[2] What was true for Augustine was also true for Francis, well into young adulthood.

Then came the appeal of war, strangely but powerfully felt by many young men, particularly in the West during the crusading era. The Frankish Latin Kingdom of Jerusalem, established as a result of the success of Pope Urban II's First Crusade, was defeated generations later, in 1187, by the great Kurdish sultan

Saladin. The Third Crusade (1189–1192) then failed in its goal of retaking Jerusalem. And once Innocent III took the papal throne in January 1198, he made it a primary goal to finish what was unaccomplished. An August 15 papal bull laid out his plans for what Christendom must do to retake its holiest places. Knights were poised and determined to defeat Saladin in the Fourth Crusade, beginning in 1202.

At twenty-one, Francis was the ideal age for a crusading recruit, but this may have been too much for him to grasp, let alone take on. His father also may have dissuaded him, knowing that his boy's constitution and upbringing didn't make for effective soldiering. Many of the men drawn to crusading were those with more native warring tendencies. Pope Urban had appealed directly to them in 1095, saying, "Let those who are accustomed to wantonly wage private war against the faithful march upon the infidels in a war which should be begun now and be finished in victory. Let those who have been robbers now be soldiers of Christ."[3] As the Fourth Crusade began, many of the men who gathered in the summer of 1202 in Venice to board five hundred ships for the East were from the regions of France well known to Bernardone— Amiens, Blois, Champagne, Burgundy—while relatively fewer were from the Papal States of which Umbria was a part.

Nevertheless, by the time crusaders were on their way to Egypt, Francis had joined Assisian forces in another, much smaller battle against neighboring Perugia. Joining this campaign was still a way to impress everyone he knew, especially his father. So in late 1202, Francis was in the Battle of Collestrada, standing alongside many—or rather, riding above most—of the boys he'd grown up with. The moneyed position of Bernardone's son was enough to afford him a horse. Within days, however, he was captured along with others and, perhaps due in part to that fancy horse, spent more than a year in a Perugian prison until being ransomed home by his father's money—an experience that sobered him, but only briefly.

"You will see: one day, I'll be worshiped by the whole world," Francis said to his fellow prisoners while in prison, endearing himself to no one.

Upon returning to Assisi, he fell quickly back into a pattern of alternating idleness, playfulness, and philandering. Vanity and excess were the surest ways of demonstrating his nobility. This was the boy Elias knew. Still, the time was short: 1204 would prove to be the year when his conversion would spark.

Francis seems to have fought against some mysterious illness during this time, and one suspects that depression may have been its name. The world didn't know of depression from the medicine of Hippocrates and Galen, just as it couldn't yet imagine demon possession in the characters in the gospels as addiction. Frequently, Francis is described as ill, without any specific symptoms. Throughout the year, he increasingly turned away from the old pursuits, even his old friends, as he lost his taste for food and foolishness.

By early 1205, feeling healthy again and still apparently dreaming of knighthood and honor, Francis joined another small army, this time of men from Perugia as well as Assisi, to support the pope in bolstering the claim of Frederick II as king of Sicily. In his first military excursion, it had been a noble steed that set him apart from others; this time he went off to battle with special armor purchased by his father. Francis was convinced that he would be successful this time, returning with honor to make something of his life. However, he made it little farther than he had before—only as far as Spoleto—and within days he was fleeing for home, either seriously ill, having seen a vision, deserting from the front, or all three. Perhaps he was simply unwilling to use the lance and sword. Everyone he knew was unimpressed.

"There's Bernardone's boy," murmured the people in town, once he returned. "Disgraceful."

CHAPTER 8

UNCLEAN LOVE

Spring 1205, Assisi to Rome and back

The year 1205 was the turning point in Francis's life, the period when his conversion burst into flame. After his return from Spoleto, old friends such as Elias could clearly see that he was not the same. Francis was losing his interest in parties and fun. He began to spend long periods of time alone—which was shocking—and he began to do penance.

At this point, untouchable people appear in the narrative of this confused young man almost like subjects in a recurring nightmare. Lepers seem to approach Francis more often than they do most people precisely because of the terror he feels when considering them—the way a dog jumps on a man because he can sense the man's fear of dogs.

Leprosy had been present in the West for millennia, but there was a dramatic rise in cases soon after the First Crusade. One Enlightenment-era expert sees the disease as punishment: "After the Christians had established new principalities of brief duration, de-populated the world, ravaged the earth, and committed horrible crimes, connected with both glorious as well as infamous deeds, they finally brought back leprosy as the fruit of their efforts." In fact, everyone in Francis's time believed leprosy to be caused by sin, and in the century of Francis's birth there were leprosariums in nearly every large town north of Rome.[1]

Modern medicine knows leprosy as Hansen's disease, a chronic infection caused by bacteria that affects the skin and nerves, leading to inflamed, withered, numbed skin; sunken eyes; and sores. Hansen's disease is not highly contagious: it is passed by fluid droplets, as when one person coughs in the face of another, but nearly 95 percent of people have a natural immunity. None of this was understood in the twelfth and thirteenth centuries, and leprosaria were run like asylums.

It was not uncommon to face a leper along the road, for they were forbidden to live in towns, and the experience was especially acute for someone as well-off, cultured, and sensitive as young Francis. Francis would shout his disgust at what he saw as human fragments and flee from their uncleanliness. One day, a leprous man stumbled up to Francis on the road, and Francis was so repulsed that he ran in the other direction. On another occasion soon afterward, a leper walked into Pietro's shop while Francis was tending it and asked for food or assistance.

"Get away!" Francis said, with anger in his voice that masked his fear. The man left and walked away toward the piazza. Minutes later, Francis chased after and found him there. He handed him all of the coins from his pockets so convicted was he that his earlier response had been wrong. From that moment on, Francis deliberately wanted to show affection for people whom society had abandoned. He was repulsed to the point of illness, and yet he wanted to love them. There was something about their suffering, pain, and loneliness that spoke to his sensitive nature—or to his own fresh needs.

Taking a leave from the shop, probably while Pietro was away on one of his trips, he left his older brother, Angelo, to care for things and traveled to Rome as a pilgrim. Throughout the Middle Ages, men and women undertook such journeys because a priest or confessor imposed them upon them as penance for mortal sins. Slowly walking barefoot to Rome while fasting was a common penitential "sentence." (In extreme cases, as described in one period penitential handbook for priests, the word *pilgrim* didn't even apply—the sinner was jettisoned, "like Cain a wanderer and a fugitive on the face of the earth."[2]) In Francis's case, this journey was most likely brought on by a *personal* sense of sinfulness, as an act of intense piety. Bishop Guido may also have suggested it.

Staying on the west bank of the Tiber, in one of the narrow, cobblestone alleys in Trastevere, Francis visited the tombs of St. Peter and St. Paul, where he left large sums of money as alms. He worshiped at St. John Lateran, Santa Maria Maggiore, and other Roman churches. He kneeled and prayed, seeking God's guidance, making confessions, and receiving the Eucharist at daily Mass. Most important of all, on this visit to the Holy City in 1205, Francis stopped for a day and begged beside people whom society had deemed disposable and ugly out front of Old St. Peter's. Here he was like the highborn young man who experiments with deprivation for only a day, feeling that he understood something profoundly when he probably didn't understand it at all—not yet. But he also exchanged his new clothing for the rags of a beggar, feeling that day what it was like to be looked upon as one with nothing.

Finally, back on the road a week or so later, he was approached by another leper. By this time, something had fully changed in Francis. He recounts the story himself; he does not tell many details of his personal life in his writings, but this one was pivotal. Instead of fleeing and shouting, Francis stopped and took the man's filthy hand in his own. He kissed it—surely as great an act of faith as any he'd ever attempted up until that point in his life.

"What had seemed bitter to me was turned into sweetness of soul and body," Francis says.[3]

He saw God in that leper. Francis suddenly perceived that each and every person, no matter how undesirable, is a representation of Christ and is to be treated accordingly. Christians have come to recognize this inspired perception as one of the most common ways of understanding the teachings of Jesus, although Francis's firsthand way of reaching it is not so common. This is the prime example of why Francis is the world's most popular saint and also the single way in which he is the least imitated. Francis came to understand that literally (in words Pope Francis preached in 2015) "to care for a sick person, to welcome and to serve him is to serve Christ. The sick person is the flesh of Christ." It is as if there should be another sacrament beyond the Church's traditional seven, one even more important than the others: the "sacrament of our neighbor," as theologian Yves Congar put it half a century ago.[4]

Francis seemed to place an extremely high regard for serving his neighbor in this way once he learned it in the school of conversion. Loving the unlovable was a matter of obedience that over time became, mystically and organically, a sacramental way of seeing and behaving. "Charity is beyond the resources of nature," Thomas Aquinas wrote in the *Summa Theologiae*. "We have it neither by nature, nor as acquired, but as infused by the Holy Spirit."[5]

CHAPTER 9

HEARING GOD

Summer and fall 1205, Assisi and Mount Subasio

Soon after Constantinople was sacked by the knights of the Fourth Crusade in 1204, small panel portrait icons began to flow into France, Spain, England, the lands of the Holy Roman Empire (oxymoron and myth if ever there was one), the Papal States, and the Kingdom of Sicily. Returning crusaders stripped the icons from churches and ecclesiastical houses in the Levant, carrying them back home. This influx inaugurated new forms of pictorial religious art in Italy as well as a new era of piety. The pope soon allowed that images could work miracles, as relics had long done, and people began seeking out images and praying before them.[1] It was into this fresh era that Francis stepped early in his conversion when he was twenty-four years old. We see him praying one morning all alone before a Byzantine painted cross icon in the ruins of an old church just outside Assisi.

"The history of human events, like intellectual and literary history, highlights certain dates; these are engraved in the cultural foundation of future generations, and sometimes in the memory of those directly involved, as fateful moments," wrote a recent biographer of Franz Kafka. This is not to suggest that what Francis heard in his heart and mind was heard by anyone other than him. Kafka's biographer continued: "At such 'historic moments,' people have the feeling of being carried on a wave and experiencing an unprecedented intensity of sensation and thought. The darkness gives way, and the long-sought path suddenly lies before them in full splendor."² It is to suggest that what Francis heard from God toward the end of 1205 while kneeling in the ruined early-twelfth-century church of San Damiano—a place all the more appealing to him because it was outside the city walls—changed much more than just him.

"Go and repair my house," Francis heard, either aurally or interiorly, one morning all alone. The words have been recorded but not the astonishment. One gets the feeling that he listened and then stood up. Setting to work almost immediately, ignoring the metaphorical angle of the imperative tense, Francis set about repairing San Damiano. His earliest biographer says, "He built a house for God; and he did not try to start from scratch, but repaired an old one and restored an ancient one."³ He moved out of the family home and began to live in the crypt of the half-ruined church while working to repair it. It was solitary work.

This is the point in Francis's life when everything begins to change in earnest. Failure and embarrassment—such as he'd undergone in Spoleto—have the power to make one pause. Talk, play, and frivolity had reigned in his life up until that point, but he now began to turn over a more receptive, active posture. How this happened, we don't know. Those are private, spiritual waters. As Ivan Illich has memorably put it, "The grammar of silence is an art much more difficult to learn than the grammar of sounds"⁴—and Francis began to learn to be quiet.

———— ✿ ————

During breaks in the work of church building (which would have been deeply therapeutic for a brooder), he trusted only one person to listen to the evolution of his spirit. That was Elias, "a certain man in the city of Assisi whom he loved more than any other because he was of the same age . . . and since the great familiarity of their mutual affection led him to share his secrets with him, he often took him to remote places, places well-suited for counsel."[5] Francis and Elias began to take long walks together, Elias listening and Francis describing his growing love for simplicity and poverty—"precious treasure," as he called it.

"Where are we going, Francis?" Elias would ask each morning.

"Seeking treasure," Francis would reply.

Elias was overjoyed by what Francis told him, Celano relays to us, which means that he was a true friend, willing to stay with Francis even through serious and significant change.

Francis would sometimes lead Elias to a cave he knew on the side of Mount Subasio, asking him to wait outside. He knew the teaching of Christ to pray in secret, and he would go in to do that, confessing his sins, imploring God, pleading "with all his heart that the eternal and true God guide his way and teach him to do his will."[6]

"What has happened?" Elias would ask when Francis re-emerged from the cave. But Francis never said much about those moments. He didn't yet have the words.

Imagine how the notion of beauty and treasure in a life of poverty must have sounded to someone like his father. What did Francis know of anything, let alone poverty? Bernardone wouldn't have been the only one to wonder this. And if, prompted by what he was now hearing from his son, he ever pondered what God wanted of him, Bernardone probably thought, *Doesn't God want me to flourish? Doesn't God want me to work hard in order to care for my family?* Many of his generation must have given thanks to God for emerging capitalism and free markets, seeing in them a kind of salvation for those living in involuntary poverty. What must they have thought when they heard a dirty-faced boy preaching about how beautiful it was to own nothing at all? Bernardone's son was dreaming of becoming what his father had worked hard to overcome.

There was a freedom in Francis's discovery of poverty, however: voluntary poverty came with the power to make a man feel more liberated than hard work could make him feel. Evangelical poverty—which wasn't something Francis invented—became central to the emergence of the individual in the West. A man might not have much control over his income and position in a town such as Assisi, but he had complete control over whether or not he kept his money and possessions for himself. This new way was soon expressed through prayer, devotion, and love, and Francis began to teach others that they could choose to fill their lives with similar pieties, emotions, and expressions.

Francis and Elias kept returning to that grotto on the side of the mountain, Elias waiting outside, Francis spending time inside.

"I am asking God to show me something," he would say to Elias upon reemerging. "I am repenting for my sins."

And every time Francis stepped out from the grotto, Elias noticed a different man from the one who had gone in.

CHAPTER 10

A FATHER PROBLEM

1206, Assisi

The divine message at San Damiano wrought other changes in Francis, centering on personal penance. Francis began to deny his body more seriously, not only removing the fine clothing his father had always provided but disdaining it and everything like it, dressing in abject rags, carrying a begging bowl, and probably mortifying himself in the manner of medieval hermits. He began to use the money he was accustomed to receiving from his father to feed the poor and satisfy beggars.

Like many influential men, Francis was affected by his father far more than by his mother. In fact, he never even mentions his mother. His father is remembered only as the one who gave him his name, *Bernardone*, which Francis seems to recall sarcastically, as a symbol of worldliness that was worth allowing to pass away. Still, the friends of Francis who wrote down the earliest source materials we possess had plenty to say about the impact of the father upon the son, and none of it is positive.

"Come on. . . . We will be good to each other. When you ask for my blessing, I'll get down on my knees and ask you to forgive me," says King Lear poignantly to his daughter Cordelia toward the end of Shakespeare's tragedy.[1] If the mature Francis ever yearned for such a reconciliation with his own father, we have no evidence for it.

Bernardone was an exacting, demanding man. Merchants of special goods—be it wool, wine, gold, or, in his case, silk and fine cloth—tended to be entrepreneurial and independent. They were also usually at odds with the Church, whose curia and clergy believed that selling goods produced by another was just like charging interest on a loan: usury, condemned by Jesus in the gospels, and universally denigrated by Christian theologians since the earliest centuries.

As Francis grew in spiritual desire, so did his attachment to penitence. This further embarrassed his father, who prided himself on wealth, position, and bloodline. He watched as his son publicly disdained all the things he treasured and fiercely protected. Then, Bernardone began to curse and ridicule his son when he came across him in town. Private, domestic solutions seemed exhausted, and he had run out of ideas. All he could see in Francis's change of habits was disgrace, and he was ashamed of his son. Francis's response to this provides a scene that could easily be taken from the pages of a medieval farce: we see him selecting a destitute beggar on the street and dressing him up to play a part in a play.

"Come with me, and I will give you some of the alms that were given to me," Francis promises the man, putting him in just the place in the city center where they are likely to cross paths with Bernardone. He puts a coat over the man's shoulders that resembles one his father wears. The man is just about Pietro's age.

"When you see my father cursing me, I'll say to you, 'Bless me, father.' You then make the Sign of the Cross over me, and bless me."

The props in place, Bernardone comes walking by. He looks in Francis's direction and begins to speak.

"Bless me, father," Francis quickly says to the beggar.

The old man then gingerly touches Francis's forehead, making the Sign of the Cross over him. "Bless you, my son," he says, just as he has been coached.

Bernardone watches this in understandable astonishment. Then, Francis turns to his father and says, "Don't you believe, sir, that God can give me a father to bless me?"[2]

One can't imagine these scenes without feeling somewhat sorry for Pietro. Yet he becomes even worse, at least according to the interpretation of Bonaventure. Bonaventure followed Alexander of Hales, his teacher at the University of Paris, into the Franciscan Order in 1243 when he was twenty-two. He eventually became one of Christendom's most important theologians. In 1257, at the age of thirty-six, he was elected the Franciscan minister general. Three years later he penned a new biography of Francis, which was published in 1263, decades after Celano's work had circulated. It was quickly named the "official" narrative. At the 1266 general chapter meeting in Paris, the assembly voted to actually destroy Celano's books so that Bonaventure's *Life of Saint Francis* (also called the *Major Legend* in the literature) might supplant all previous attempts. The friars believed that Bonaventure had utilized the most up-to-date materials, evidence, and testimony, and they wanted to rid themselves of controversies beginning to arise over competing interpretations. (Thankfully, some of Celano's books survived, but only in convents and monasteries outside of the Franciscan Order—fewer than twenty, mostly in Cistercian scriptoria!)[3]

In Bonaventure's telling, Bernardone becomes greedy and cruel, violent and selfish. Bonaventure introduces this narrative in order to downplay Francis's own faults in the relationship. A saint wasn't supposed to show obvious faults—but surely, by any objective standard, this son was disobedient to and disregarding of his father.

———————

In early 1206, Francis stole bolts of fabric from his father in order to sell them and use the money to repair his falling church. He rode with the goods to nearby Foligno, knowing that he couldn't pass them off in Assisi, and he sold the horse, too, walking back with the money.

There is no question that what Francis took wasn't his. It was Bernardone's, and yet he doesn't admit it as wrongdoing. "Francis was never a good moral theologian," as an expert once put it.[4] Neither were his first biographers, for they gloss over the incident, even turning it into an example of sanctity: "Arriving at the church, the new soldier of Christ, aroused by piety and great need, entered with awe and reverence. He found the poor priest, kissed his holy hands, and offered him the money, explaining what he hoped it would be used for."[5] It is ironic that this sequence of events provides the most iconic scenes from the life of the saint before his order was founded.

To his great credit, the priest knew better and refused to accept the money. Yet, under the influence of Francis's growing ability to persuade, the priest allowed the young man to take up residence within those walls. That is where Bernardone finds him a month later. It takes a month because Francis—described in heroic terms by Celano, who compares him to Daniel in the lion's den—was cowering in a secret compartment he built for himself. When he finally emerges, feeling a surge of new confidence, especially in his poverty of appearance, the real drama begins to unfold.

Bernardone, with the town looking on, quite literally drags Francis back home, locking him in what amounts to the family basement. It isn't concern over the money but embarrassment over his son's erratic behavior that moves Bernardone. Elias, too, may have believed that Francis was crazy at this point. In any case, a father was legally justified to control an errant son, and Francis lies there for days until his father leaves on a business trip and his mother sets him free. Then, when Bernardone returns, he castigates Pica and goes again to San Damiano to look for his son, who is there, emboldened by the church once again, declaring that this time he will not be moved.

Pietro's mind then turns toward the money and safeguarding his property. By law, he is entitled to recompense, and by nature, he desires restitution of his pride before everyone. At Pietro's insistence, Bishop Guido of Assisi—whom Francis has become accustomed to visiting for spiritual advice and counsel and to whom he is now somewhat accountable, having taken up residence in one of his churches—summons Francis to a public meeting. Also present is much of Assisi, in the Piazza del Vescovato, having heard from the local gossip that Bernardone would finally be confronting his upstart, much-changed boy. Pica is probably there, too. Guido presides because it is clear that the Church is now responsible for Francis since he is sleeping under its roof. People come to see a show and are not disappointed.

"As everyone knows, my lord, my son has stolen from me," Bernardone says.

But Francis does not admit it. There is a willful pride in him, a refusal to honor his father that goes unnoticed by those who want only to repeat the pious legends. The good bishop insists that Francis respond and that there be no more pilfering from his father in order to do the work of God.

"An unholy work it would then be," the bishop pronounces.

"Alright, then, let me return to you everything that is yours," Francis says to his father, removing all of his clothing.

"Take it all," he says, impudently adding without regard for Pietro's feelings what many already know he believes, "because my only father is my Father in heaven." He probably imagines that he is acting like Christ, who at thirteen said smartly to his worried parents, "Why were you searching for me? Did you not know that I must be in my Father's house?" (Luke 2:49). (Many Franciscans would eventually leave their parents behind in this bold, arrogant fashion. Salimbene of Adam quoted two other sayings of Jesus to his own unhappy father: "No one who puts a hand to the plow and looks back is fit for the kingdom of God" [Lk 9:62] and "Whoever loves father or mother more than me is not worthy of me" [Mt 10:37].)

The crowd must have been hissing and cheering. Always drawn to good theater, Francis continues to play his part with aplomb. He tosses the clothing at Pietro's feet. Guido, in his own embarrassment, removes his linen rochet and drapes it over Francis's shoulders. If we are to believe the fresco in the nave of the Lower Church of the basilica in Assisi that depicts this scene, painted fifty years after the events took place, there were other clerics present as well. Then, since his father wants him to be a man and start a family, Francis uses a literary allusion to describe the bride he was taking.

"I will run after Lady Poverty!" he declares, and suddenly, some in the square understand what Francis has been saying over the previous months.

"Have you seen her whom I love?" he adds, to no one in particular.

"I am seeking her who is wiser and richer than all others." Some think he is out of his mind, recalling and pining for a girl from his youth. But "Lady Poverty" has become the personification of the young man's conversion—toward God and away from his father's way of life.

Francis would do penance at the guidance of Bishop Guido, but beyond that, he would attend and serve only Lady Poverty in the future. She is, for him, the "queen of the virtues."

Perhaps he has in the back of his mind the fourth-century saint Alexis, the son of a Roman senator, who fled from his arranged wedding, saying that God and poverty were his true loves, and became a beggar. Just as theatrically, Francis "throws himself" at Lady Poverty's feet as he abandons his father, asking her to be with him, to be faithful to him, as he would be to her, and to be the path for him to God, just as the Son of God was born in her glory in that manger.

"I want to shout it to the whole world!" he cries.[6]

This "Lady" was almost one and the same in Francis's mind with the female image for God in the late Hebrew scriptures, Wisdom, as well as the Gospel of Christ embodied in the beauty and simplicity of the Blessed Virgin. She stood in opposition to the seeking after fortune that seemed to fill his father's heart. But that makes his outburst seem rational. Clearly, it was not, but rather a flood of emotion and feeling. French lyric poetry inspired this new calling as much as anything, a fact not lost on those who heard him that day, including the children who pelted the new fool with mud and stones.

A French *fabliau*, or "comic tale," also from the thirteenth century, curiously mirrors the situation between Francis and Pietro in Assisi. The ribald tale imagines a priest, the priest's lover, and the priest's mother, whom he detests because she is always nagging him for money and attention. The priest prefers to lavish his income and time on his paramour—"his girlfriend's everything to him, / he loves her more than kith or kin," the mother accuses him before the local bishop.[7]

The bishop tells her that he'll summon her son to come and answer the accusation. Scene two, then, provides the real parallel to the case of Francis and Pietro: Two hundred onlookers, both clergy and lay, are present, plus the bishop and mother. Before the priest arrives on the scene, the mother misunderstands the bishop when he says what he plans to do to her impudent son. In fact, she thinks her boy is about to face hanging. "She flushed, her heart began to pound," it says. So she quickly decides to abandon the complaint altogether and trick the bishop, instead, in order to save her son's life. "Your Holiness, so help me God,

/ my son is that fat priest you see!" she bellows, lying, pointing to a scapegoat with a collar in the crowd. The bishop then reprimands the innocent priest, who begins to protest but is quickly cowed into accepting any punishment for fear of excommunication. How different was Francis's outcome before the bishop of Assisi! The ridiculous tale has a sense of justice that is strangely absent in the pious legend, in which the ends justify the means.

There was more than a touch of the rebellious child in Francis's divine inspiration and in the recusant Francis's flaunting disregard for the Fourth Commandment. He decided that it wouldn't be possible to serve his both earthly and heavenly fathers at the same time—which troubled no one who retold the story of Francis in his own century. What is most disturbing is that he seems to have come to this decision entirely on his own, with the Holy Spirit as his only teacher. Even Pope Gregory IX, in his papal bull making Francis a saint after his death, would praise him for rejecting his father's authority. "After the example of our father Abraham," Gregory preached on July 16, 1228, referring to the story in Genesis chapter 12, "this man forgot not only his country and acquaintances, but also his father's house, to go to a land which the Lord had shown him by divine inspiration."

Francis's conversion was wrapped up in rejecting his earthly father and everything he stood for. It was an act of God as well as Francis's volition, and it was strangely a turning from love—the need to love and be loved—toward a desire for a love that is truer.

CHAPTER 11

DON'T TOUCH ME

1207–1208, in and around Assisi

On the subject of Francis's self-actualization, if we should even call it that, it is important to note that we have almost no written evidence. There must have been many interior monologues, but he left no musing letters or searching poems about his conversion in retrospect. All we have is this: "When I was in sin, just the sight of lepers was like acid to me," Francis wrote later in life, remembering those early days. "But the Lord led me among them . . . and all that was acidic turned to sweetness in my soul and body."

Then, "Shortly after that, I got up and left the world."[1] That he did when he left his father behind and soon found his way to a lepers' colony, where he undertook what would become the second part of his spiritual work.

The absence of other documentation about interior struggles is entirely in keeping with the customs of Francis's era. A person rarely ever reflected on parchment or paper. From antiquity to the late Middle Ages, writers such as Cicero, Augustine, and Hildegard are the exceptions rather than the norm. Francis's musings were in dialogue with what a Christian might call the movement of the Spirit within, and they went unrecorded.

But one could see it on his face, which was both resolute and dreamy. He had the features of a sensual Italian. Celano, who knew Francis firsthand, nonetheless modeled his first biography of Francis after famous lives of saints from the past. In such accounts, every man looks about the same. So according to Celano, Francis was "of medium height, closer to shortness." His head was of average size. His hair, black. His eyes, "moderate." Nose, "thin and straight." Ears, small. Teeth, "even, and white." Lips, "small and thin." And his build was described as slender and straight.[2] That's not what we see on the wall of the Upper Church of the basilica in Assisi where the famous Giotto fresco cycle has Francis standing tall, his hair almost blond, his countenance beautiful. But in the Lower Church, in the Cimabue painting mentioned in the prologue, we see a short man closer to Celano's description and probably more reliably swarthy like an Umbrian peasant. His eyes are large for his face, black, and matched by ears that are not at all small. His nose isn't thin and straight; it is a Roman nose. The mouth, however, is small. With his dark eyes, full lips, and angular nose, Francis wasn't the northern European that he appears to be in Giotto's idealization. And he was often smiling—we know that from the stories about him—yet we rarely see a smile in the art, completely distorting a proper view of the man.

Sometimes it is by following a ghost, rather than appearances, that we come to see what is real. Just ask Hamlet, who meets his dead father on a rooftop one evening and hears from him what Hamlet knows must be true, if only he can then "see" it played out. Francis's friends related to him in this way after his death. The Poverello had an apparition-effect on them, their memories, and their interpretation of real events, in ways that seem both true and false all at once.

The early biographers—Celano, Bonaventure, whoever penned *The Legend of the Three Companions*, and other anonymous friars who immortalized Francis with bucolic and fantastical anecdotes of wonder working—were not simply making things up from nothing. The raw material of Francis's life was from early on imbued with wonder and awe. If only, in addition, we had the notes he exchanged with friends like Elias or Clare or wrote to his mother while stuck in that jail in Perugia. These are all lost, tossed away without thought that anyone would one day desire to see their contents. Fantastic things *did* happen, and although the stories about those actualities were often inflated, they had truth about them.

From this time in his life, we have other scenes from Francis's conversion and echoes of the charismatic and romantic qualities of his early years. We see signs of Francis pining for privacy, occasionally leaving friends like Elias at arm's length, as he desired to spend more time alone. Time spent in leprosaria was time away from all his old friends, none of whom were willing to follow him to such places. Perhaps that was part of their appeal.

Thomas Hardy wrote in *The Return of the Native* of his character Clym, "He had reached the stage in a young man's life when the grimness of the general human situation first becomes clear; and the realisation of this causes ambition to halt awhile." Francis recognized the grimness of the human condition that sought only for what his father sought, and his ambition ceased, replaced by a new one.

He needed space and time in order to maintain his equilibrium. A converted troubadour, he no longer wanted to sing for women, nor did he desire a stage with crowds. He increasingly yearned for a stage with the One or the many, that is, the creatures with which he also conversed, finding in them a comfort that was not possible with human companions. These lines from Keats, written to Poesy, could just as clearly communicate Francis's confessional prayer in these hours: "Should I rather kneel / Upon some mountain-top until I feel / A glowing splendor round about me hung, / And echo back the voice of thine own tongue?"[3]

His self-isolation couldn't have been easy for his friends. And Elias, no doubt, was disturbed to be kept at arm's length.

A wolf is a pack animal, but there is also the solitary wolf that stands apart from others of his kind, for reasons ultimately unknown to scientists. Some are more aggressive and stronger than their brothers—otherwise they couldn't survive living alone. Others seem more lonely than aggressive and scavenge for their food, satisfied to eat the leftovers of the pack if it means they are able to spend time in solitude. Francis was this latter sort of lone wolf—often to the deep disappointment of his closest friends.

If Francis played an instrument, he played it, like King David, alone to God. He sang in the woods and by the riverbanks. The ascetic strain was strong in him in these early days, in the sense of Heraclitus's idea that the wisest soul is the driest one. Like a man who keeps abusing himself after a time of penance is supposed to be finished, he had difficulty accepting the love for which he yearned. What Rainer Maria Rilke wrote of the Prodigal Son, away from home and alone, was just as true for Francis: "Sometimes he would spend whole nights in tears. . . . How often he thought then of the Troubadours, who feared nothing more than having their prayers answered."[4]

His recognizing and rhapsodizing about beauty came a little while later, once this intense period of purgation was over. Celano, in his *Second Life* of Francis, tells us, "Often, without moving his lips, he would meditate within himself. He drew external things within himself, and they would lift his mind to even higher things."[5] This might seem impossible for a biographer to discover, but he did have the testimonies of Francis's friends such as Giles and Leo at hand when he was writing his account. Still, these sorts of experiences require no friends.

"Isaac went out in the evening to walk in the field," one of the oldest biblical texts reads, and the ancient rabbis really had no idea how to translate the word that has come down to us as *walk*. Genesis 24:63 contains the only instance of it in the entire

Torah. Many have suggested that the Hebrew word means "ponder" or "meditate," not just "walk"; with this interpretation, the verse tells us that Isaac was known to go out at night to be alone with God in the fields. So did Francis, and he was often followed by a friar, which is why we know about it.

He was trying to discern what was next. He abused himself with asceticism. Why should he be any better off than the lepers whom he cared for? Now come the scenes of extreme fasting as well as nights of self-imposed standing in prayer—he was discovered doing this one evening in Bernard of Quintavalle's house only a few months later. At other times, we see at second- or thirdhand Francis beating his chest in the way artists have depicted saints such as Jerome doing, with a rock in the desert.

It is tempting to imagine how the writings of one of the most famous ascetics—albeit from the Eastern wing of the Church—could have influenced him during this time. There is no evidence that Francis read the fourth-century saint Basil the Great, but the spirit and concerns of the two men are similar. Basil's creed, stated in the opening lines of his most famous work, speaks directly to what Francis was attempting to do in 1207: "'Come to me, all you that labor and are burdened and I will refresh you,' says the Divine Voice, signifying either earthly or heavenly refreshment. In either case, He calls us to Himself, inviting us, on the one hand, to cast off the burden of riches by distributing to the poor, and, on the other, to make haste to embrace the cross-bearing life of the monks by ridding ourselves through confession and good works of the load of sins contracted by our use of worldly goods."[6] Basil had the same "burden of riches" as Francis, and more so, growing up as he did in a wealthy, and richly Christian, home. There was much to be jettisoned, much to replace with Christ.

Francis probably visited the priest of San Damiano, whom he knew and trusted, for the Sacrament of Reconciliation during these months. But most of all, he continued to visit the caves of the Carceri in a gorge upon Mount Subasio, two miles above Assisi. This barren place—which he'd already experienced for years with Elias by his side—became a third home away from home for him. Everyone knew that hermits occasionally lived there, so the caves were a logical place for a lonely, questioning man to stay until he figured out what to do next. Also, no one needed to be compensated for their use. From San Damiano to the leprosaria to the caves he went.

The name *Carceri* means "isolated place" in Latin or "prison" in Italian. Mount Subasio can be "a fierce reflector of the sun," as Henry James once put it, praising the view of it from a place of repose below in the valley of Spoleto, but it is also a place of deep shadows.[7] Recesses upon a mountain that saw snow throughout the winter, they were usually damp, leaving them rarely occupied. As a twenty-first-century person might light a candle in an ancient gesture of a prayer intention, so Francis would visit a cave. He continued to take Elias with him and leave him outside while he went in to pray.

Thieves also sometimes made their homes there, and according to the tales of *The Little Flowers of St. Francis*, Francis was in frequent contact with these men and women. Not unlike Pope Francis who has in recent days said, "Don't let yourselves be robbed of hope, it is time for redemption,"[8] Francis often told them that salvation is about this life, not just the one to come. With their rock-hewn cells for sinners and ancient oaks full of birds, the Carceri were just right for Francis. Those caves were ten feet wide and six to eight feet high at the tallest points. When he slept there, he would lie down in niches in the rock.

Francis knew of other caves and grottoes in the lives of the saints. Anthony the Great, the founder of Western monasticism, lived in caves in the desert of Egypt. In places as diverse as Ethiopia, Bulgaria, and Greece, monks and hermits have sheltered in caves, sometimes hewn out of the side of mountains, often accessible only by ladders, pulleys, and baskets. Caves have also been central to religious reform more broadly, as when a young tradesman named Muhammad began to receive revelations from Allah in a cave called Hira outside Mecca in AD 610. St. Benedict retreated to a grotto in Subiaco around the year AD 500 in the mountains of north Lazio, forty miles east of Rome. Known to history as *Sacro Speco*, or "Holy Cave," it was simply an empty, deserted place. (In 1218 Francis likely visited the monastery later built around that cave, which explains the presence of one of the earliest fresco paintings of him upon its walls.) The legends of Benedict at *Sacro Speco* include him responding to temptation by throwing his naked body in thorns. Similar stories would later be told of Francis throwing himself into snow.

CHAPTER 12

FINDING THE REASON

1208–1209, Assisi

Sumptuous feasts were common at Bishop Guido's residence beside the church of Santa Maria Maggiore in Assisi. Pheasant and goose raised fat in Perugian pens were stuffed with mushrooms and truffles imported from Norman-controlled France. There was succulent veal glazed with honey and the best of the vegetables from local markets: turnip, carrot, and rutabaga—all prepared by a team of cooks and servants, functioning as was common throughout Western European private estates until only a century ago.

Also at the bishop's table was the aristocracy from town, elite imperial representatives traveling outside of Rome and Naples, and visiting prelates and emissaries from the Holy See.

Less than a quarter mile from the bishop's palace was Francis's childhood home, where Pietro would dine alone with his wife, Pica, serving him. Members of the rising merchant class would occasionally join Bernardone, and they, too, had plenty. These were men who were a few rungs down the class ladder from the bishop, yet they, too, ate to satiety every evening. Wine, oil, and bread were the essentials at their table and at the table of anyone who had plenty to eat and drink. In Bernardone's case, this included fine wines carried back from his travels to Champagne and Burgundy.

Just down the street was the recently restored church of San Damiano. Francis had purchased and begged for stones, mortared them together, and patched the holes. The work was rough-done (this was not a man accustomed to working with his hands), but Francis was moving quickly. He also began to eat quickly—when he ate. What a change this was for him for whom even leftovers from a lavish table were once not good enough. But soon after leaving his father's house, Francis began practicing the rule of eating whatever was available, without wanting otherwise. He would later tell his friars that they should be willing to eat what was put in front of them. So a potato might be eaten uncooked, with only memories of how one's mother once used them to make her gnocchi. Well-set tables were in their past.

After repairing San Damiano, Francis turned his attention to another falling chapel, San Pietro, located below the city and recently abandoned by local Benedictine monks. He enjoyed the physical work, taking his conversion, so to speak, into his own hands, adding muscle to what was otherwise stirring emotional stuff. The third chapel was of ancient, or at least early medieval, origin. Francis would rechristen it Portiuncula and begin to spend much of his solitary time there. The seventeenth-century, Mannerist-style basilica that now surrounds the tiny chapel has taken the chapel's original name of Saint Mary of the Angels.

Restoring Portiuncula, two and a half miles south of Assisi, took place "in the third year of his conversion," according to Thomas of Celano, putting it at 1207.[1] All the while, Francis was going about town and in and out of its surrounding fields and valleys dressed in a hermit's habit, carrying a staff. He was often singing in full voice and mostly songs from his childhood. Unidentified with any established religious order, he was his own somewhat unpredictable man.

Then something strange but understandable took place. As often happens, an idiosyncratic and personal sort of radical otherness or individual piety, perhaps counterintuitively, began to appeal strongly to others. Here was a genuinely unique man, one who might, in contrast to everyone else, have something worth imitating.

Over the winter and spring of 1208, Bernard of Quintavalle, a prominent Assisian, began to observe the young man he'd long casually known and his strange evolution of personality and purpose. One day, Bernard invited the now twenty-seven-year-old Francis over for dinner and asked him to spend the night. He knew that, otherwise, Francis would sleep on the floorboards of San Damiano or in a cleft of rock somewhere.

They dined together and then, after fixing up a room in his home where Francis might spend the night, Bernard lied to Francis, saying that he was leaving him for the evening. In reality, he kept watch over his guest through a peephole. What he witnessed next is what convinced him that the conversion of young Francis was sincere and his commitments real: there was Francis awake during the night, on his knees praying.

The next morning, Bernard surprised Francis: "I want to join you in what you are doing."

"You do?"

"Yes. How may I do that? What should I do?"

Francis was, to say the least, surprised. This was a man closer to his father's generation than to his own, and suddenly Francis was the teacher. He said to Bernard what was then his creed, "Sell everything you have and give it to the poor."

And so they did, together, that same day, on the streets of Assisi. Francis would thereafter refer to Bernard as his "firstborn." Bernard's decision to join him was significant since he came to Francis possessed of wealth and reputation—one of the most respected men in Assisi—and was willing to leave it all behind.

Next came Peter Catani, another well-known figure in town. Peter had studied at the university in Bologna and was a canon lawyer at the Cathedral of San Rufino in Assisi.[2] He and Bernard were friends and had talked about the work of Francis before either of them felt certain that it was genuine. The same day Bernard gave away all his goods, he sent news to Peter, encouraging Peter to join them as well. Peter did, and Francis would come to trust him, too, like a brother.

In the winter months of 1208, Francis was still attired like a hermit who lived in the mountains. This changed after April 16, when, together with Bernard and Peter, Francis heard a passage from the Gospel of Matthew read aloud one Sunday at Mass by the priest of San Damiano. They sat there that morning mostly uncomprehending of the lessons, which were, of course, read out in Latin. So the three men approached the priest once the solemnities were concluded.

"Father, may we speak with you?" Francis asked.

The priest nodded.

"Will you explain the gospel to us? We caught only a few words," Francis went on. Those few words they had understood were enough to tell them that this teaching was essential to their lives.

"I will be happy to, Francis," the priest responded. He knew him by name, but then everyone in town knew this strange young man. "Let me tell you what I read." And the priest proclaimed the day's gospel to them in plain Italian:

> Then someone came to him and said, "Teacher, what good deed must I do to have eternal life?" And he said to him, "Why do you ask me about what is good? There is only one who is good. If you wish to enter into life, keep the commandments."
> . . . The young man said to him, "I have kept all these; what do I still lack?" Jesus said to him, "If you wish to be perfect,

go, sell your possessions, and give the money to the poor, and you will have treasure in heaven; then come, follow me."

Francis took a step back, wide-eyed, his mouth open like a fish.

"That is what Our Lord says in Matthew's gospel, chapter nineteen," the priest explained. "Then there is this, which is related to it," he added, turning to a reading from Luke's gospel, chapter 9, translating again for Francis and the others: "Then Jesus called the twelve together and gave them power and authority over all demons and to cure diseases, and he sent them out to proclaim the kingdom of God and to heal. He said to them, 'Take nothing for your journey, no staff, nor bag, nor bread, nor money—not even an extra tunic.'"

Francis looked at him like a man who has suddenly remembered where he left a treasure hidden and now must get to digging. He was like St. Anthony in the desert who, according to legend, upon hearing the same scripture read aloud in church took it as God's word directly to him—he got up immediately and left to go and give away everything.

"This is all that I want!" Francis shouted too loudly. "This is what I desire more than anything!" But before he could thank the priest and run away, the good father added one more passage, again from Luke: "Then Jesus told his disciples, 'If any want to become my followers, let them deny themselves and take up their cross daily and follow me.'"[3]

Possess and carry no money, nor any sort of sack of things for later, including food and extra clothing. Carry no staff. Do penance and deny yourself. Take with you only what you wear, and keep it simple—this is what Jesus tells his disciples in Matthew 19:21, Luke 9:1–3, and Luke 9:23. Francis heard these words as if they were said only for him. He may not have understood the Latin, but once he heard it in language he could understand, as Celano says, "he committed everything to memory." That was the way of medieval men and women, and from that moment on, he knew those readings as he knew his own heart.

"This will be our Rule!" Francis declared.[4]

Within days, Francis had replaced that hermit's habit with a rougher fabric one—so rough that the wearing of it was both a rejection of sacerdotal clothing and another kind of penance. He essentially put on dirty sackcloth that was given to him, another discard from a nearby monastery. His leather belt was then exchanged for a simple cord. Shoes were traded for sandals; sometimes he wore them; often he didn't. Nothing on his person was permitted to be of a quality that it could be coveted by anyone else. He looked despicable, as he felt he should. "Dirty, contemptible, unlovely," as one contemporary put it.[5]

Then the fourth friar came. He was Giles, a crazy fool after Francis's own heart, and he arrived exactly one week after the original three discovered their Rule of Life. Giles, as we've seen, was also a native of Assisi. He had known Francis growing up and was another witness to his conversion. For a time, he was, like Elias, one of the old companions puzzled by the changes going on in him. But after Bernard and Peter formally joined in Francis's religious work, Giles walked out of the city through the iron east gate that leads down to San Damiano, looking to join them. Francis met him there and led him down to the plain—home to outcasts of all kinds—to the tiny Portiuncula chapel that Francis already thought of as their holy place. There Giles heard their Rule, such as it was; he, too, loved it immediately, and Francis declared him a brother. Francis would later refer to Giles as "the knight of our Round Table!"

Where was Elias? His parents had died, leaving him without familial commitments. And so—just as Francis's movement was taking off—Elias left Assisi to get an education. He was living in Bologna, unaware of all that was happening in his friend's life.

The men built a small, makeshift dwelling beside Portiuncula and called it their temporary home. There they established a base of operations, dressing and living as peasants but praying the Divine Office and going out into the fields and surrounding towns each day to share their Rule with anyone who would listen.

A few weeks later, Francis and Giles headed off to the March of Ancona. There was something about that region that seemed important to the two of them. Perhaps Giles knew of some ready converts there. With the Apennines in the way, there was no easy way then to travel from Assisi to Ancona, so they walked north to Rimini and then southeast along the coast of the Adriatic. Singing French songs along the way, Francis and Giles fed off each other's joy and playfulness. They didn't exactly preach (those days were very soon to come), but they continued to share their simple Rule with people wherever they went. Francis usually did the talking.

"We have sold all that was ours in the world and given the money to the poor," Francis would explain with a big smile, "in order to follow Christ completely."

Giles would stand to one side, gesturing to those passing by, saying, "What he says is very good. You should believe him."[6]

By the time they returned, three more men had come to join the group. John of Capella had watched Francis sweep churches in Assisi, asked if he could help, and then asked what else he might do. Francis had told him to give away everything to the poor, which John did, releasing his cows, but keeping one behind for his family with Francis's blessing.[7] We know almost nothing about Sabbatino and Morico, who are recorded in the sources as the next friars. By this point, they formed a merry band of seven, a jolly but serious group of men. And rather suddenly, they were noticed in town wherever they went.

Throughout this time, and while forming the principles that would guide his new religious life, Francis remained close to Bishop Guido of Assisi. The two talked often. At first, it was always at the instigation of the young man seeking an elder's advice. But soon the bishop was coming to see Francis.

Once, Francis was praying in his cell at Portiuncula when the bishop made the two-mile journey from his home inside the city walls down into the valley to see him. *Just a friendly visit,* he thought to himself, as he strolled into the small campus of cells that were now surrounding the little chapel and knocked briskly on a door. Without waiting for an answer, Guido stuck his head inside.

He saw Francis at prayer, and there was something about the way he was praying that was deeply unnerving to witness. "I couldn't move," Guido later recounted. Then, as he told it, "By the Lord's will, I was quickly pushed outside by some force and dragged backwards a long way."

"I was stunned," he said, and walking to greet some of the others who were standing nearby outside their own cells, he quickly confessed his wrong.[8]

CHAPTER 13

THE SLAUGHTER

July 22, 1209

Six months before Francis was to seek the blessing of Innocent III for his fledgling order, the pope began the Albigensian Crusade, his slaughter of heretical lovers of poverty. The Cathar heresy had become a thorn in the foot of the lion of the Church, and he would have no more of it.

From the time of the First Crusade onward, popes were as concerned about pockets of heretics in Europe as they were about removing Islam from the Kingdom of Jerusalem. In 1095, Urban II, former monk and prior of Cluny, desired a world in which the papacy was universally esteemed, honored, and served. That notion grew with each occupier of the Holy See and in Innocent III found a man of theological acumen as well as determination to return the papacy to its position of world leadership.

Francis's understanding of all things turned to the spiritual and to ideals. He had no politics. The Son of Man had said, "Blessed are the meek," but also "I have not come to bring peace, but a sword" (Mt 10:34), and that was confusing. Christ told Pilate during his Passion, "If my kingdom were from this world, my followers would be fighting" (Jn. 18:36). And Christ's example was the ultimate teaching, deeper than words: the Lord turned the other cheek, forgave, and prayed for his enemies.

Pope Innocent III was, by necessity as well as inclination and in contrast to Francis, a deeply political animal. He was also filled with a sense of divine mandate for protecting the Faith from those who might harm it or lead others away from it. There were cancers that had to be rooted out or else they would spread, and it fell to God's representative on earth to handle the task. Just as Joshua had done, so would Innocent do: "On the day when the LORD gave the Amorites over to the Israelites, Joshua spoke to the LORD; and he said in the sight of Israel, 'Sun, stand still at Gibeon, and Moon, in the valley of Aijalon.' And the sun stood still, and the moon stopped, until the nation took vengeance on their enemies. Is this not written in the Book of Jashar? The sun stopped in midheaven, and did not hurry to set for about a whole day" (Jo 10:12–13). One day in July 1209, it was also as if the sun stood still for twenty-four hours, enabling the pope's mercenaries to slaughter the enemies of God.

These enemies, the Cathars, lived in pockets that were difficult to reach, which was their primary defense. And had they kept their heretical ideas to themselves, Innocent might have left them alone, as several previous popes had done. But Catharism had grown in popularity in the decades leading up to that day.

Their teachings were always insidious and disruptive. Central to their theology was the way in which they belittled the Godhead, saying that since God can contain nothing that is not good, God did not create the devil or his demons. There are, therefore, two competing forces in the universe, each eternal and uncreated, and God is just one of them. God is the ruler of all that is spiritual and good, while the devil rules that which is evil—the material, physical world. This theological and existential dualism extended logically to the second person of the Trinity, causing Cathars to believe and teach that Jesus Christ was never fully man, for how could he be, since that would be to partake of the material world—the domain of the devil? In most respects, these ideas matched those of a religion with third-century Persian roots, Manichaeism—the heresy with which Augustine had struggled in the fourth century. By the late Middle Ages, these ideas were common.

Nearly twenty thousand crusaders—men recruited from throughout France, Germany, and Lombardy—set out from Lyons early one morning in late June and moved through Montpellier en route to their primary destination, Béziers, the Cathars' Languedoc stronghold. Béziers was a town of about twenty thousand people situated on a bluff above the River Orb about six miles distant from the Mediterranean Sea.

The hordes of soldiers surrounded Béziers on the afternoon of July 21, 1209, ordering true Catholics to hand over any Cathar sympathizers. Not a single person was turned in by his neighbors, and even the Catholic priests in Béziers prepared to defend themselves or to shelter the most vulnerable from what was about to take place. The following day, July 22, every single man, woman, and child in Béziers was killed by the sword. Even the abbot of Citeaux, Arnald Amalaricus, took part in the massacre. The infamous quotation "Kill them all. The Lord will sort them out" has its ultimate origin with Arnald, who responded thus on the eve of the Béziers murder spree to a crusader concerned about how to tell true Catholics from Cathars. The punishment of the heresy was divine, he believed, and the vengeance with which it was carried out wasn't simply justified but was divine as well.

In order to understand why a pope would feel justified in ordering the killing of these errant Christians, it is essential to grasp the medieval understanding of the soul: It was the animating component of every human body, an eternal spark of the Divine, and something as real as a beating heart or limbs with joints. A breathing human being possessed a soul as surely as it did skin and a face, and the health of one's soul was deemed far more important than whether one kept breathing. Souls preexisted bodies, and they survived them as well.

"They burned them with joy in their hearts," recalled a Cistercian monk who was there at Béziers.[1]

After Innocent III's death, Honorius III, who followed him, continued the fight against the remnants of Catharism with equal enthusiasm. Gregory IX did the same by initiating the Papal Inquisition in 1231, making it permissible under canon law for secular authorities to burn convicted heretics; this was aimed primarily at rooting out Cathars in hiding.[2] The second pope after Gregory, Innocent IV, was responsible for bringing the crusade to an end with the mass burning of 220 resistant Cathars at the foot of their fortified castle in the commune of Montségur, once again in the mountains of southern France. That was in March 1244, after a nine-month siege.

Francis knew what had happened in Béziers before he ever considered traveling to Rome to see Innocent III. He knew that thousands of men, women, and children had been cut in half, decapitated, and burned alive. His naiveté toward the Holy See had surely vanished. The haughtiness repulsed him, just as the lowliness of men once had. As Virgil wrote in his first *Eclogue*, "Rome carries her head as high above other cities / As cypresses tower over the tough wayfaring tree."[3] The cardinals and even the pope he now saw for what they were: men of various, conflicting priorities.

Meanwhile, more men came to join Francis almost every month, and he accepted every one. The brothers now numbered twelve, including Francis. At one point, looking at a crowd assembling to greet them as they approached, one of Francis's friends from the original twelve, Masseo of Marignano, stopped and turned back to look at Francis.

"Why you, friar?"

Francis ignored him, or perhaps he didn't hear him at first.

"Why you, Francis?" Masseo repeated, asking an impertinent question that only a friend could ask honestly.

"Why do they want to follow you?" Masseo said for a third time.

"What do you think?" replied Francis, finally.

"I don't know. You aren't beautiful. You aren't wise in the ways of the world. You haven't any nobility of birth. So why does the world seem to run to follow you, to listen to you, to obey you?"

"I think that God usually uses the lowliest of creatures to reveal himself to the world," Francis said.

The two men then walked on in silence, until they reached that waiting crowd. But Masseo would tell this story until he died. This was the moment he became convinced that the friar he followed was genuine.

CHAPTER 14

SKIRTING HERESY

Winter–spring, 1210

Sociologist Max Weber once defined charisma as a "certain qual-ity of an individual personality, by virtue of which he is set apart from ordinary men and treated as endowed with supernatural, superhuman, or at least specifically exceptional powers or quali-ties. These are such as are not accessible to the ordinary person, but are regarded as of divine origin or as exemplary, and on the basis of them the individual concerned is treated as a leader. . . . How the quality in question would be ultimately judged from an ethical, aesthetic, or other such point of view is naturally indif-ferent for the purpose of definition."[1]

Francis wanted no part of such exaltation, which is why Weber's definition works best for explaining the ascendency of someone like Adolf Hitler in early-twentieth-century Germany. But the question lingers: How did little Francesco Bernardone, the frivolous son of a cloth merchant, become *St. Francis*?

He hadn't yet formally founded anything. He and his friends were an informal gathering of committed, reforming Christians, nothing else. At the same time, only a few years after the pub-lic separation from his father, the Friars Minor were beginning simply and quietly as "little brothers," committed as *mendicants* (meaning "beggar") to voluntary poverty, chastity, and obedi-ence. They would take up no catechism but, from the start, had a detailed spiritual practice. Sharing the good news of their Rule, practicing simplicity in manners, and embracing a life of impermanence came first for them and would always remain as important as the threefold formal vows.

There is no reason why the average Umbrian observer in early 1210 would have understood those first efforts toward spirituality as distinct from the spirituality of cloistered monastic life, on the one hand, and from the other contemporaneous spiritual movements that were frequently getting into trouble with the pope and curia, on other. In these first months, there were many who thought of Francis and his friends as nothing more than the *gyrovagues* condemned as the fourth and most miserable kind of monks in St. Benedict's Rule. "These spend their whole lives tramping from province to province, staying as guests in different monasteries for three or four days at a time. Always on the move, with no stability, they indulge their own wills and succumb to the allurements of gluttony," wrote Benedict in the opening chapter.[2]

It was inevitable that, once Francis had gathered like-minded men around him, he took on a certain air of authority. Even before his efforts were formalized into anything recognized by the Church, Francis acquired a reputation as a man not to be easily contradicted. One reason for this is that authority used to attach itself naturally to men who were perceived to be in communication with God. But how surprising this transformation was in Francis: he went from village fool to instructor of bishops and priests in less than two years. He was still trying to figure out what he was doing, where, and how. And his behavior was still just as puzzling to those who knew him.

In the midst of singing spiritual songs and talking about his new guidelines for happy living, he would spend hours admiring the work of bees, praising their industry and the excellence of their work. In rainstorms, he would stop what he was doing in town in order to seek out worms on the road, forced from their holes by the rushing water, and gently place them back in the grass and soil. This didn't keep him from exercising that new authority, but it did mark his authority—and his new movement—as unique.

Above all, we see him in these early days as a man with a profound inner sense of the need for reform.

He was living at the little chapel (Portiuncula) of St. Mary of the Angels, in the Spoleto valley with his first companions. He would leave in the morning to walk into Assisi carrying only a broom. Sometimes he would preach to the people if they gathered around, willing to listen. At other times, he would walk into a church and stand appalled that the floors and surfaces were not clean. Lax about his own appearance and presentation but fastidious about the care taken for those places where the Body of God was to be consecrated, Francis used his broom to sweep up either before or after the sermon was done or without even preaching at all.

He was no monk, but this practice of his was some small evidence that he had absorbed something of Benedictine tradition, which—going back to Benedict's Rule—decreed that all things in the monastery were sacred, even the floors. Characteristically, Francis extended the principle by sacralizing a wider range of human experience than that which might be found within a monastery. Leo, Rufino, and Angelo—who were among the next men to join him—watched as Francis urged local clergy to keep their churches clean, reminding them of the importance of preparing a place for the celebration of the divine mysteries. It was startling how rapidly Francis had become someone to whom people might listen.[3]

On the other hand, once they became aware of his practices and religious work, there were some who were worried about what Francis was up to. He was impetuous, peripatetic, and exuberant in how he expressed, and urged his brothers to express, their new way of life. This reminded many of a range of faith expressions disapproved by the Church, from heretical movements to recently born liturgical expressions, such as the Feast of Fools on January 1, that were frequently condemned by bishops, abbots, and popes. When Francis rolled in the snow or danced in the streets—and he did—was he mocking God? Dancing is joyful, but it is also without any important purpose. Was he rejecting the discipline and decorum of the Church? Prelates rarely understood the theatrical qualities or potentials of the faith they practiced and preached.

———————

We don't actually know how much Francis was influenced, subtly and behind the scenes, by religious movements that flowered in the generations before him. The similarities of their charisms to early Franciscanism are, at times, uncanny. The Waldensians and Humiliati, both condemned by popes during Francis's lifetime, were two of the more prominent examples in the decades before Francis was born. In both movements, men and women practiced lay preaching, corporate prayer to interrupt the day's work, individual Bible reading, and banding together for private and public expressions of faith outside the walls of parish churches in ways that made the ecclesiastical hierarchy nervous. They also placed great emphasis on personal poverty as a duty and a gift rather than a curse or accident of circumstance. This was what troubled the authorities most of all. Commitments to poverty have always made the papacy worried; how could they not, given the ways in which St. Peter's successors steered the Holy See away from Jesus's praising of the birds of the air? Preaching poverty was understood as a critique, however subtle, of the medieval Church.

Waldensian founder Peter Waldo sparked his religious conversion when he gave away his property and possessions in 1177, just a few years before Francis's birth. In 1179, he and his first followers traveled to Rome, seeking approval from Pope Alexander III and the curia. Does this sound familiar? It is precisely the pattern of Francis's early conversion. The Waldensians called themselves "the poor men of Lyons" after the town in France from which Waldo came. Francis's insistence on the moniker *Friars Minor*, or "Little Brothers," is again similar. In contradistinction to Francis's experience, however, Waldo and his movement were condemned as heretical in 1215 at the Fourth Lateran Council—the largest ecumenical council in the history of Christendom, where nearly one hundred archbishops were in attendance, more than four hundred bishops, and at least eight hundred abbots of monasteries, in addition to the patriarchs of both Jerusalem and Constantinople.[4]

From the twelfth to the fourteenth centuries, the line between orthodoxy and heterodoxy was easily and inadvertently crossed. Peter Waldo, Dominic of Guzmán, and Francis were all advocates of reform and gospel poverty, taking the Christ of Judgment known and feared in the cloister out among the people as the Suffering Servant. But only Waldo was deemed a heretic. Personality and style matter as much as stated opinions. From the start, Waldo was a vocal critic of the Church and its teachings. He actually dared to quote St. Peter in response to demands that he recant: "We must obey God rather than any human authority" (Acts 5:29). In fact, all the heresies that were popular in the twelfth and early thirteenth centuries were characterized by a deep anticlericalism and zealotry and led by charismatic figures seeking freedom from the power of the Church. So for Waldo and his followers, personal poverty was combined with preaching against the excesses of the hierarchy, condemning their lifestyle as similar, even, to that of the harlot of the book of Revelation. They began their spiritual revival by disputing a Catholic dogma that they believed obscured the truth—namely, the doctrine of transubstantiation. In this regard, Francis's early years of formation were quite different from those of Waldo and the Waldensians. One can imagine that he learned from their mistakes. But he was also, simply, a simpler man.

Another contemporary prophet, the Calabrian abbot Joachim of Fiore, inspired all these reformers and zealots. Joachim was a pioneer and a puzzle.[5] His voluminous writings were mostly published during his lifetime, dictated to numerous disciples and scribes, disseminated throughout the monasteries and darker, contemplative corners of Christendom. His statements were marked by quixotic features that make for a man inspired by the Spirit—including contradictions often within the same discourse, a preoccupation with the end times, a desire to synthesize all knowledge into one system, and a lack of fear of recrimination from those in power, even when confronting political leaders. For instance, he preached that the importance of ordained clergy may be coming to an end and that what the world really needed was more contemplatives living ordinary lives of Gospel-inspired significance. Most of all, Joachim taught that the classic view of God taught by the Church's theologians (such as Peter Lombard in his *Sentences*) was condemnable because it didn't seem to allow for God to be intricately involved in human history. He insisted that God's ways can be known by human minds through examining history. Lombard won, and Joachim's ideas were also condemned at the Fourth Lateran Council.

Joachim died when Francis was twenty-one years old. One of Joachim's primary ideas was the notion that new orders of Gospel-inspired people would usher in an "age of the Spirit" to replace what was staid and stale in the institutional Church. He said that Benedictine monasticism had ushered in this era but that it was soon to find its fullest fruition. Old-new ways of religious life were on the cusp. There was a distinct monastic character to what was about to happen, and yet it would take some new forms and character. "A prophet foretells the future: he can also create it," according to one expert; men such as the Franciscans (the connection to Joachim's prophecy was not lost on Francis) rushed in.[6]

By the thirteenth century, the path of penitents, reformers, and sincere believers was well worn. Francis stands in a century-long line of individuals who claimed divine inspiration for doing something other than what was presented by Mother Church. Still, his life was different from the lives of these others, and the way of his Friars Minor combined the religious and the real in palpable ways that were easily felt by the men and women whom they served and lived among. People needed what Francis was offering, which was, above all, a direct experience of God, and he offered it in a way that took little or nothing away from the institutional Church.

Although he never wandered into theological discussions, Francis would make some provision in his spiritual "Testament," his last and most important writing, for distinguishing between true and false faith, since he knew that apostasy could be dangerous. In it, he asks his friars to be sure that each one of them says the Divine Office correctly and that those unfaithful to "the Catholic faith" be reported to the cardinal protector for their order. No doubt the Cathar heresy was on his mind. A reformer needn't fall into their pits, and the best way to avoid doing so was to steer clear of criticism. But Francis's own rediscovery of the Gospel unfolded without any specific reference to the canons, politics, and sacramental finery of the medieval Church. If he ever paused to consider these institutional things, we know nothing of it.

Elsewhere in his writings, he urges people to observe the sacraments and show due reverence to priests, also counter to the practices of the Cathars, who denied the relevance of both. The Cathars—who survived in many places in and out of southern France long after July 1209—were even ordaining their own deacons and bishops. Above all, Francis's close identification with the created world was his way combatting with life and practice the most prevalent heresy of the day: dualism. Cathar biblical interpretation began with dualism—identifying a spiritual battle essential to the structure of the world itself. The spiritual was at war with the material. A Cathar, unlike a Catholic, was taught to separate from creatures whenever possible. This is one reason, in fact, why Francis was not a vegetarian. To abstain from meat was to participate in the Catharist heresy, rejecting a part of the creation given to humankind by God.[7] Francis responded to dualism by moving far in the opposite direction.

What also always kept Francis safe from charges of heresy—which were never attached to him during his life or afterward[8]—was his continued respect for the clergy and for authority. He was skilled at avoiding the crush of reporting and accountability to those in ecclesiastical power, but he also never criticized them. In fact, he praised priests whenever he could, which made him and his friars quite unlike the Waldensians and Cathars. And the paternal relationship he would soon cement with the Holy See saved him and his friars from Benedict's charge of disruptive wandering, for which the Waldensians were condemned a generation earlier.

CHAPTER 15

SHOWING THE POPE

Spring 1210, between Assisi and Rome

Certain figures in history have persuaded others to join them, not by argument or intellect, persuasion or power of personality but by their willingness to be trampled for a cause. The great leaders of nonviolent twentieth-century movements, Mohandas Gandhi and Martin Luther King Jr., were such figures; their followers saw the forthright honesty with which they approached problems and how they were willing to die for their efforts. So they, too, put their lives on the line. This is discipleship by imitation.

Jesus seems to have had no such followers during his lifetime. The crucifixion scene and the thirty-six hours afterward, during which the eleven remaining disciples cowered in fear and uncertainty, demonstrate as much. Scholars have suggested that Christ's followers were confused and disappointed, having misunderstood the purpose of his mission and the meaning of his message.

There was no way to misconstrue what Francis was about.

By the end of spring 1210, he knew that he wanted to walk to Rome with his eleven spiritual brothers to see the pope. It had become necessary to ask permission to do what he had already started. His ministry was taking on a life of its own. As Joachim of Fiore had recently foretold, "Spiritual men will be called to descend from the contemplative to the active life," preparing themselves for holy work through prayer and ascetic practices but then interceding for and inspiriting the lives and souls of all people.[1] But Francis knew, as anyone involved in religious life at that time knew, to be careful—and to ask permission. So, spurned by nearly everyone he had known and loved, with a few new quixotic friends, Francis took to the road, intent on explaining his spiritual vision to the most dynamic, powerful, and brilliant pope that Christendom had seen since Gregory the Great: Innocent III.

The people of Rome, never known for being happy with their bishop-rulers, had only just welcomed the Holy See back in May 1188 in the figure of Pope Clement III. For half a century, popes had felt unsafe in Rome, and Romans had taken to sometimes violent rebellion for the right to elect their own local magistrates and officials. With the calm, negotiating Clement III, the Church finally and gracefully backed down, retaining only the appointment of a Roman governor as its exclusive prerogative. Elected in January 1198, Innocent III, Clement III's nephew, came two popes later.

In Innocent, Francis would find a sympathetic ear, if not an entirely kindred soul. Innocent had been a student in Paris. He was a theologically and spiritually sensitive leader who had written a treatise in praise of voluntary poverty. In fact, one of the members of the pope's curia even told of the new pope removing commerce from St. John Lateran upon taking the holy office. The anonymous author compared his pope to Jesus chasing the money-changers from the temple.[2] Francis probably knew little of this, but he knew what needed to come next.

"Let us go and see the Holy Father," Francis said to the small band gathered around him. "We will show him who we are and what we are doing. He will understand."

Cathars, Waldensians, and other, smaller unorthodox groups were running afoul of Innocent III at exactly this time, mostly because they were disliked by the clergy wherever they went.

The popularity of their lay preaching infuriated priests, whose flocks were the ones attentively listening. And then it was easy to assume that anyone preaching poverty was doing so for ulterior motives. They were pocketing what was being given, many supposed.[3] Poverty was a convenient weapon in the Church: if the clergy and prelates were not accusing the new spiritual movements of extolling poverty only to keep for themselves what was to be given away, these new preachers were blaming the Church and its hierarchy for robbing from the poor. From the start of his papacy, Innocent III worried about every new spiritual movement that espoused personal poverty as important for its members.

In the days before superhighways and trains, one traveled mostly on foot, following rivers. The Tiber, immortalized by the ancient Romans with a god, Tiberinus, originates on Mount Fumaiolo, 4,200 feet above sea level in the Apennine Mountains of what used to be Tuscany until Benito Mussolini redrew the boundary between Tuscany and Emilia-Romagna in order to make his home region, Romagna, the Tiber's source. The ancient river's yellowish waters gently make their way through Umbria, then Lazio, into Rome. The Tiber splits the city of Rome, giving it much of its character and much of its history, before heading out to the Tyrrhenian Sea at Ostia.

Bernard was there with Francis along the road by the Tiber. So were Peter Catani, Giles, and the others. They walked for two or three weeks until they arrived at St. John Lateran in Rome, asking to see His Holiness.

Theirs was a raw, unschooled spontaneity. Francis was more like a John the Baptist than a St. Paul. He lived his life a world apart from the universities that schooled men such as Innocent III on a silver-plated path to the hierarchy. Young men in Paris and elsewhere, usually promised to become bishops and cardinals, learned the arts of lecturing on fine points of scripture, disputing the interpretations of others, and preaching. Theirs was a liberal arts curriculum, steeped in rhetoric. Compared to these, Francis and those who joined him in the first few years were rough edged.

Francis had no intention of creating a school of thought, commenting on matters in the Church, or exegeting the holy scriptures; he didn't do much more than simply repeat the words of the Gospel. Most of all, he seems to have wanted to embody the teachings of Jesus and to welcome anyone who said they wanted to do the same. There's absolutely nothing theoretical and almost never an argument about him. His faith did not need explaining to anyone. It was quite easily visible.

When he wrote it was never in order to be read. He did not, in fact, write much; others were usually jotting down what he said. Francis was never composing. I imagine one of Francis's brothers queried him on the road to Rome, "We will really be able to meet His Holiness, Francis?"

"I hope so!" Francis replied.

"What, then, will we say to him?"

"We will tell him about our lives of poverty. We will tell him that we want to live as Christ instructed the disciples."

"Perhaps we should write it down?"

"Good idea, brother. Let's do that. Prepare a pen—and let's remember the sentences from the Gospel that were revealed to us."

Throughout his life, Francis's writings often functioned as instructions jotted down for his own purposes and to share with his brothers, who were trying to replicate his ideals in their lives. At other times they were a record of a joyful, zestful moment in their lives, as when Francis composed and sang a song on the spot. Or they were private letters; we have a handful of those. So his writings are more a biography of the order than an autobiography.

For his part, Innocent is a more complicated figure than he is usually portrayed. When Lothar of Segni was elected to the Chair of St. Peter on January 8, 1198, Francis was almost seventeen. A cardinal-deacon, an expert in canon law, and a theologian of no small reputation, he was thirty-seven, about the same age as Francis's father. He possessed a powerfully sincere commitment to personal faith. It has never been explored just how fertile the spiritual ground in the Church of ca. 1200 became *because of* this pope rather than in spite of him (as is the *de rigeur* perspective). As witness to this, consider the subtlety and practicality of his teaching to clergy and bishops, as their pastor, on how to pray. Francis did not—indeed, probably could not—teach this way: "Saying the prayers aloud should be combined with devout emotion, because, like a breath blown on charcoal, expression engenders devotion. Listen to what the psalmist says about this: 'I cried out to him with my mouth; I praised him with my tongue.' You, therefore . . . when you pray, stand before the Lord our God remorseful, humble, and devout, without movement, without laughter, without scoffing. Do not shout too much or hurry too much. Pronounce distinctly so as to be understood."[4]

Someone in Innocent's curia wrote an anonymous record of his sayings and deeds at precisely the time when Francis was walking to Rome to see the pontiff. It is full of biographical details but also hagiography, such as "while the [papal] election was being celebrated . . . three doves came down on the place in which the assembled cardinals were sitting."[5] There is also a story of Innocent's struggle to win over the Roman people and to consolidate his power within the papal lands through negotiation, truce, decree, ambassadors, and then force. When this account turns to spiritual matters, the author says that "among all the pestilences, he hated venality the most."[6] It was well known that the curia, clergy, bishops, cardinals, and even popes were for sale. Innocent shared something in common with the heretical groups he was then stamping out: he also wanted to clean up the Church.

The scene where Francis and his ragtag band meet this brilliant, relatively young, pope is one of the most unusual in Franciscan history, never portrayed satisfactorily on a fresco wall (or, yet, in the movies!). It is absurd to try to imagine Francis in the loggias of Roman basilicas—almost like picturing him posing in front of the Egyptian pyramids. Marble, gilt, ornamentation, Corinthian capitals, velvet, tapestries, and every sort of beautiful object seem apart from him, not his proper surroundings at all. If we need a cultural reference for imagining Francis before the pope, we should anachronistically look to the sandaled, toga-wearing Gandhi meeting Winston Churchill in prewar London.

Francis came with his first Rule, which was in fact little more than the simple pastiche of gospel passages that had spurred each of the first friars to turn their lives around. Some people found religious movements or institutions by starting with firm convictions as to how things ought not to be rather than how they ought to be; they come out of the establishment, convinced that change is necessary or values need to be rediscovered. That wasn't Francis. He knew nothing of what he was about to change so dramatically, and in that naiveté he unconsciously reveled. All he wanted was a simple adherence to the teachings of Jesus—almost as if to say, "Why is this so difficult?" And for the rest of his life he would jealously protect those original sentences.

They are lost to us. The original Rule hasn't survived. This is a fact of history and one that strangely receives little comment in the scholarly literature. Why wouldn't some of the early observers, if not the friars themselves, have safeguarded a copy? Why wouldn't it have been preserved, as were most manuscripts, codices, and books—even those of pagan, heretical, and foreign religious movements—in a monastery scriptorium somewhere? I can only imagine that the reason is practical: the first Rule was scribbled down on scraps, if it was ever written at all, and not committed to vellum or parchment. That would have been too costly. As Francis himself puts it in his "Testament" at the end of his life, "The Most High revealed to me that I should live according to the ways of the Gospel. I had this summarized simply, with some few words, and then the pope confirmed it for me."[7] The summary itself sounds ephemeral. Most importantly, the three gospel passages were lovingly taught and passed along as a sort of "oral Rule." So, the Rule of 1209—the one explained to Pope Innocent III that summer of 1210, called the *Proposition vitae* or "primitive Rule" in the annals of Franciscanism—didn't exist materially. Instead, it is the Rule of 1221, the one known as the *Regula non bullata*, "the earlier Rule," that is the first Rule for which we have records.

Innocent III was faced with judging whether the ephemeral nature of their Rule reflected a similar fleetingness of their actual commitments. The members of the papal curia who met Francis and the others surely regarded the men as of little importance for the future. But Innocent was wise. Franciscanism began simply and organically as a growing crowd of evangelical lovers of poverty. They stood in opposition to money and property. Poverty was their only real creed, and Innocent knew that such love and commitment could be dangerous—or useful—to the Holy See.

Conspicuous disorganization ruled, and as Francis and the other brothers encountered members of the curia in the loggias of St. John Lateran while waiting for an audience with the Holy Father, the officials thought, *Just another ragtag bunch. Only a matter of time before they try to turn people against us.* Cardinal Ugolino, Innocent's older cousin—who would come to know Francis and the Franciscans well in the years to come—was there, too, and also took notice of these unusual men.

When Innocent III received them, Homobonus of Cremona might have been on his mind, and maybe even his lips. Born Omobono Tucenghi in Lombardy, Homobonus stands out in the history of sainthood for two reasons: he was a married man and a layman. When Innocent assumed the Chair of Saint Peter, one of his first official acts was to canonize Homobonus as "the father of the poor." But Homobonus's championing of the poor is not the only similarity he had to Francis: he was also the rich son of a tailor and cloth merchant. And he used the inheritance he received from his father to continue their successful business, donating the profits to support those who were called to live a life of poverty.

When Innocent III heard Francis's story, he may have said, "You have told me who you are. Now tell me, what of St. Homobonus? Why not imitate him?"

"Our work is grounded in poverty, Father," Francis may have replied, "but there is more to it than just that." He had yet to articulate, even for himself, all that Franciscanism would entail.

A few of his companions knew, as Francis did not, what an unusual thing they were doing. For his part, Innocent III was bemused and charmed by what he saw and heard that afternoon. *These men might be useful in convincing others to take on more meaningful lives of faithfulness to the Church*, he thought to himself. Importantly, he saw in their hearts faithfulness, not rebellion. So he blessed their idealism; Francis took this blessing back to Umbria as a hearty endorsement.

CHAPTER 16

WHERE TO LAY THEIR HEADS

Second half of 1210, in the plain below Assisi

As a student of the Gospel, Francis did the opposite of human nature as much as possible. Despising power, eschewing glory, ignoring his appetites, and consistently acting against his own interest became essential to his creed. For Francis, the animal human nature was something to convert into something more glorious, more original. But he also displayed a strange combination of intense vanity and brutal self-honesty and self-reflection in these early days.

For example, one day Francis was making his way through the center of Assisi with many people following him, watching. Just then, a poor woman approached, begging alms.

"Take my coat, madam," Francis responded, removing it from his shoulders and giving it to her. That's fine, to be expected—but then Francis turned to the crowd that had gathered around him.

"I am sorry, everyone. I must tell you: That good deed I just did for that poor woman? I did it simply to find praise in your eyes," he painfully confessed, exposing his vanity for all to know.[1]

In the months after his return from Rome and the audience with the pope, Francis's mind turned naturally to building a community of faith. Standing in the monastic tradition, he was nevertheless a feeling and an opinion apart from the great communities that Sts. Pachomius, Basil, and Benedict had started with their own brilliant work. There were twelve in the spiritual brotherhood when they visited Innocent III at St. John Lateran, but by the time they returned to Umbria, their numbers had probably swelled to twice that number. They needed a place to live together that was deliberately poor and either free or lent; those concerns took them far out of town. Heading down the valley through a forest of oak trees (which Francis the old troubadour loved but which have long since vanished), they returned first to the dilapidated chapel devoted to St. Mary of the Angels that they already knew. But they were now too many for that place.

In the autumn of 1210, with the number of brothers growing, Francis knew that the group would need somewhere to stay beyond the lean-tos they'd hastily constructed from found materials around Portiuncula. They needed somewhere where they could not only sleep but also cook meals for a growing number and perhaps even pray together as an assembly when it was raining. Francis thought immediately of *Rivo Torto* ("Crooked Brook"); it was another ruin along that small road leading from San Damiano into the valley. A mostly abandoned lazar house, or lepers' colony, Rivo Torto became the would-be friars' new home.

"We don't need proper beds," Francis said. "Why should we?" Worn-out rags over chaff was how one of his friends later described the accommodations.

"It is easier to get to heaven from a hut than from a palace," he added.[2]

The men would head out each morning with destinations in mind and work to be done and wouldn't head home until darkness approached. Given that they might journey an hour or more to where they would spend the day—four to six miles, of course on foot—and then an hour home, the brothers returned (like commuters in any era) at dusk or after dark, except for in the height of summer.

They soon began to speak to people according to Francis's instructions. He instructed his brothers to greet people by saying "God give you peace." This language, which might be delivered and received banally today, was highly unusual in his lifetime. Some of the friars even complained that people were puzzled and upset upon being greeted this way.

"May we greet them in some other way?" they asked Francis.

"Let them ask about it," he replied, "for they don't yet know the way of God."[3]

Francis's preaching was of a sort that people were unaccustomed to hearing. What usually passed for sermons in his day were the largely incomprehensible Latin exercises given in parish churches and the brimstone-filled exhortations of traveling preachers, bordering on heretical nonsense, that most people tuned out like the negative daily news. Francis, in contrast, possessed fervency and yet joyfulness, heroic exhortation and yet inspiration. He, the sources all tell us, filled people with wonder. They wanted what he seemed to have.

Then he added songs to his sermons and encouraged his brothers to do the same. Like sugar to help the medicine go down, music was a way to usefully communicate and ease the acceptance of their penitential message.

"We are minstrels of the Lord," he began to say. "This is what we want as payment: that you live in true penance. . . . The servants of God must lift people's hearts and move them up to spiritual joy."[4]

What could Francis possibly have had to preach about? Dominic was founding his movement at this same time, also focusing on preaching, but Dominic was intent on raising up an educated cadre of preachers. They would soon become ideally suited for providing catechetical instruction and even inquisitional work on behalf of the pope. Dominic's preachers were well-schooled, often brilliant, decisive men. Francis's, in stark contrast, were deliberately "lesser brothers." They were quite literally and intentionally weak and small. Who would want to listen to them? What could they have to say?

That's just it. People listened, at first if for no other reason than that their preaching was so incongruous. Francis began to preach about conversion, about the Christian life. That he understood well. He also began to hear confessions. The brothers' joy and dancing were not just odd but contagious. "To dance is to celebrate the body, to discover a new kind of freedom which is spirit filled. . . . The healed person leaps for joy. This leap into the future is the essence of dance," an Indian Christian wrote not long ago.[5]

Much of what was happening was new, but not all. Francis did not create the friar, in contrast to cloistered monks, out of thin air. There were precedents. One was the founder of a small religious order active in Tiron-Gardais in northern France a century before Francis first preached in Umbria. A biographer of this Bernard of Tiron recounts his activities: "They went about barefoot; in villages, castles, and cities they preached the Word of God; turning men aside from the errors of their life, and, like useful and very powerful battering rams, aided by the force of divine power, they smashed down the walls of infidelity and vice. . . . And although they did not raise the bodies of the dead, they did what was even greater, that is, they gave life to souls dead in their sins, and joined them, revived, to the God of true life."[6]

There were a number of others, too—preaching, leading, forming small religious movements—in the century before Francis. Robert of Arbrissel, Norbert of Xanten, Stephen Harding, and Peter Damian are just a few examples. And there was Heimrad of Hasungen two centuries earlier. Just as peripatetic as Francis and as committed to poverty, Heimrad was distrusted by most of the Church authorities of his day, who were always trying to get him to join a monastery. Together, these men, whose reputations for penitence and a desire for spiritual reform would have been known to Francis by the time he returned from listening to the pope and curia, might be called the proto-Franciscans.

Meanwhile, at Rivo Torto, everything they were doing felt new.

One of the friars was assigned to cook for everyone. He knew nothing of cooking, which by the twelfth century was rich with spice and flavor and passed from mother to daughter. He was also repeatedly told by Francis to refrain from even attempting to make the food interesting. The sense of taste went unvalued. One might blame Adam and Eve, who, according to St. Jerome, followed their stomachs to the original sin committed at the tree of the knowledge of good and evil. Walking in the garden of Eden with God ceased as a direct result. So, for the friars, a cabbage soup was not to be adorned with turnips or leeks.

Francis rebuked friar cook one day when he saw that he was putting up beans to soak.

"Are we having beans tonight, brother?"

"No. These are for tomorrow. I find that if I soak them for a day they tender up nicely and are more enjoyable to eat."

"Absolutely not," Francis replied. "Take no thought about to-morrow, our Lord said. Throw them away," he said, applying the gospel principle—as usual—quite literally.[7]

Within several months, the friars began to outgrow Rivo Torto. Francis accepted every man who came as a new friar, and their movement increased rapidly. Lepers were even an active contingent, knowing that they, too, would receive assistance and care, living, as they often did, as permanent residents in this new spiritual community. Francis felt blessed by all of this, but the community required more space. They were sleeping almost literally on top of one another. And they missed having easy access to a chapel.

Real community requires proximity—something often forgotten in the twenty-first century when one usually experiences community as the whims of emotion rather than as a physical reality. But Francis knew that in order to really be brothers, the men would need to remain close together. He asked for help from Bishop Guido, who had nothing to offer, except to suggest that Francis talk with the abbot of the Benedictine monastery of Mount Subasio. The Benedictines owned Portiuncula, which Francis and his earliest companions of course knew well. Then, the abbot granted the group the use of that little chapel and its immediate grounds on permanent loan. It would become Francis's favorite place on earth.

Quickly, the brothers moved across the valley and begin to construct simple dwellings. The little huts they built around the chapel were made of mud, straw, and branches of trees. A stone or brick home was preferable and more stable and could easily become two-storied, but for these very reasons as well as the fact that Francis never expected to be anywhere for very long, he opted for simpler materials. "He taught us," the anonymous author of one early account recalled, "to make our huts poor and usually of trees, not stone, and to construct them of rough appearance, not only because he hated pride in dwellings but because he hated choice things."[8] They cultivated a hedge around the perimeter and declared Portiuncula the motherhouse of their new order. The huts where they slept and often prayed made their first convent. And Francis still had the Carceri caves to which he could retreat whenever he felt the need.

How different a cave or a little chapel was from the housing of traditional monastic life! Even in Benedict's day, in the early years of the sixth century, monastic houses already existed, yet Benedict did not choose them. Seven centuries later, both Portiuncula and the Carceri were a departure from the Benedictine and Cistercian monastic houses, so essential to the landscape and environment of medieval Europe; in these established houses, the use of servants—inherited from the ethos of the Roman Empire—had essentially been replicated by the use of lay monks to cook, clean, and perform every sort of manual labor.

Up until this point in his life, there is an endearing, almost dangerous, simplicity about Francis. *After* this point, Francis often seems to take on a subtle, somewhat stubborn acknowledgment of what was wrong about the late medieval Church. His attention to living out the Beatitudes is joined with attention to the other, sometimes contentious and even angry, aspects of Christ's teaching. One translator of Virgil's *Eclogues* has written that "Virgil's pastoral world sometimes . . . mirrors the disturbances of his real world, the Waste Land of the dying Roman Republic."[9] For Virgil, it was mid-first-century BC Rome, awash in anarchy and confusion, a time of civil wars following the assassination of Julius Caesar. For Francis, this Waste Land was a corrupt Christendom rife with wars and conflicts, many of them religiously motivated. Both poets had their moments of praising the pastoral and bucolic as well as of concern for human anguish and need.

CHAPTER 17

AN ANTITHEOLOGY FLOWERS

1211–1213, in the plain below Assisi

It was likely around this time, in the winter of 1211, that Elias caught back up with his old friend. He was one of those who had known the old troubadour and was more than curious about the new man he had become. Several years earlier, after spending those afternoons waiting outside of caves and clefts of Subasio as Francis went inside alone to pray and do penance, Elias had left Assisi to get an education. He worked as a notary for a time in Bologna and was teaching children to pray the psalter when he began to hear what was happening with Francis.[1]

He might have heard some of the story from Bernard of Quintavalle, another acquaintance from Assisi, when Bernard came to Bologna in early 1211 as a holy fool. Sent by Francis, "Bernard sat in the public square of that city and sat down where as many people as possible would see him. He looked the outcast. He knew that he was reproachable in their eyes. And the children were the first to see his unusualness; they began to mock him and make faces as if at a lunatic," recorded one text.[2] Within a few days, a Franciscan community was founded in Bologna.

After returning to Assisi and observing how many men were feeling drawn to Francis's new spiritual movement, Elias became convinced that theirs was actually serious and important work.

One afternoon around the time of Elias's return, Francis was walking in the diocese of Narni (today's Terni) in Umbria and arrived at the village of San Gemini. He began to preach in the city square, telling the people who gathered about the kingdom of God. Three of his fellow friars were with him.

When Francis was done speaking, a godly man from the village offered Francis and the others hospitality in his home. They gratefully accepted. When they all arrived at the man's home, the man introduced Francis to his wife, who was suffering from a serious ailment attributed by some local clergy to a possible demon possession. The caring husband urged the visiting holy man to intercede on behalf of his wife. Not surprisingly, Francis refused. He was often afraid of being noticed—or, to put it another way, of being at all remarkable. But there were some who saw this as a mistaken form of humility that stood in the way of doing what was right.[3]

It was true that Francis was often his own worst therapist, badgering his psyche to examine every motive, seeking to find something, anything, pure in it, and then often turning away. First, it was a turning away from family, from domestic life and the quiet experiences of living rooms; then he turned away from monastic life and its alternative securities. And throughout his life, he turned from heaven itself, postponing paradise, which he experienced in the moments of solitude that he permitted himself, only to turn back toward the world, wanting to find God there instead.

Here in the diocese of Narni was a sick woman, offering an inescapable aspect of God's world, right there before him. The people of the village joined in the pleading, for everyone knew of the ailment of the suffering woman and the reputation of Francis as one who could help. Finally, Francis relented by asking the three friars who accompanied him each to take up a place in a corner of the house. Francis stood in the fourth corner.

"Together," Francis said, "let's pray to God for this woman, asking him to shake the devil out of her! From each corner, offer up this prayer to God." This was Francis's way of involving all the friars present but also his strategy to give the devil nowhere to hide in that house. It worked, and the woman was cured.

Elias wasn't one of the three friars with him, but he heard about what happened; three months later, after Elias had come to Portiuncula and caught up with his old soulmate, Francis was again making his way through Narni and San Gemini, this time with Elias at his side. Perhaps Francis had forgotten about the woman or perhaps he was simply trying to avoid bringing attention to it once more, but the woman who had been healed called out when she saw Francis walking by.

"Francis!" she screamed.

Francis kept walking, motioning to Elias to ignore her. The woman (whose name we do not know), like the prostitute in the gospels, ran up to Francis and kissed his feet.

"You freed me; you freed me!" she said, weeping with joy.

At this, Elias took hold of Francis's shoulders and turned him around, insisting that he stop, greet the woman, and bless her once again, bringing praise to God for what God had done through him. This was a role that Elias would often play in Francis's life in the years to come.

———————

The years 1212–1213 saw the real golden years of Franciscanism, the flowering of its charism and commitment in Italy and throughout the western world. Portiuncula buzzed like a beehive with friars coming and going out in pairs on missionary journeys, doing their work in towns and rural settings, praying the hours, laughing, eating, and caring for each other and those they found in need. Francis led by a kind of divine inspiration that unnerved many around him.

On one occasion, while standing in a field with Elias, Bernard, and Angelo, he suddenly asked Elias to say something quickly and without premeditation, whatever the Holy Spirit gave him to say at that moment. Shocked, Elias after a couple of seconds indeed began to speak.

"Thank you, brother," Francis interrupted; turning to Bernard, he said, ". . . and now you?" Bernard then began to say what quickly came to mind, until Francis silenced him, too. Then Francis asked Angelo to do the same. This holy experiment was repeated at other times and in other places.[4]

Throughout these days, however, the brothers did not study together. Francis insisted that they make no provision for keeping or copying books. Some have called him anti-intellectual for this, and he was. He had no interest in the subtleties of theology or in speculating about who God is apart from what one discovers in life and prayer. It is easy to contrast him with two now-prominent figures from the century before him: Bernard of Clairvaux and Hildegard of Bingen. Both advised prelates, wrote theology, and sent letters to heads of state. By comparison, Francis was always a humble Umbrian boy. He found his contentment in other pursuits. Even when visionary experiences (which we know of from the accounts of others who believed they witnessed them) captured him, he—unlike the equally attuned Bernard and Hildegard—didn't describe them or use them to teach others.

He trusted his heart far more than his head, and in this he stood in the prophetic tradition of Joachim of Fiore more than in the rationalist mode of the Scholastics to come. A better description of Francis than *anti-intellectual* might be *antitheological*. Rowan Williams has recently used this term to describe the writings of the fourteenth-century English anchoress Julian of Norwich: "Julian's immense appeal to most readers is that she represents in some sense a theology that leads into contemplative awareness; uninterested in winning arguments and consolidating formulae, she speaks repeatedly of what she sees and what is 'shown.'" Williams goes on to say that Julian's writings are full of theological themes: she is aware of doctrine, and she is much more than a poetic or devotional writer when she speaks and writes about God. But Julian is antitheological in the sense that she never sets out to settle conundrums; in fact, to Julian the puzzles and paradoxes of theological discourse are perhaps "the result of our failing to grasp that the entire logic of salvation depends on the basic fact of unconditional and unconstrained love."[5] The same might be said of Francis. As the great medievalist of the last century Étienne Gilson once summarized the thought of Thomas Aquinas: "Theology is the science of the truth necessary for our salvation; but not all truths are necessary for that purpose."[6] If this is so, there were many, many fewer of these necessary truths for Francis than ever for St. Thomas.

Francis's teachings and emphases resemble those of the Buddha, two millennia and half a world away. In one of the more memorable stories of the Buddha—the parable of the arrow—a monk is deeply troubled by the Buddha's lack of response regarding a certain number of "unanswerable questions" regarding the nature of the universe and the ultimate meaning of life. "I will renounce all of your teachings if you don't respond," the monk tells him. But rather than capitulate to the threat, the Buddha explains that he doesn't intend to speculate about such things; then he tells a story about a man who is shot by a poisoned arrow and then spends all his remaining energy insisting upon answers to questions of who shot the arrow, where it came from, and what sort of arrow it is. In the end, the man dies. The point is this: life matters; speculation that doesn't relate to life is at best pale in comparison and, at worst, irrelevant.[7]

Francis was guided so much by his heart, rather than his head, that he intentionally spoke little. For example, other preachers and reformers contemporary with Francis laid out specific instructions on how to care for lepers, including how to preach to them. One of these was the French Dominican Humbert of Romans, ten years younger than Francis and the fifth master general of the Dominican Order. Humbert wrote and said things that wouldn't have occurred to Francis. For example, why go to see lepers? Because they don't come to sermons of their own accord. What is one supposed to say to them? Don't allow your afflicted condition to weaken your resolve for virtue. Suffer with patience, as we are told to do in holy scripture.[8] Prepare your soul and look toward heaven. In contrast, Francis tended to speak rarely as he ministered to people. The founder of a preaching order, he nevertheless acted most often in place of words.

Even in the area of what today is called pastoral theology, Francis showed little to no interest. Peter Lombard's *Sentences* was the theological work that most preoccupied students in the early thirteenth century, and Lombard's work was not entirely an armchair sort of theology; it remained relevant for centuries precisely because it was relevant to faith as lived in one's life. All of Book Four (there are four books in all) is devoted to the sacraments; to study it was to engage with questions such as how the sacraments were first instituted and why there are seven and then move on to more practical matters such as the roles of exorcists, acolytes, and deacons, and when a marriage begins to exist between a man and a woman. Still, one never sees Francis engaging such questions.[9] This is because, ultimately, one cannot read about something and do that thing at one and the same time.

It is one of the tragic ironies of Francis's life that this aspect of his thought and personality struggled to endure after his death. In fact, it all but died away. The mainstream Franciscan perspective became that of Bonaventure and Duns Scotus. Bonaventure was of the opinion that only a saint could walk in Francis's shoes and do what he did; so unless you were graced with the stigmata yourself, you shouldn't expect to be able to follow Francis to the letter of his rules of simplicity. Scotus, a Scotsman born in 1266, rhapsodized beautifully on metaphysics, praising the study of *ens inquantum ens*, "being qua being." He was also a realist, in that he argued for the reality of universals—like the "forms" in Plato's thought—saying that all individual expressions of universals have their meaning only through their participation in the perfect form of their ideas. Such a cerebral, heavenly approach was diminishing to actual human and creaturely existence, in Francis's view. There is nothing untoward about ideas such as Scotus's: he shared them with most of the great theologians of the Church, including Thomas Aquinas; but in light of the first five years of the Franciscan movement, it is surprising that anyone with Scotus's preoccupations could be cut from the same cloth.

Bonaventure, who was the real giant among early Franciscan theologians (as well as author of the "approved" Life of Francis in 1260), wrote a much-neglected classic work entitled *Itinerarium Mentis in Deum*, or *The Journey of the Soul into God*. This is the book of Bonaventure's that is said to be most "deeply impregnated with the spirit of Saint Francis." One reason for its neglect over the centuries by those who are drawn to the spirit of Francis is the simple fact that its author attempts to write about what Francis sought only in real life. This theological-mystical text sees Bonaventure literally ascending Mount La Verna in order to absorb the setting and spirit of Francis's mystical experience but then reproducing it in Scholastic tones. It is a work of speculation, "an intellectual activity of the higher reason beholding in various objects their relation to God."[10] But for Francis, direct experience of God was never an activity of the intellect—the mind—but rather a receptivity to human experience and an openness of the human heart. This anthropological difference is essential for understanding him, as compared to the theological giants of the Church who predate him and the Scholastics like Bonaventure who, in the decades after his death, shared his loves and convictions.

Any plan for explaining or duplicating Francis's essentially unique method of calling others to conversion in theological terms was doomed to fail. To paraphrase the twentieth-century Austrian philosopher Ludwig Wittgenstein, one should speak as clearly as possible about what can be expressed in words, but of ultimately ineffable things, it is best to remain silent. For Francis, as for Bonaventure, divine revelation and religious experience add knowledge. But Francis didn't feel it was appropriate—or perhaps accurate—to speak of this knowledge. And he did not journey to God in his mind, or at least he didn't speak of it. He never presumed to preach about how one might achieve ecstatic union with the Divine. His way was always to ask people to begin their journey of conversion, to follow the Christ of the gospels. What comes on that path is, for everyone, unique.

CHAPTER 18

THE WOMAN

1212, Assisi

In a journal entry from 1899, a teenaged Virginia Woolf mused, "I was thinking the other night that there's never been a woman's autobiography. Nothing to compare with Rousseau. Chastity and modesty I suppose have been the reason."[1] She was right, and what was true in Victorian-era England—the chastity and modesty part—was even truer in late medieval Umbria.

A woman like Chiara (Clare) Offreduccio wouldn't write about herself, nor would she have been taught to even think much about herself. We have letters from the hand of Clare, of religious advice penned to other women, but they throw little light on her own life and its radical originality in the matter of religion—which is unfortunate, for a high-born young woman wasn't supposed to leave hearth and home in the middle of the night to join a group of misfit men gathered outside town, as Clare did.

Clare was the daughter of Offreduccio of Favarone, a nobleman in Assisi. She was raised with great privilege and entitlement. In fact, in 1198, when Assisi was embroiled in riots between those with established wealth (the *boni homines*), and merchants (the growing class of *popolo*), Offreduccio and his wife Ortolana fled with the family across the Tiber to live in Perugia, fearing their position might be overrun by the peasant fervor in their hometown. Once the riots—the same ones that destroyed the Rocca Maggiore—were over, the family returned to Assisi with enough resources to acquire one of the most prominent properties beside the Cathedral of San Rufino. There was a clear demarcation in medieval Assisi between the upper and lower parts of the city and surrounding area, corresponding to the upper and lower classes of society. Wealthy families like Clare's made their homes in relative peace near the fortress and basilica in the upper city, behind protective walls. It was outside these parts of town, with those in perpetual need, that Francis consistently made his home after his conversion, and it was there that he would later be buried.

Clare was the nobleman's daughter. Francis was the rebel merchant's son. Surely he, then seventeen, threw some of the rocks during those 1198 riots. At the same time, she, even at age four, began to realize there were conflicts between people and that her status was somehow at the center of the troubles. By the time she reached her teenage years, steered toward the right sort of marriage, Clare had become increasingly disappointed with what she saw of domestic life. When the theologians of late antiquity talked Neoplatonically about the "prison" of the body, enslaving the heavenly soul during this life, they might as well have been describing the lives of women in domestic shackles throughout the medieval centuries.

Most importantly, Clare was the daughter of Ortolana, a woman who understood what it was to be a pilgrim in this life. Of noble birth and means, she had visited Jerusalem, Santiago de Compostela, and the relics and holy places of Rome in her extraordinary desire to deepen her own faith. She and her daughters heard Francis preach in town when Clare was fifteen, sixteen, and seventeen. They all knew what Offreduccio wanted for his girls, and Ortolana reassured Clare that a spiritual life need not cease after marriage. Clare knew as much, watching her own mother, and yet, stubborn and determined, she wanted something that still remained out of her mother's reach.

"I feel God stirring in me," she said to Ortolana.

"I know, my dear. I know."

What happened next was one of those blessed coincidences, if one may call the death of a parent a holy event. Clare's father suddenly died, and the disruption caused by his death made possible her flight in the middle of the night a few months later. Nearly eighteen and probably already pledged to marry, she arranged with Francis through an intermediary (Bishop Guido?), to accept the life that he was preaching about. She, too, wanted to know God in ordinary life. Her joining the movement appealed deeply to Francis's imagination, which was receptive to every way that gospel simplicity and evangelical poverty might upset societal norms.

Our imaginations quickly run to the sexual possibilities of a relationship such as Francis and Clare's, but the sources offer little to justify assuming a romantic infatuation between them—either before or after she arrived at the Portiuncula on Palm Sunday evening in March 1212. A century later, Boccaccio's *Decameron* would put the private sexual practices of late medieval men and women—including nuns who happily break their vows with priests, servants who have sex with their masters' wives, and monks and abbots who pray one moment and copulate the next—on hilarious parade. But that wasn't the life that Francis and Clare led. Sexual activity was simply unimportant to them.

There was drama, however. Clare's entrance into religious life was nothing short of cinematic.

She was accompanied by an aunt and another friend from her family that night, as they walked hurriedly from the family home beside the Cathedral of San Rufino down into the Spoleto valley. Several hours later—by then it was early morning—the men of the house, led by a furious uncle, chased after them. Ortolana had given her tacit permission; one imagines her watching from a window, praying with her rosary. But her permission wasn't enough. When the men came pounding into the

Portiuncula campus, horses sweating and weapons drawn, they were quickly surrounded by concerned friars with their hands in the air. No one needed to explain what was happening. Francis had known that Clare was coming, and hours earlier the friars had circled around the teenager while he welcomed her, prayed over her, and then cut her hair. Two of Clare's cousins, Rufino and Sylvester, already friars, were there looking on.

"Welcome our new 'brother,' Clare," Francis told them all with a grin. He called her a brother for lack of a more accurate and appropriate term. She was one of them as soon as she arrived and was tonsured—until a few days later, when it became obvious that having women live among the men wouldn't exactly work.

Her uncle shouted for her, and Clare stepped out of the little chapel. She looked straight at him and dramatically removed her veil, revealing her shorn hair. It was already too late.

When Clare's sister Catherine attempted to join her three days later, the men tracked Catherine quicker, caught up with her, and actually beat her until she was unconscious. Clare found her sister and nursed her back to health, giving her a new Christian name, Agnes, after the famously courageous virgin martyr-saint of Rome. Agnes became the second sister-brother. Then their youngest sister, Beatrice, arrived the following day. Ortolana had raised a spiritual brood!

When Francis and Clare looked into each other's eyes that Palm Sunday evening, they were sharing an understanding of the freedom that brought them together—freedom from what enslaved their parents. Like Francis, Clare wanted to do penance and begin a genuine life of conversion. Like him, she wanted to leave worldly pursuits and domestic promises behind. One thinks of the popular American monk and writer Thomas Merton, who toward the end of his autobiography, summarizes what it felt like, at twenty-six, to leave the world behind and enter the cloister: "Brother Matthew locked the gate behind me and I was enclosed in the four walls of my new freedom."[2]

What became the formally written Rule for Franciscan men in 1221 was in 1212 a succinct, memorized, internalized set of teachings from the gospels about poverty and freedom that Francis called their "book of life . . . hope of salvation . . . and key to paradise."[3] Is it any wonder that Clare and so many others ran toward this new way of life?

With three and not just one, Francis and the friars quickly found that they needed a place to house the sister-brothers. Suddenly, they had *women*. A few years later, Ortolana even joined them in religious life.

The tradition of "double monasteries" or "double houses" existed at that time within monasticism, particularly in Anglo-Saxon England and Gaul, but it had been mostly discredited in the West by the early thirteenth century. Although the Second Council of Nicaea forbade them in 787, they persisted in some places within Benedictine monasticism, with an abbot or abbess over a house of both sexes worshiping and living side by side. Later, in the fourteenth century, Bridget of Sweden would reinvigorate the idea for her new order of Brigittines, separating the sexes at meals, in church, and in their enclosures, but keeping them under one roof and one abbess.

But for Francis, Clare, and the other friars, the time they all spent as "brothers" was fleeting, probably only a few days. The considerations of the world crowded in, and everyone realized that women and men could not live together in asexual spiritual harmony, at least not in their time and place.

So after a few brief and false starts, Francis turned to the first church of his conversion, San Damiano, adding to the renovations he'd made seven years earlier what was needed to accommodate a small community. Soon, they were able to call it a convent. One can still see the inspiration and handiwork of Francis in the rustic, simple style of that first church he loved and made paradigmatic for his movement.

"I am *la pianticella* ("the little plant") of our Father Francis," Clare began to explain. She knew her gospel and was comparing herself to the mustard seed in Jesus's parable. The group of women who gathered around her became known as the Poor Clares.

Within a few years Clare and her sisters were obliged, by Cardinal Ugolino more than by Francis, to observe rules that were not imposed on the men. They were to be enclosed, for sure, but also not to walk outside except for on special occasions or if a pending disaster were to require it. Even the dead body of a Poor Clare was to rest within the walls of the convent, not beyond.

And the sisters were to live a life of religious silence—a rule instituted most likely "due to the clerical fear of female chatter. After all, these women spent a great deal of time together, away from male oversight. It was important that they did not talk, especially not about doctrinal matters."[4]

An iron grille separated Clare and the other Franciscan sisters from the outside world. Confessors and physicians were permitted to visit as required, but only through grates and slats. In some cases, foot-long iron spikes were attached to this outside grilling making it impossible for someone to come any closer to a vowed sister.

Clare responded to the restrictions with disappointment at being unable to participate in most of what drew her to Francis in the first place. She was unable to preach the Gospel and do most charitable work. By 1220, when Pope Honorius III named Cardinal Ugolino the official "protector" of what became the Second Order, the Poor Clares, the cardinal wrote a Rule for her that was mild by comparison to Francis's ideals, basing it on St. Benedict's Rule. This frustrated the true and sincere penitent more than anything else. Clare responded with years of pleading and prayer, even a hunger strike. She petitioned to at least be permitted to fulfill the prime aspect of the Franciscan charism: poverty. The cardinal eventually relented, and in abject poverty and rejection of worldly hope, she remained until her death a source of inspiration and a spiritual mother to the friars who were to oppose Elias's extravagances in the years to come.

CHAPTER 19

FINDING HIS EQUILIBRIUM

1213, Assisi

"Stand on my neck and mouth, brother, while repeating after me
. . . ," Francis started to say one afternoon to Bernard at the Portiuncula campus. He had committed some small sin and insisted on being punished for it. Bernard flatly refused.

"I cannot do that, Francis. I *won't* do that."

"By holy obedience, then, brother, I command you to abuse me!"

After further hesitation, but finally relenting, Bernard placed his sandaled foot upon the mouth of Francis just enough to be felt by his friend, but not so much that it would hurt him in any way. Francis closed his eyes, imagining some great blow, squeezing his lids tight. The other friars stood watching in stunned silence. There was a certain psychology at work here—an understanding of how the mind sometimes desires one thing even though the body pulls toward another. But it was just a typical day among the brothers of Francis, followers of Christ.

If they were not learning from Francis's words and example, they were watching and listening to other characters in the compound. The fourth friar, Giles, provided a lot of unusual experiences, never for entertainment's sake. He was as offbeat as Francis, only on different subjects. Giles spoke in rough, bucolic metaphor, learned from years spent growing up on a farm, of what it was like to struggle with temptation. He said, "Our flesh is like pigs that eagerly run to the mud and take delight sitting in it." And, another day, "Our flesh is like flies that love to wallow in horse crap." And "Our flesh is the devil's lovely dark forest. He doesn't despair of reaching us, so long as he sees that we still have flesh." He placed little hope in the body to do what is right without a great deal of help from the spirit.

"But that all sounds hopeless," someone said back to Giles. "What then is a friar to do in order to overcome temptation?"

"If we borrow an animal, we make as much use of it as we can. So should we do with our flesh. But first we have to divest ourselves of fleshliness."

"How?"

Giles's wisdom was always expressed in language that was homely, blunt, and brief: "By using whatever means necessary to correct yourself. A beast can bear heavy loads, and we must feed the beast well. But a beast will not go along the road correctly without the rod of correction. So it is with the body of any penitent," he replied. Giles learned these lessons, if not the language with which he expressed them, from Francis.[1]

The friars formed a merry band of men doing serious work. One might find Giles and other friars making baskets, giving spiritual direction, cutting wood, or preaching sermons. One of the reasons why so many people came to join them in their work over that first decade was that they made such a distinct impression.

If Francis envied other men at this time, the objects of his envy were neither monks in their cloistered cells piously mumbling from their prayer books nor bishops in their palaces. He would have envied hermits, who were free to spend most of their days under only the sky, in solitary prayer of the most personal, intense kind. His conversion seemed, at times, to be so complete as to have turned his personality completely around. He who had been an outgoing lover was fast becoming a man drawn to introversion and quiet. These desires intensified in him a few years after his movement was underway; he again had yearnings, if not to flee, then to be increasingly alone with God.

Had he made a mistake in taking on followers, like a mother hen with chicks? Now he was surrounded by brothers as well as new responsibilities. The privileges of monks he had always questioned in his heart, but a hermit might live according to the precepts of the gospel passages Francis had "heard" from God as essential for his life, and still be free to wonder. The stone cloister, the sacristy, and the scriptorium didn't hold much interest for his freer spirit. One also imagines that he would have shrunk under a vow of obedience that was strictly and daily tested. But the life of a hermit held out a different appeal: a hermit might be even better positioned than a mendicant friar to live out the precepts he was already composing in his Rule, without the encumbrance of spiritual brethren who could sometimes be all too present. Silence has its blessings; as the American poet John Berryman wrote, "I am so wise I had my mouth sewn shut."[2]

Had he made a mistake taking on followers? He pondered this question for weeks before doing what he knew he should do—and what the spirit of his Rule dictated he ought to do: he asked two of his friends for wisdom. One imagines that he selected these confidants carefully, which is the only evidence we have to suggest that Sylvester, the first priest to join the order, was among those he trusted most; and then of course he sought out Clare, who was always close to his heart. The story of his consultation with the two of them is told in *The Little Flowers*:

> He called Brother Masseo and said, "Go and find Sister Clare and Brother Sylvester and ask them to pray on my behalf to God, and to ask God if I should preach or devote myself entirely to prayer." Masseo did as he was told. Now, Sylvester

very often received immediate answers to his prayers and he did, this time, as well. He quickly said to Masseo, "Tell Brother Francis this. God has brought him this far so that a harvest of souls will come about as a result. Many people will be saved through him." Then Masseo went back to Clare, to see if she had received an answer as well. She had. She told Masseo that God told her exactly what he had told Sylvester. At this, Masseo rushed back to Francis.

At this point we see the value Francis placed on hospitality and religious ritual, despite the informality that characterized many aspects of his life and work: "The saint received him with love, washing his feet, preparing food for him to eat after his long walking." Francis serves his brother in these ways before he ever asks him for the word of discernment he has received: "Once Masseo was done eating, Francis asked him to sit with him in the forest outside. He knelt down beside his brother Masseo and said, 'What does Jesus want me to do?' 'He wants you to preach wherever you are, for God did not bring you this far for yourself alone, but for the saving of many others.'"[3]

Clare and Sylvester confirmed what Francis perhaps didn't want to hear: a friar was what God wanted him to remain. Nevertheless, Francis's response to this confirmation of God's desire was, characteristically, immediate. One gets the feeling that there would be no more moping about. Henceforward we see him impatient with any friar who prays too long in secret or neglects his duties to preach and work by pleading a special commitment to silent meditation; he saw such meditation as Yeats would later characterize it: "A man in his own secret meditation / Is lost amid the labyrinth that he has made."[4]

This was when Francis began to compose, by repetition in his preaching, what would become the first written Rule—not to be committed to paper for several more years. We know that its vision dazzled those who heard it. When Francis and the friars began going out in twos to preach in cities like Bologna, their simplicity, clarity, and precision about the meaning and purpose of a Christian life caught the sophisticated completely off guard.

As for the unsophisticated, the spirit of early Franciscanism revealed to them a way of joyful living that they never expected would be available to them; an active, personal faith that brought structure and meaning to everyday life outside a cloister or hermitage was a revelation. Until they heard Francis's gospel message, they had thought religion to be simply the meeting of obligations, which were minimal and without any real comfort or impact upon one's life. To hear that a depth of meaning was possible and that someone they respected might expect something of them often brought them joy that bordered on dumbness.

CHAPTER 20

THE FRANCISCAN
MOVEMENT IS BORN

1213–1217, from Portiuncula to Syria

"Alright then, let's go," Francis replied to Masseo after hearing from him the discernment on his behalf from Sylvester and Clare. Leaping to his feet, with Masseo running after him, Francis also grabbed Brother Angelo to join them. The three ran down the path leading from Portiuncula to the south with a spiritual passion that even they didn't quite understand.

It was then—just moments after Francis and Masseo had been eating together at table—that the Poverello first did something that would become iconic for his life. He would repeat the action, but never with the same spontaneity. Told that God wanted him to preach wherever he went, Francis led his brothers excitedly for three-quarters of an hour until they had almost reached Cannara, seven miles directly south of Portiuncula. He promptly stopped at the sight of the first audience he encountered along the path: a gathering of swallows. Francis began to speak while Masseo and Angelo watched in stunned silence. Telling the birds of God's glory, which of course they already knew about because they sang so sweetly of divine things, he related to them as kindred creatures.

"Sing, sisters," he told them. "Praise the Lord for what he has given you." And as he talked the birds seemed, strangely, to listen. After five or ten minutes of this, some citizens of Cannara standing nearby began, one by one, to observe what was taking place. Many of them, once Francis was done preaching, asked Masseo and Angelo how they could join the brothers in their work, even though they were married, raising a family, or occupied with financial responsibilities.

"Don't hurry away with us now," Francis said, overhearing what was going on. "I will advise you on what to do soon."[1]

From that moment in the spring of 1213, Francis began to plan the organization of what would become the Third Order: a way for men and women to follow the principles governing the brothers' way of life without necessarily sharing in all of their vows. After that first encounter on the road, the number of men and women deciding to become "Franciscan" became so great that Francis felt the need to stop their progress—or else figure out a way to accommodate them without tearing families and communities apart. If everyone leaves their nets behind, there is no one left to put fish on the tables, let alone raise the children. There are ways to live in solidarity with us, Francis said, without leaving your work, responsibilities, and families behind.

Besides, growth in numbers was never his goal.

"If it were possible," Francis said one day, "I wish the world would only rarely get to see Lesser Brothers, and should be surprised at their small number!"[2]

Many of the friars, including Elias, were surprised at this statement, until Francis explained that being poor involved resolving to be not only without resources but powerless in other ways.

"We are poor as Christ was poor," he said, "which means that we are humiliated, despised, rejected, small, insignificant—and if we cease to be those things, we cease to follow Christ."

Francis instinctively knew that the effectiveness of his spiritual movement could be ruined if it grew to great numbers: not everyone was cut out to live this sort of abject poverty, and people would not listen to the message of their preaching if their poverty was not complete. He and Elias would be at odds on this point in the years to come.

Francis preferred to keep Franciscanism, as it came to be called, tied to its gospel simplicity—a crowd of people on the way of conversion more than a spiritual movement with any organizational structure or planning. Conspicuous disorganization was the rule—except for the clearly laid out intention of not establishing anything definite.

The preaching to birds continued in this vein, a distinctive feature of Francis's unique charismatic gifts. Unlike other nature poets and singers who take pastoral subjects such as harvest time, milking, hearth and chimney, shepherding, pastures and ploughmen, Francis sang and spoke to and of wildness. He praised what was wild because it was what he knew and where he was. His nature preaching didn't stop with swallows: soon he was observed preaching to fields of flowers ("Praise the Lord, Sister Flowers . . .") and then in like manner to cornfields, vineyards, forests, and piles of stones.[3] Speaking of God to wild things may have seemed natural to him because he had no interest in the commerce of domestic or mercantile life, which he'd deliberately left behind. What was wild was holy to him in its simplicity, uncomplicated by human beings, and therefore closest to the Divine. He remained a man of the road, walking many miles every day.

At about this time, some of the friars began writing down and carrying copies of their Rule with them, even before Francis asked in the Rule of 1221 that they do so. It was wise to carry the Rule, for even as late as 1219 and in a place as familiar as France, friars were accused of heresy,[4] not necessarily because of what they were saying but because the Albigensian Crusade was still fresh in people's minds. Many Cathars had fled underground.

The friars were always careful, however, and there are no stories of any among the first generation being confronted by inquisitors. But their Rule did become increasingly definitive for what it meant to be a follower of Francis, which they believed was equivalent to being a Christian on the way of salvation.

One defining occasion, witnessed an unnamed friar deciding to carry a copy of the Rule on his person right up until the moment when he was murdered by a group of Saracens somewhere in Syria. Before dying a martyr's death, the anonymous friar was allowed to kneel before his companion (the friars always traveled in twos), which may have in fact been Elias, and confess his sins, measuring himself against the Rule's principles.

"I want to confess, before God and you, where I have failed in the light of these holy principles," the man began. And once he was finished listing his failings—centering mostly around a failure to keep fasts—one of the Saracens abruptly lopped off his head. Celano adds that this obedient young friar was a happy man during his life, "but finished even more happily."[5]

The order's missions to the Middle East had become central to their work by 1217, and after this traumatic event, Francis made clear his own intention of visiting there. So he sent Brother Elias to lead a group to the Holy Land. Only a most trusted friend could take on such an important mission for the future of their message of salvation. Within a few weeks of his arrival, Elias was made the first provincial minister of Syria.

CHAPTER 21

BROTHERS SHOULD BE LIKE MOTHERS AND SONS

1215–1217, in and around Assisi

In cool Portiuncula the community lies in darkness, the night office finished, the last candle long extinguished. Every friar should be asleep, or at least silent, in his cell. A bell is rung before dawn, calling all of them to Matins, but Francis, always with a touch of the disobedient son, is out walking. A boy friar is following him—at a distance.

This seems to have been a common experience, or at least it became an iconic one, for the tale appears more than once. It must have become common knowledge among the friars that their founder was rarely nestled in a cell for very long. Knowing him as they did, they would have considered Francis alone in a cell destabilizing. Theirs was not meant to be a well-ordered Carthusian charterhouse or Benedictine abbey.

To many friars as well as monks since Benedict, the cell was the warmest and most comfortable of places. There were stories of monks chaining themselves to their cells, believing that they would learn everything they had to learn right there. With only the sounds of a summer wind and the occasional nightingale, a friar could rest deeply in the short night hours. In the winter months, the additionally allowed wool blanket made emerging before that Matins bell unthinkable. Even for the original twelve friars, for whom poverty was to be exact and extreme, their cells were as near to a personal space, something to call "mine," as they ever possessed.

More often than not, Francis cut short his rest in the night to get up and pray like a monk—and to go out walking. He taught that a friar was to pray the hours of the Divine Office each day, but he often prayed the night hours away from his cell, off on his own.

As he stood in the darkness, he prayed the simple words of the Hail Mary, which he instructed the friars all to know by heart. One reason Francis advocated the Hail Mary was that he loved the genuflections and prostrations that were its common accompaniments. A friar could "do" the prayer, genuflecting with the words of the angel to Mary, "Hail Mary, full of grace, the Lord is with you," and moving to a full prostration during the prayer's second half. There was a cardiovascular quality to early Franciscan piety, and this is what we might imagine the boy friar observing when he spied on his master in the middle of the night not far from Portiuncula. He reported back certain things he witnessed in those dark hours, and many of them became legends of the saint.

There was a tug and shove within Francis when it came to religious community. He showed great love to his brothers and built small communities of friars wherever he went, but then he also often went out and avoided their company. "We must not ever live in large numbers in the same place," he once said. "It is more difficult to be faithful to Lady Poverty in a multitude."[1] This was one of many ideas that he was either testing with his life or learning by experience.

On the side of intimacy, "motherhood" developed as a theme in Francis's spiritual instruction. It was one of the ways in which the physical life—the experiences of the senses and the life cycle of human beings—became part of how he understood God. A century earlier, Bernard of Clairvaux had imagined Christ in similar, feminine terms. This might have been in Francis's mind: that Christ is like a mother, to use St. Bernard's metaphor, awaiting the embrace of her sons, as contrasted with the more masculine understanding of God the Father.

But more important to Francis was motherhood as it was demonstrated in the life of the one who bore Christ and sang the Magnificat. One expert has explained that "the role of Jesus as Mother for the Cistercians is exemplary, [but] for the Franciscans it is spiritual and mystical. Spiritual motherhood refers not to what Jesus has done for us but rather what we become when the compassionate love of God takes root in us."[2] This sort of spiritual mothering always shows itself in how one lives one's life. If Francis could see God in the face of a wolf, how much more he could see it in that of a mother giving birth or nurturing her children.

In a short message, "A Rule for Hermitages," from 1217 that someone fortunately preserved, Francis explains to his brothers that they should take turns caring for each other as mothers and sons care for each other. This metaphor is probably borne out of Francis's relationship with Elias and quickly becomes the model for the sort of intimacy expected in all of the brothers' friendships.

"We should live together in threes or fours, no more," he writes. "Two of us should be 'mothers.' And two of us should be 'sons.'" Francis wants to preserve the intimacy necessary for a friar's spiritual development. (The same principle made it into the Rule of 1221.) Then, alluding to the story of Mary and Martha welcoming Jesus in their home, he says that it is possible to take turns caring for the physical needs of the other, leaving time and space for all to meet spiritual needs, as well.

These are the teachings of a man who had been deeply disappointed by the relationships in his own family home, particularly in the way his father had related to him. Elias had watched as that disappointment played itself out years earlier. How telling, then, that Francis wants to find a way of caring for others that is exclusively understood as motherly. A brother who is a "mother" to "sons" is instructed to protect them from commotion outside the home they share together. And "sons" are to keep themselves in a posture of attentiveness, listening, and reverence to what their "mothers" say is good for them.

"Take turns in these roles," Francis instructs, "by mutual agreement."[3]

He had practiced this motherhood in his own relationships for years in caring for the sick. His nurturing, protecting, and consoling of those ill with leprosy was quite motherly. He would cradle them in his arms and love them as a good mother loves her children. "Little children, let us love, not in word or speech, but in truth and action" (1 Jn 3:18), a verse from the epistle at the end of the New Testament, would have made sense to Francis, had he known it.

There is even an account from Clare showing her own relating to Francis as "mother." The story is so incredible that it must surely be genuine. Clare recounted a dream to her sister Filippa in which she sees herself coming to Francis with a bowl of hot water in which to wash his hands. (One imagines that the friars around him, even without an understanding of germs, wished he would clean himself after caring for the sick.) In the dream, rather than accepting the gift of warm, clean water, Francis instead offers Clare his breast, saying, "Come, have a suck." She does so. Then he offers the other breast to her and she sucks again, remarking that it seems to be the most nourishing nectar on earth.[4]

Some, but not all, of the friars would have been comfortable enough around Francis—their sometimes stringent leader and founder—to comfortably call him "mother." Brother Pacifico, for example, was able to address him as "*Carissima mater*," or

"Dearest mother," holding and kissing his hands, seeking a word of guidance or some comfort in body or spirit.

On the other hand, Francis also looked to accept the love of a "mother" from another brother. "Elias was the one that Francis chose for the role of mother to himself," Celano tells us.[5] Only the most trusted and confident of friends could take on such an honor—and responsibility.

CHAPTER 22

WHEN IN ROME . . .

1215–1218, Western Christendom

We know it as the Fourth Lateran Council of 1215, when Pope Innocent III gathered thousands of cardinals, archbishops, bishops, priests, abbots, and dignitaries from throughout Europe, including a few monarchs, to discuss the future of the Church. It was a defining moment for western Christendom. To Francis, it was a gathering of experts with whom he felt only the simplest sort of kinship. Many of them were his brothers in faith, and he was there to listen.

Innocent's bull calling for the council was issued on April 19, 1213; the lead time required illustrates how long it took for word to travel and for people to journey across lands frequently embroiled in military conflicts, as well as the seriousness of Innocent's intended reforms. This, the largest-ever ecumenical church council, was from the beginning intended to be a watershed moment.

The attendees gathered at the Basilica of St. John Lateran, the pope's own church, on November 11.[1] Crowds outside, which included many who couldn't get in, were so immense that they resembled the surging, disruptive hordes that occur occasionally at today's European football matches. A few prelates who were caught in these scrums were even said to have suffocated to death.

"Before I die," Innocent began his opening sermon, "I would like to complete the work I have begun."

Either Francis was there in Rome or he received secondhand reports of what was said. If he was in the audience, he understood little, especially when they were discussing theological matters in Latin. But he was good at gleaning the gist of things. Canon 21, for instance, *Omnis utriusque sexus*, contained some essential guiding wisdom to be followed by priests and others who take spiritual responsibility for others. Francis would follow its teachings carefully, and he heard Innocent instruct that every Christian should make a confession and receive Communion at least once a year. Francis would go further, instructing those following his way—including members of the new Third Order—to gather congregationally once a month for a meal (the Mass) and to help out those among them who were in need.[2]

The pope also defined transubstantiation in the Eucharist with refined clarity, and as a result, Francis's own relationship to Christ's Eucharistic presence became a profound aspect of his teaching for the rest of his years.

Most of all, Innocent called for a new crusade, the Fifth, since the Fourth had ended disastrously and in dissension among competing Christian groups. He called for reforms among the clergy and in the churches that would leave fewer cracks in the masonry where heretical seeds may take root.

"I want to wake up the people of our nations," he preached to the thousands gathered. "Their princes and kings need to rise up and fight for our Lord. We must revenge the injuries done to our Crucified Lord—and liberate the Holy Land!"

There were fewer kings and princes there in the Lateran than clergy. "We priests may not be the ones to fight, but like the sons of Mattathias, the priests of old Israel, we can be instrumental in freeing the temple from the ungodly," said Innocent.

To bolster his case, the Holy Father told his audience that he was quoting from the book of Lamentations, but then interspersed the verses from chapter one with his own interpretive gloss. The pope said, "In the Lamentations of Jeremiah Jerusalem pitiably cries out to us for the physical passover. . . . 'Alas! Lonely sits the city once great with people! She that was great among nations is become like a widow. . . . Zion's roads are in mourning, empty of festival pilgrims; all her gates are deserted. Her priests sigh, her maidens are unhappy—she is utterly disconsolate! Her enemies are now the masters, her foes are at ease, because the LORD has afflicted her for her many transgressions; her infants have gone into captivity before the enemy.'"

Then he continued, "The holy places are all profaned, and the sepulcher of the Lord which used to be revered, is now defiled. Where Jesus Christ the only begotten Son of God was adored, Mohammed, the son of perdition is now worshipped."[3] The message was clear and urgent. Something had to be done.

In the midst of this portion of the opening sermon, Francis also heard Innocent quote a Hebrew prophet, using a metaphor that would become central to Francis's own work and ministry and, later, to the iconography of his life and legend. "The holy places in Jerusalem, and throughout the Holy Land, have been defamed. We cannot allow this to continue," Innocent repeated. Then he quoted from Ezekiel, chapter nine, verses three and four, a passage that depicts an odd, mystical scene: "Now the glory of the God of Israel had gone up from the cherub on which it rested to the threshold of the house. The LORD called to the man clothed in linen, who had the writing case at his side; and said to him, 'Go through the city, through Jerusalem, and put a *Tau* on the foreheads of those who sigh and groan over all the abominations that are committed in it.'"[4]

Francis had the Latin translated. As often happened, hearing the Word of God struck him with an immediate literal sense of application, even when the verse or the speaker was probably intending a metaphorical meaning.

Innocent went on to explain his view of the scripture, which was not original but had been offered by earlier Christian theologians including St. Jerome: "The *Tau* is the last letter of the Hebrew alphabet and has the same form as the cross. The cross was constituted as a *Tau* until Pilate decided to add his infamous inscription above our Lord's head." He explained that those who are marked with this particular sign will receive the mercy of God, for they mortify their flesh and conform their lives to the crucified Savior.

Innocent meant this as a statement of Christian salvation as distinct from the faith of those who were holding the Holy Land captive. He was also perpetuating a crusader tradition that preceded his papacy. For a century, crusaders had marked themselves with the Sign of the Cross, even prostrating themselves on the ground in cruciform shape before undertaking their holy journey with armaments. Witness the opening lines from "The Rite for Receiving the Sign of the Holy Cross for Those Setting Out for Jerusalem":

> First of all, the mass of the Holy Cross should be sung, just as it is set forth in the book of the sacraments, and once it has been sung, those who are going to depart ought to prostrate themselves in the shape of the cross, and let these psalms be sung: The Lord rules [Ps 22], May the Lord have mercy [Ps 66], Sing to the Lord [Ps 149], The Lord has reigned [Ps 96]. Amen. Savior of the world, save us whom you redeemed through the cross and blood, we beseech you, our God, to aid us. Kyrie. Christe. Kyrie.[5]

No matter how erroneous the notion may seem from this distance, the devout crusader—and there were many—looked upon this duty as a way of *imitatio Christi*, "imitation of Christ."

Some of the Church fathers suggested that the physical representation of the written letter *Tau* was no accident: as the last letter—or last "word," so to speak—of the Hebrew alphabet, the

Tau, like the Cross of Christ, is the Law's fulfillment. (*Tau* is also the last letter in the Hebrew word for "truth"; not a jot of holy scripture was considered incidental.) But never mind all of that; Francis heard the pope's words as an exhortation to Christians to mark themselves with the sign of *Tau* as their cross, and thus was the distinctive Franciscan cross, without a head post, born.

———— ✺ ————

The next few years would see hundreds of crusade preachers traveling western and northern Europe exhorting men to join the fight. One of these was Conrad of Speyer, whom Caesar of Speyer studied with in Paris earlier in the decade and then followed to the Levant soon after the Fourth Lateran Council was over. It was in the Levant that Caesar met Elias, whom Francis had earlier sent to the Holy Land to become provincial minister of Syria; Elias welcomed Caesar into the Franciscan Order. Caesar's reputation for preaching was well established before that time. Even before the turn of the century he'd spent years preaching among the Waldensians, persuading many of them away from their excesses and back to orthodox faith. He was impressed by their commitments to poverty and reform, however, and found the message of Francis of Assisi appealing.

It may have been in Rome at the council that Francis met the mendicant friar who would be known to history as both his parallel and his opposite: Dominic of Guzmán, founder of the Dominicans. The two were exact contemporaries, and their meeting has been immortalized in paintings and frescoes since a few generations after their deaths, but we do not know for certain that they were ever actually acquaintances or friends.

Celano has Francis and Dominic meeting one another, probably in 1220, at the Roman palace of Cardinal Ugolino. Other stories circulating after their deaths imagined Dominic stopping in Assisi to sit in on a general chapter meeting on his way to

Rome.[6] We can only suppose. Perhaps they even exchanged a glance when Innocent III declared that no new religious movements were to be permitted, saying "so whoever wants to become a religious must join an order that is already approved." The two men may have first met late one evening in the church of the Lateran, during the Council, while each was praying earnestly in the cool darkness, introduced to one another by the Virgin Mary herself, as a source from 1260 tells it. Regardless of when or how they met, they held similar commitments to poverty and preaching, but they were also very different men.

Innocent III's older cousin, Cardinal Ugolino, saw Francis again at the Lateran Council. Their friendship deepened in the years following, beginning a few years later, in 1218, when Ugolino was a papal legate in Tuscany and they met each other in Florence. Francis in fact asked to see the cardinal.

"I was just in Arezzo, lord cardinal," he said, "and there were devils assaulting our work from every side." Violence and civil unrest had upset Francis.

"There is trouble everywhere," Ugolino told him.

"So I am leaving with some of my brothers on a mission to the French," Francis said.

"I don't advise that," the cardinal said. "Not now. I think that you must remain close to home. There are too many bishops who want to examine your work and it is at greater risk if you are far away."

Francis was not yet accustomed to this sort of thinking and advice. He listened to Ugolino and returned to Portiuncula. For the first time since his discernment regarding the future of his religious life, when he'd asked the advice of Sylvester and Clare, Francis changed his course on the advice of another man. From this moment on, the cardinal was his protector and advocate in Rome. A year later Ugolino also became dean of the Sacred College—and Brother Pacifico, a singer whom Francis brought to faith and named for peace, went to France in Francis's place.[7]

Innocent III died the year after the council, and Honorius III was elected to replace him. Soon thereafter, Honorius noticed the rapid growth of the Franciscan Order and made inquiries as to what was behind it. The extraordinariness of Francis, their founder, and the fact that he seems to accept almost anyone, someone told the pope.

So Honorius wrote a letter to the Poverello. It was the first letter ever written by a pope to Francis, who felt the weight of the leaden papal seal as he cracked it open.

"I forbid admittance of anyone to the profession of your order, if first he has not undergone a test of one year," the Holy Father instructed.

This is not unlike what Pope Francis said to a room of more than a thousand formation directors of religious orders in the spring of 2015: "There is the discernment to know [when] to say no."[8] In that case, new vocations were at a low ebb and Pope Francis was reminding those who discern vocations not to act out of desperation, taking any and all, without regard to their suitability or stability. In Francis of Assisi's case, his pope's reminder seemed necessary because the tide was so high and the number of fish was making the fisherman nervous!

CHAPTER 23

BROTHER MUSLIM

1215 to summer 1219,
western Europe to Egypt and the Levant

Between 1209 and Christmas 1216, houses of friars were established throughout Italy in university towns, hill towns, and far-flung places—including Bologna, Castelvecchio, Celano, Cortona, Messina, Milan, and Teramo—as well as in Santiago de Compostela in northern Spain, where a few friars had traveled with Francis in 1214. It was while praying in Santiago that Francis first "received a revelation," *The Little Flowers* says, telling him to found many more places for followers of the way to organize and live. Before the end of winter 1217 came plans for the first era of sustained Franciscan missionary activity: missions to France, Germany, Hungary, the Kingdom of Jerusalem, and Spain, once again, were decided upon.

Above all else, Francis wanted the friars to practice hospitality wherever they were sent. They were to welcome spiritual seekers to find life in the way of Christ's humility and love. This proved challenging for some, including Francis's best friend, Elias.

On one occasion at Portiuncula, at about this time, Francis, Masseo, Elias, and the others were praying the Divine Office together in chapel when they heard a loud knock at the door. The friars jumped from the rapid, loud sound of it.

Masseo went to the door and opened it. There stood a young man.

"Where are you from, son? You've obviously never been here before or you wouldn't knock so rudely!"

"How is someone supposed to knock?" the boy replied.

"Knock three times," Masseo replied, and then he added something that sounds similar to what one reads in Benedict's Rule, "and slowly. In fact, then wait for as long as it might take a friar to say an Our Father. And even then, if a friar hasn't yet come, knock quietly once again."

"Well, I'm in a hurry," the young man responded, "and I knocked that way because I need to see Brother Francis. He's in the woods praying, and I don't want to disturb him. So, could you send Brother Elias to help me? I have a question, and I have heard that he is wise."

This happened years before Elias became minister general, but already he was recognized as Francis's vicar, or deputy. Masseo left the doorway and went to Elias, asking him if he would speak with the young man.

"I'm busy, and he needs to learn some virtue," Elias replied curtly, putting Masseo, then, in an awkward spot.

Masseo didn't know what to do or what to say to the young man. If he said, *Brother Elias can't come just now*, he'd be lying, but if he told him the truth the man would see a bad example. Masseo stood and pondered his options, perhaps longer than it takes a friar to say an Our Father. Then, the young man knocked again, just as he had the first time. At that, Masseo returned to the gate and told him, "You didn't knock the way I told you to!"

The young man said, "If Brother Elias will not come, will you please go and tell Brother Francis that I have come, since I don't want to interrupt his prayers? Would you ask him to send Elias to me?"

So Masseo went to the woods and found Francis deep in prayer, his face lifted up to the sky. He told him what was

happening. Without moving, Francis replied, "Go tell Brother
Elias to go to the young man immediately, as an act of obedience."

Again Masseo was stuck in the middle. And when Elias
heard Francis's order for him, he was furious, as well as embarrassed. He stomped to the gate and flung open the door.

"What do you want!?" he yelled at the young man.

The man answered him, "Be careful of anger, brother, because it can darken the soul and cloud the mind."

Much later, when Francis returned from the woods, he
found Elias and scolded him, saying "Only a too-proud friar
would drive someone away. I fear that your haughtiness will lead
you into trouble."

"No, Francis. I am sorry," Elias said.

But Francis added, "He was an angel. You should treat every
man who visits this place as a divine visitor."[1]

Francis began sending friars to the Holy Land—as pilgrims
called it—in 1215. Giles went first and had enough success
to justify sending Elias in 1217 as the first provincial minister
of what was by then a large enough following to require some
semblance of orderly governance. Elias was already there when
Francis finally made his way to the holy places two years later.
That visit witnessed the most important event in Francis's fifteen
years of religious life up until that point. When Francis returned
to Assisi, he brought Elias back with him.

"When the First World War was over, the muddled and martyred peoples knew nothing about each other, or rather, they
knew the wrong things," wrote Klaus Mann early in the last century.[2] The same could be said, and more, about the misinforma-
tion about Muslims that was rampant among European people
in the centuries of the crusades. By the ninth century, for example, it had become common for learned people in the West

to believe that the Prophet Muhammad had started not simply a new religion but a new, monstrous race of men.[3] The most common visual image of a Muslim among Christians was the Arab Saracen, and the darker color of his skin contributed to the impression of his demonic monstrosity. Images of Muslims and of the prophet that proliferated throughout Italian, German, English, and French lands anticipate the similar caricatures that have become so controversial in our own day. Joachim of Fiore supposedly designated one of the heads of the Apocalypse's seven-headed dragon as Saladin, the first sultan of Egypt. And the Benedictine monk Matthew Paris, twenty years younger than Francis, revealed the majority opinion in his most influential historical work when he depicted Saladin at death with a blackbird flying from his mouth, representing his evil soul.[4]

It was shocking, then, that Francis wanted to sit down with the current sultan in Egypt, Malik al-Kamil. But this wasn't simply to practice the sort of hospitality that Elias had learned a few years earlier at Portiuncula: Francis was there as a pilgrim.

Since Francis was so readily seen as a saint and since saints by definition desire martyrdom, his first biographers interpreted his visit to Sultan al-Kamil behind enemy lines during the Fifth Crusade as an attempt on Francis's part to be killed. But an important variable was missing from that equation: those thirteenth-century biographers were men of thirteenth-century prejudices, which included the assumption that a Muslim would kill any Christian who professed his faith.

Francis had attempted his first trip to Egypt by boat back in 1212, but the ship he was traveling on sank off the coast of Dalmatia, just across the Adriatic from where it had set sail in either Bari or Brindisi. Recovering from the wreck, he had set out on foot past Venice, across the Po River valley, through southern France and into Spain, where he soon fell ill and had to return to Assisi. Other matters closer to home then occupied his attention, so he sent out many of his brothers on mission trips, including sending Elias ahead of him to the Levant. But finally, in May 1219, he booked another sea passage and this time made it out of the Adriatic, across much of the length of the Mediterranean Sea, to Damietta in Egypt, near the eastern mouth of the Nile. There he remained all summer long.

Crusading forces of Franks, Germans, and Frisians had arrived in the Nile delta exactly one year earlier. Their fleet sat in those ancient waters as they set up a camp that they then occupied for eighteen months.

Egypt was a land rich with associations. It was in the Nile delta that the ancient Israelites dwelt, toiled, and then miraculously fled from Pharaoh. And it was in Thebes, in the region of Upper Egypt, that the first Christian hermits had taken up residence back in the third century. Francis was a genuine pilgrim— in contrast, say, to the later Tuscan poet, Petrarch, who wrote a complete travelogue of the sites of the Holy Land without ever actually visiting the places in person. Francis wanted to walk where Moses, David, and Jesus had walked.

"Rise up, O Lord God, and let your hand be raised up, lest you forget in the end. Perfect my steps upon your paths, so that my footsteps are not moved. Make wondrous your mercies, you who make safe those trusting in you," were the words of the rite for receiving the cross, recited by and on behalf of departing crusaders throughout that century.[5] But Francis saw the Christian knights and soldiers gathered near the Nile—recuperating and preparing for battle—and there was little piety in evidence there. Most of the men who undertook to fight the infidels did not go for spiritual reasons; or if they did, they were unable to sustain them. Two of the antiphons from that rite make more sense from this distance. First, there was the rite of repentance, to put a soldier's soul in its right place with the Almighty: "May the days of repentance come for us, for the redemption of sins, for the salvation of souls." This was followed by the words said over the weapons of war: "Let us commend ourselves to the power of God in diligent long-suffering through the weapons of righteousness."[6]

Francis taught that a Christian should not even touch a weapon. One wonders what he thought he would say to the crusaders. For him—and, he believed, according to Christ—power and violence always went hand in hand; therefore, to follow Jesus in nonviolence was to agree to a tangible powerlessness. Francis heard the stories of the crusaders' losses as well as their thirst for glory. But we have no contemporaneous account of those conversations. Francis urged the crusaders to abandon their planned attack, although none heeded his advice. That's not what soldiers do.

Only this letter from the following spring survives, offering a picture of the scene of what happened when Francis went to see the sultan. It was penned by a crusader, James of Vitry: "When their master, who is also the founder of their order, came to stay with our army, he was not afraid to go into the camp of our enemy burning with zeal for the faith; for several days he preached the word of God to the Saracens, but with little success. However, the sultan, the king of Egypt, secretly begged him to pray to the Lord for him so that, by divine inspiration, he might adhere to that religion which was more pleasing to God."[7]

Al-Kamil was a young man. He'd become sultan just one year earlier, after the death of his father in September 1218; he then remained in the post for twenty more years. Over the course of that summer when Francis and one other friar visited him, al-Kamil repeatedly led attacks on the crusaders' camp in the delta and sank several of their ships in the Nile. In fact, al-Kamil's dramatic success at Fariskur on August 29, 1219—when thousands of Christian knights were killed and perhaps another thousand taken prisoner—probably immediately preceded the visit from Francis. Perhaps the Sultan expected a peace negotiator rather than a mendicant.[8]

Two friars visited Sultan al-Kamil. Some sources refer to them just that way, simply as "two friars," without proper names. Others tell us that Brother Illuminato was the one with Francis. Celano indicates that they were captured, insulted, and beaten by soldiers on their way, and one assumes that he's talking about Muslim soldiers, even though it isn't made clear. In his biography of Francis, Bonaventure paints a heroic picture, using colors not seen in this scene before. Bonaventure has Francis challenging the sultan and his imams to a miracle contest, including trial by fire. This version was then immortalized—as was every major scene of Bonaventure's framing of Francis's life stories—in frescoes on the walls of the Basilica of San Francesco in Assisi and again by Giotto in the Basilica of Santa Croce in Florence.

Various other sources have Francis preaching overtly to convert the sultan. The notion that Muslim rulers were easy converts to Christianity was popular among crusaders and their clergy. For example, Oliver of Paderborn, a German cleric who was also present at the siege and victory at Damietta, wrote of a contemporary sultan "believed to have been baptized" before he died who "ordered the followers of Christ to be released whom he found in chains in the fortification which he attacked." Oliver went on to write letters to a king in Babylon and a doctor in Egypt encouraging them to convert to Christianity—with no discernible results.[9] It does not appear that Francis's example inspired men like Oliver but rather that the various scenes of Francis and the sultan were imagined through the lens of a worldview that saw Muslims as weak-minded adherents of a flimsy faith.

It is far likelier that Francis and al-Kamil simply talked, without miracle pyrotechnics or grandstand preaching—Francis sharing the joy of his faith and discovering that the sultan's faith, too, was a lively one. They would have found many things in common. Both men knew the customs of international trade.

Al-Kamil was a *hafiz*, one who knew the Qur'an by heart. The concluding paragraphs of *sura* two—the longest in the Qur'an, and one that reverences the scriptures of the Old Testament as well as prayer, fasting, and pilgrimage for all people—may have been on his mind, including its dictates on how to be faithful to God when communicating with a foreigner. The paragraph is about ethical principles of trade and commerce, but the morals are more broadly applicable: "If you are on a journey, and . . . if you decide to trust one another, then let the one who is trusted fulfill his trust; let him be mindful of God, his Lord," the prophet recorded, followed immediately by "Do not conceal evidence: anyone who does so has a sinful heart, and God is fully aware of everything you do."

If al-Kamil quoted the holy scriptures on these matters, Francis would have agreed. Both men knew what it was like to be a stranger and an outsider. There was plenty of common ground between them. "Grant us your forgiveness, our Lord. To you we all return! . . . Pardon us, forgive us, and have mercy on us. You are our Protector, so help us against the disbelievers," *sura* two concludes.[10]

The purpose of Francis's mission was to speak loudly, through his actions, against the crusading movement itself. The idea that Francis defended the crusading movement, even to the extent of making the Great Commandment condition, is absurd; this is suggested in one late-thirteenth-century collection of stories about Francis, which has him quoting Jesus from Matthew 5:29, "If your eye is an occasion of scandal, pluck it out, and cast it away," and then saying to al-Kamil: "It is for this reason that Christians have acted justly when they invade your land and fight against you, because you blaspheme the name of Christ and you have tried to keep people from worshipping him. But if you wish to recognize, confess, and adore the Creator and Redeemer of the world, we would love you as ourselves."[11]

The Siege of Damietta ended on November 5, 1219, with a victory by the Christian forces. By that time, Francis and the other friar had moved on, probably to the Holy Land itself, where they met up with other friars, including Elias, who were already there. After visiting Jerusalem, Bethlehem, Damascus, and Acre, they traveled home by ship from Egypt to Venice, as many of the crusaders would do. They carried with them a gift from the sultan: a horn used in the Muslim call to prayer, which can still be seen in Assisi today.

Between Venice and Umbria, they probably spent time among the Camaldolese monks of Tuscany. It was there that Francis may have composed or dictated the beautiful Latin poem, the twenty-seventh of his "Admonitions":

> Where there is charity and wisdom,
> there is no fear or ignorance.
> Where there is patience and humility,
> there is no anger or disturbance.[12]

Many centuries later, this verse would inspire the most famous prayer-poem ever attributed to a saint of the Church, even though it wasn't actually composed by one. I'm referring to the so-called "Prayer of Saint Francis," which cannot be traced back any earlier than 1912 and which was written anonymously.

Francis returned home in the spring of 1220 with Brothers Elias, Peter Catani, Caesar of Speyer, and Illuminato; the last was then also among the few with him upon that mysterious mountain, which would transfigure him four years later. A little more than one year later, in July 1221, the final battle of the disastrous Fifth Crusade was won by the sultan and his forces. The hawks were sorely disappointed. If they thought well of the little poor man from Assisi beforehand, now they surely despised him. Pacifism was uncommon, even heretical.

At the Fourth Lateran Council when Pope Innocent III had called for this crusade, he concluded his sermon with these words:

> Remember what Moses is recorded as having spoken to the sons of Levi, "If any man is the Lord's, let him be joined to me. Let every man put his sword upon his thigh: go out and back and forth from gate to gate through the middle of the camp, and every man kill his brother, and his friend, and his neighbor. And the sons of Levi carried out the command of Moses." May you henceforth similarly carry it out: so strike, that you heal; slay, that you may give life, by the example of him who said, "I will kill and I will give life; I will strike, and I will heal."[13]

Those were his words when talking to cardinals, archbishops, bishops, priests, and abbots; imagine what he said when addressing knights and kings!

Quietly, but clearly to anyone who was watching, Francis disobeyed. Extending care for his neighbor to a leader of another faith was a radical gesture and one that would inspire the next century of Franciscans who would take up missions to encounter Persians, Syrians, Mongols, Indians, and Ethiopians.[14]

While Francis was away throughout the summer of 1219, a crisis of authority began to brew among the friars back in Italy. *Who was in charge? What if Francis died? What would we to do next, if the worst were to happen?* This is when Cardinal Ugolino begins to loom larger.

Up until the middle of 1219, "the life of the whole Order revolved around him, and where he stayed or journeyed was its capital," explained one expert from a century ago. But this changed upon Francis's return from the East.[15] Many of the friars were no longer willing or able to follow him as far as his nonviolent intentions took him in meeting with the sultan. And Francis's long-standing practice of doing first and asking permission later—if at all—was an uncomfortable stance for those less tuned to divine inspiration and more adept at listening to their superiors.[16]

Only one month after Francis left by boat for Damietta, Ugolino began obtaining papal bulls recommending the work of the friars around the world and sending them to secular clergy and other religious leaders throughout Europe. That was in June 1219, while Francis was talking with the knights and soldiers in the Nile River delta. At the general chapter meeting of 1220, despite Francis's safe return from abroad months earlier, Ugolino presided over all of the proceedings. A year later, at the 1221 general chapter, a number of special seats were set up for visiting bishops from various territories of the Church. No longer Francis's fraternity, the Franciscans had become the Church's order.[17] Francis must have felt like an earthenware jar forced to travel between iron pots: he was definitely going to be injured.[18]

PART THREE

I have toyed with an idea—the idea that although a man's life is compounded of thousands and thousands of moments and days, those many instants and those many days may be reduced to a single one: the moment when a man knows who he is, when he sees himself face to face.

—Jorge Luis Borges
This Craft of Verse

CHAPTER 24

FRANCIS RENOUNCES

1220–1221, throughout Italy

The experience with al-Kamil cemented in Francis a confidence in mediating conflicts. The ordinary position for a religious leader faced with two conflicting and potentially dangerous parties was one of unarmed neutrality. Self-protection or, what was worse, taking the side of the more powerful of the two and naming it a churchman's responsibility to steer clear of the ways of the world were also the norm. But Francis had grown in his ability both to mediate and to know which side needed championing.

A few years earlier, an incident occurred while he was passing through the town of Gubbio that strangely presaged this new confidence. A fearsome wolf, made crazy with hunger, was devouring both animals and human beings. The people of Gubbio were terrified and took to carrying weapons with them wherever they went, but even weapons did not keep them safe from this creature. Before long, they stopped going outside the city gates altogether.

Francis was told of the situation and decided to walk out to meet the wolf. The people warned him in the sternest of terms, "Don't do it, Brother! The wolf will kill you, as it has others before you!" But Francis walked out to meet it. A few local people accompanied him part of the way, but then said, "This is where we stop."

"I will go on," he replied.

With the townspeople watching, the wolf bounded toward Francis with its mouth gaping. Francis made the Sign of the Cross, and the creature slowed. "Come here, Brother Wolf," Francis said, naming it a friend and a kindred creature. "In Christ's name, you must not hurt me or anyone else." Then—so the story goes—the wolf came and lay down at the saint's feet.

Francis brokered an agreement with the wolf that it would stop hurting the people of Gubbio and in return, the people would feed it for the rest of its days. "Give me a pledge of your agreement," Francis said. And the wolf held out its paw, putting it in Francis's outstretched hand. Then, together, they walked into the market square where all the people were assembled. Francis preached a sermon, saying that God allows awful things to happen sometimes because of our sins, and that the fire of hell is far worse than the dangers posed by a hungry wolf. A wolf may be able to kill our bodies, but hell is something truly frightful. One animal shouldn't be able to keep a town in a constant state of fear and trembling. "So come back to God," he said, "and do penance for these sins of yours, and God will bring freedom to both you and this wolf now and in the next world."

Then he announced the pact that Brother Wolf had agreed to. The people also agreed. The crowd was amazed and shouted praises to God for bringing Francis to their part of the world. From that day forward, Brother Wolf was fed by each house in the town and he harmed no one. When Brother Wolf died of old age two years later, the people of Gubbio were actually sorry to see their symbol of peace and kindness go.

Now, the wolf of Gubbio may actually have been a man. The Italian word for wolf is *lupo*, and there are local legends that Francis converted a criminal in that region who became Friar Lupo, who later traveled with Francis to Spain.[1] If that is so, the incident is even more telling of the sort of person Francis was becoming. He was soon putting himself between competing princes and city magistrates, siding with those without power and protecting them as best he could—and not always quietly. Always, though, he continued to teach that the best way to avoid problems of all kinds was to follow Christ on the proper way of true and absolute poverty. Nothing owned meant nothing to be protected, nothing stolen, and very little at risk.

As Francis's personal assuredness grew, so did his religious order, and the demands of running it increased proportionally. The first leaders of the First Order of Franciscans were as follows:

Francis of Assisi	1209–1220
Peter Catani	1220–1221
Elias	1221–1227
John Parenti	1227–1232
Elias	1232–1239

In other words, something happened in 1220 that caused Francis to renounce his leadership of the movement he founded. He wasn't pleased to step aside. He was either exhausted, exasperated, or both.

The Franciscan tree had spread widely, with fruit-heavy branches extending throughout the earth, as Celano explained in a metaphor that doesn't conceal the stress caused by great blessings. Francis, however, used a different metaphor—the biblical one of a shepherd and his sheep—and by the winter of 1220, he saw friars who were a danger to his flock. "They may not mean to cause it harm, but they will," he said.[2] "Who are these brothers of mine who don't seem to value holy peace and unity among us?" he wondered out loud. "Who are these who are so puffed up with their own virtue and intelligence?"

He was no longer capable of leading by personal inspiration; there were too many friars in too many places around the world. He couldn't even know each brother by name any longer. So, at the Portiuncula general chapter meeting in September 1220, Francis stepped down as the friar in charge. Exhausted and changed from his journey to the East, he turned the leadership over not to Elias but to Peter Catani, a lay brother with broad experience, naming him the order's first vicar general.

Many of his closest friends were deeply saddened, though not exactly surprised because it had become clear that Francis's idealism was burning out in the majority of friars, like a flame seeking and no longer finding oxygen. The first decade had been a time of following his ideals, which were almost pigheadedly willful at times but which had turned into something of a wistful memory of loving passion by 1220. And many of the friars were already preparing ways to move the order along, beyond the "founder's stage."

But Francis retained a desire to influence and lead, as evidenced by one of his more powerful writings, penned soon after he renounced. In this open letter, most likely written as a response to some particular question posed by a contemporary in secular authority, Francis addressed the broader concerns of all who are appointed to positions of leadership:

> We should all reflect and understand that our day of death is coming soon. I plead with you: do not ever forget the Lord our God, even though the cares of the world and its many concerns preoccupy your attention. We should never turn from God's commandments. For if anyone leaves him, and turns from his commandments, he will be cursed and "in the iniquity that they have committed they shall die." When that day of death comes, all that you believe is yours will be taken away from you. The punishments of hell are greater for those who were the most powerful and world-wise in this life.

Therefore, I desperately plead with you, my worldly superiors, take time to set aside the cares and preoccupations that consume your attention, and receive the holy body and blood of our Lord Jesus Christ with passion, remembering him and his holiness. Then, may you foster this same honor to the Lord among the people who are entrusted to your care. Every night you could announce, via messenger or some other simple sign, that your subjects might take time to offer their prayers and thanksgivings to the one, all-powerful God.

If you fail to do this, please know that "on the day of judgment you will have to give an account" before your Lord, God, Jesus Christ.[3]

Francis continued to instruct his brothers just as a religious superior would do, which complicated the transition in leadership. And the superior (although Francis refused to use that traditional word for the role) whom Francis chose was almost too Franciscan of a Franciscan: he was meek to a fault.

On one occasion, Francis reproved one of the brothers too severely and thought it necessary to confess this to Peter, his new vicar general. "I want a severe penance," Francis told him.

"Do as you please, brother," Peter replied, unwilling to be the one held responsible for whatever Francis had in mind for himself.

"Then this is my penance," Francis said. "I will eat with my Christian brother, this fine leper." He gestured to a man who had come to the friars for care. Then Francis set a table for himself and the leprous man. They shared a finger bowl, though the leper's hands "were deformed and bloody, so that whenever he put them in the bowl, blood dripped into it," says a source from about 1250, showing that even then it was common knowledge that diseases are probably transmitted by bodily fluids. Peter and the other brothers witnessed this, but no one dared say anything out of fear of the man who was still their holy father.[4]

There's no doubt that actions like these led to Francis's increasingly fragile health.

But it was Peter Catani who died suddenly, of natural causes, six months after he assumed leadership. Quickly, into the vacuum of charismatic and inspired leadership stepped Cardinal Ugolino, Innocent III's older cousin, whom Francis had respected and trusted for years. Honorius III had named him "protector" of the order in 1220. The good cardinal set out to establish closer links between the friars and the Roman curia.

Elias also stepped into the vacuum as the order looked to Francis to appoint another vicar general. Quietly fuming over not having been chosen the first time around, Elias took this occasion to remind Francis of his value, and Francis tapped his old friend, putting his trust in yet another layman. Elias had proven himself an excellent administrator in Syria and the Holy Land; and while Francis often had trouble making decisions on behalf of others, Elias was always decisive. He quickly became more familiar with Cardinal Ugolino, and together they made plans for what they might accomplish in the future.

At this point, Francis began to truly disengage from organizational politics, leaving those concerns to Elias, whom he was accustomed to relying upon. Francis turned his attention to what he viewed as more important: soon he was healing a crippled boy in Tuscania and a paralytic man in Narni, as well as talking with birds and stones and trees—confusing people again as to whether he was a man of God or some sort of fool. Celano does not necessarily distinguish between the two when he exuberates, "O how beautiful, how splendid, how glorious did he appear in the innocence of his life, in the simplicity of his words, in the purity of his heart, in his love for God, in his fraternal charity, in his ardent obedience, in his peaceful submission, in his angelic countenance!"[5]

The world around Francis moved on rapidly without him. With Innocent III's death in 1216, the strongest papacy in the last five hundred years had been brought to an abrupt close; before he died, he had looked kindly upon Frederick II of Hohenstaufen, a move that would later prove disastrous for the Holy See.

Frederick II was born in the March of Ancona (then part of the Kingdom of Sicily, encompassing lands to both the north and the south of the Papal States) on December 26, 1194, making him about thirteen years Francis's and Elias's junior. He was already king of Sicily when he was orphaned at three; he then became a ward of Innocent III.[6] At the age of fifteen he was strategically married to the widowed Constance of Aragon, queen of Hungary, but he became a notorious philanderer even in the midst of her court in Palermo. At seventeen, he was crowned king of Germany (also known as king of the Romans) in Mainz, uniting the kingdoms of Sicily and Germany and posing a looming threat to the papacy, which would have preferred a more dispersed balance of power.

As Frederick's power increased, so did his desire for knowledge. His court gradually filled with mathematicians, astronomers, and physicians. He would found the University of Naples in 1224 at twenty-nine. He kept Arabian horses, studied classical falconry, spoke at least seven languages, and feasted on exotic delicacies. Men representing every known religious tradition were recruited for conversation: Frederick liked to discuss and debate, and he enjoyed these arts as competitively in middle age as he did riding and hunting as a younger man. He learned Arabic. He studied philosophy and jurisprudence with Normans, Jews, and Muslims. Caged monkeys sat in his court.[7] He was a heretic of the grandest sort, poking fun at Moses one day, Jesus the next, and then the Prophet Muhammad.

The archbishops of Germany had long favored Frederick over against Otto of Brunswick, whom Innocent III had crowned as Holy Roman Emperor at St. Peter's Basilica in October 1209, only to excommunicate him a year later for invading Tuscan lands that the pope wanted to remain papal. Otto's family had always opposed Frederick's House of Hohenstaufen, but it was to the advantage of the Holy See to keep rivals battling one another so that no single party might unify the throne. This divvying up by foreigners of what we now know as Italy went on well into the modern era, leading Ippolito Nievo to write in *Confessions of an Italian*, the great nineteenth-century novel about Italian independence, that his people "had been put in this world as spectators, not actors."

Kingship could be as divinely imbued in the late medieval imagination as the papacy, and many sovereigns, including Frederick II, sincerely believed in their godly purpose. Scripture was even at times on their side, for it is told over and over in the Bible how kings were chosen, made powerful, and supported by God. And in the New Testament, St. Paul writes, "Let every person be subject to the governing authorities; for there is no authority except from God, and those authorities that exist have been instituted by God" (Rom 13:1), a text discussed a century earlier by the writers of the Concordat of Worms of 1122.

That agreement reached at Worms between Pope Calixtus II and Holy Roman Emperor Henry V stated that kings had the right to invest bishops only with secular authority ("by the lance") in their territories, not with sacred authority ("by ring and staff"). This was a reforming moment for the Church, which wrested control back from the state, since emperors had previously held it as their divine right not only to name prelates for sacred functions but, when necessary, to appoint the bishop of Rome. Now prelates were accountable to their kings only regarding worldly matters, such as in a time of war.

But who was in authority when a sacred ruler was at war with a secular ruler?

In 1220, a few years after Honorius III succeeded Innocent III as pope, he crowned Frederick II as Holy Roman Emperor.

Frederick's son was made king of the Romans, and both father and son remained almost continuously in the Kingdom of Sicily, where their power was most concentrated, for the next fifteen years. One of the reasons Otto of Brunswick had earned the ire of Innocent III was Otto's insistence that the pope annul the Concordat of Worms. But Frederick, likewise, once he became emperor, felt justified in supposing that he ruled by divine mandate.

Even so, this was the same Frederick who had shocked everyone by committing to Honorius to lead the Fifth Crusade to retake the Holy Land and then failing to do so. He probably did it to curry favor and then quickly regretted it.[8] The occupiers of the Holy See would remember the promise, however, and following the demoralizing final defeat at Damietta in 1221, which brought the Fifth Crusade to an abrupt end, Honorius publicly blamed Frederick for failing to keep it.

All of these power struggles between popes and kings, minister generals and cardinals, happened without Francis paying much attention. He was mostly oblivious and blind to politics. Then came this scene—one of the most poignant in all of his life.

"Elias, may I say something?" Francis was sitting on the ground, suffering from problems with his eyes that would soon become serious, tugging on the tunic of his friend. Elias was in a chair, as the friar in charge, presiding. The general chapter meeting of 1221 was about to conclude.

"Yes, Francis?"

"I believe we should send friars to German lands, to bring them the Gospel. We were badly treated there once before, but I think they are a devout people to whom we should return. Will you ask the brothers who among them may want to go?"

Elias turned back to the crowd and relayed Francis's message. As he did, he referred to Francis with the honorific, "The Brother."

"Any brothers wishing to go," Elias added, "should gather to my left as we conclude the chapter." Some ninety friars assembled there in minutes, anxious to take a journey at the suggestion of their founder. His leadership wasn't at an end, after all. Caesar of Speyer would lead that group to Germany in 1221, with tremendous success. With him were Thomas of Celano and Jordan of Giano, who left a personal account of the scene some years later.[9]

CHAPTER 25

THE KNOT UNRAVELS

1222, all over Europe

The issues that split the order apart were simple ones. Most of the disagreements centered on the founder's ideals regarding poverty. Francis never missed an opportunity to make his point about owning nothing, maintaining lowliness, and giving no thought about tomorrow. Sometimes he made the point by begging for food outside while his brothers were being dined by Cardinal Ugolino. At other times, Francis would destroy or throw away something that had been given to the brothers.

On another occasion, in Cortona, Elias had gone to great trouble to locate a new tunic for Francis and to convince him to wear it.

"It was given to us by a man of God," Elias said to his friend, adding, in order to make the newness and value of the cloak palatable to the idealist, "He said it was of no value at all."

Francis put it on. But the next day an old man came to where the friars were staying, weeping about his dead wife and his feeling of desolation. Only Francis was there.

"Take my tunic," Francis said to the grieving man, "on the condition that you never surrender it to another unless he pays you twice the value of a new one." The old man went away warm and grateful.

When Elias and the others returned and Francis told them this story, they immediately ran out and searched for an old man wearing Francis's tunic. An hour later they confronted him on the road.

"You are wearing our minister's coat!" Elias said, demanding, "We must now have it back!"

The old man remembered what Francis had said and did as he had promised. He refused to let it go, not unless they paid him enough for two tunics. Somehow, Elias came up with the money (friars were not to have any) and paid the old man; he returned to where they were staying and placed the tunic back on Francis's shoulders. Francis simply smiled.[1]

Besides the doctrine of absolute poverty, the other central issue that caused the split was how to train a friar in the way of salvation. To Francis, the answer was, rather simplistically, to have him walk beside you. But the order had grown to such a size that this approach was no longer possible. Many of the friars—who by now included men from a dozen distant lands and hundreds of priests—began to insist upon more. They wanted real theological training, a program of study, books, and other accoutrements. This desire for training, in effect, became a further test of the strict poverty doctrine. Were Francis's minimalist ideals still reasonable in a religious order of multiple provinces in many countries requiring friaries and schools and comprising nearly three thousand men?

Meanwhile, far away from the Franciscan epicenter, a young monk began taking notice of the friars ministering near his monastery in Coimbra, Portugal. Similar to Francis in appearance, temperament, and desire, Fernando Martins was also brilliant. Born in 1195 to wealthy parents who supported his desire for religious life, Fernando was educated at the finest schools and became one of his era's most erudite theologians by the age of twenty.

He was guestmaster of the canons regular of an Augustinian abbey in the capital of the Portuguese kingdom, where Franciscans had recently settled a new friary, when news reached Coimbra that friars had been martyred in the Kingdom of Morocco. They had been sent by Francis after his mission to see the sultan and had met with a less-than-friendly reception. They also didn't possess Francis's tact and generosity. Led by Berard of Carbio, they had traveled from Italy by sea to Seville and spent months in Spain and Portugal before continuing to Morocco. Fernando may have met the five while they sojourned in Portugal before continuing to their final destination. In Morocco they preached relentlessly, with only Berard speaking the barest of Arabic, and so were viewed as insane. Eventually they were imprisoned and beheaded, in late January 1220. News reached Portugal and Umbria by late spring. The five—Accursius, Adjutus, Otho, Peter, and Berard—were rapidly sainted, and the fast-growing movement had its first international heroes. King Afonso II of Portugal ransomed the bodies, and they were brought to Coimbra to the Monastery of Santa Cruz. There they were buried with great ceremony.

Fernando was moved by the stories that came back of the public witness and death of these martyrs, and within days he was asking his superior for a transfer from the Augustinians to the Franciscans. Permission was granted, and Fernando took a new name, Anthony, in honor of the great desert saint of early Christian Egypt, for whom the small friary in Coimbra was also named. Then, also rapidly, Anthony of Padua gained permission to follow in the footsteps of the martyrs and travel to Morocco. But martyrdom cannot accommodate the mundane, and growing seriously ill from the long sea journey, Anthony soon desired a return to Portugal. When the ship was forced to abandon Portuguese ports due to bad weather, Anthony traveled to Sicily, then on to Tuscany, and finally to a cell in remote Romagna, where he resumed his theological studies. Within two years, he emerged as a shining light in the order.

It was Anthony whom Francis warned not to teach theology to the friars in a way that it quieted the voice of God in their souls. Many a theologian would have bristled at such advice or would have been baffled by it, but not Anthony. He was a true descendant of Francis, even though their natural aptitudes and leanings were different. Francis had long taught that "you know only as much as you do," and Anthony understood that perfectly.[2]

Francis's demeanor had changed since his return from Egypt. He often seemed sad and disappointed in a way that was new to those around him. We could name this for what it likely was— some form of depression—but of course there was no such thing in the Middle Ages. He began to find new friends and turned to three friars—Angelo, Rufino, and Leo—spending all of his available time in their company. Elias couldn't help but notice this. These three companions were relatively inactive in the daily goings-on of the order,[3] and Francis was probably drawn to them for precisely this reason: they were outsiders, with no desire to lead or influence.

A former knight, Angelo forged a natural bond with Francis. One of the original twelve who stood before Innocent III in 1210, Angelo had known Francis as a young man, but he had faded from view as the demands of the order grew. Now they rekindled their friendship, sharing a love of music, particularly singing, and walking around Umbria while composing songs.

Other characters wove in and out of Francis's life during this time. For example, Brother Pacifico began to interpret his dreams, and Francis often brought them to him. One featured a beautiful woman wearing filthy clothes—a dream that Francis shared with many of the brothers, some of whom believed it to be Lady Poverty. But Pacifico said that she represented Francis's soul, and the clothes were the despicable little body in which that soul was encased.[4] This interpretation was too dualistic for Francis's taste, yet it fairly portrayed the gradual diminishment of the friar's health after years of poor maintenance.

Another close friend, Caesar of Speyer, returned with Celano and others from the German province just in time to attend the Pentecost general chapter meeting of May 1221 in Assisi. There, Caesar approached Francis to beg a favor.

"Holy father, will you allow me to step down as provincial minister?"

"Of course," Francis said, knowing the contemplative heart that Caesar possessed and how ardent was his desire to return.

Meanwhile, the Franciscan spirit continued to thrive in other quarters as Francis's influence grew and the order spread. Elizabeth of Hungary, the daughter of King Andrew II of Hungary, was learning Franciscan spirituality five hundred miles and half a world away from Umbria. Friars had arrived in Thuringia in 1221, the year of Elizabeth's wedding to Louis IV of Thuringia, to whom she had been affianced since toddlerhood. That spring before her marriage, she began to pray the hours and practice a generous hospitality in the spirit of the Rule. Her husband, a second cousin of Emperor Frederick II, would take up his knighthood and die in the crusades in 1227, leaving his widow, still only twenty, with three children. The following spring, Elizabeth would formally join the Third Order, which in her case involved making full provision for the welfare of the children before renouncing all other possessions. Her estate would be used to found a hospital, named for Francis (by then a saint), and she would spend the rest of her days working with the sick and outcast there, tending to them as she had heard Francis tended to lepers. She died in 1231 at twenty-four, from a disease contracted from one of the patients she nursed, and soon became a saint almost as important to the late medieval Church as Francis.

CHAPTER 26

PURCHASING THE FIELD

1223, in and around Assisi

"I am your small, humble servant of God," Francis had written in a 1220 letter to some king or prince—perhaps one involved in the Fifth Crusade, since that year was the one in which the Poverello's mind was often turning to matters of power and responsibility.

"I wish you good health and peace," he said, in salutary, respectful fashion, like a religious man who wants to be heard rather than dismissed. Before long, however, we have this: "Do not ever forget the Lord our God, even though the cares of the world and its many concerns preoccupy your attention." And then: "For if anyone leaves them, he will be cursed and in the iniquity that they have committed they shall die," he said, quoting the prophet Ezekiel. For, "When that day of death comes, all that you believe is yours will be taken away from you. The punishments of hell are greater for those who were the most powerful and world-wise in this life."[1]

As Francis was addressing such words to powerful people throughout Europe, who were increasingly drawn to him as a man of influence, he didn't seem to imagine that the same words might come to haunt his old friend and ally, Elias, his vicar general. For Elias's part, the old notion of "be careful for what you wish for" comes to mind.

Elias noticed that friars Angelo, Leo, and Rufino became Francis's closest confidants and companions at the same time he was himself taking on more responsibility within the order. Francis was also growing increasingly ill, the result of poor self-care that was now too late to reverse; he began to slow his daily activities and before long the three companions also became his nurses—and scribes.

It was time to take their thumbnail Rule and add to it—something that even Francis accepted as necessary, given the tremendous growth of the order. The gospel exhortations that they presented years earlier to Innocent III and which had existed since then as a mostly memorized, oral Rule were no longer sufficient to speak to the variety of responsibilities and concerns of a friar. Also, if Francis were really to remove himself entirely from leadership and make himself as "small" as he desired to be, he needed to leave behind a clear, written account of the way of salvation for a friar.[2] Thus, Francis composed the Rule of 1221, or *Regula non bullata*, with the help of a few friends and with the final approval of the Pentecost chapter meeting.

Exhaustive compared to what had existed before, this Rule laid out Franciscan poverty, chastity, and obedience in detail, directions for praying the Divine Office and fasting, Honorius III's instructions for a year-long novitiate, how to correct a brother at fault, and many other topics of daily relevance. There were, however, a few sections in which Francis felt obliged to include something that was, to say the least, somewhat uncomfortable for him. Most of all, there was this in chapter 12 about avoiding the company of women: "The brothers should always, wherever they are or wherever they may go, carefully avoid looking at and being in the company of women. . . . A woman should never be received into obedience by any brother; if spiritual counsel has to be given to her, she may then go and do penance wherever she desires."[3] This didn't match what had taken place in the not-too-distant past, when Clare had made her profession before

Francis and some of the other brothers at Portiuncula. But now, it seemed necessary to accept some new realities—or, at least, Cardinal Ugolino said it was.

This Rule of 1221 is preachy and disorganized, as one might expect from the hand of Francis.[4] It also values the contributions of lay brothers, emphasizing that there are no reasons why they should aspire to become clerics—a point with which Elias was in exact accord. And, just as in that 1220 letter to the anonymous king or prince, Francis makes it clear that power can corrupt; he even tells his brothers that they should disobey an order that is unfaithful or unholy.[5]

————— ✦ —————

This first formal Rule appealed in different ways to the two separate parties developing within the order. One party desired institutional structures and plans for continued growth and influence, while the other wished to remain low in every respect—in visibility, with regard to ambition, and in expectations other than faithfulness to the Gospel and the Rule, two sources which they tended to conflate. The former were no longer satisfied with the values of the evangelical crowd that were in place under Francis's leadership. He had little interest in growing a formal movement, only in following the Gospel and Rule and being certain that the Rule was in step with the expectations of the Holy Father. But the dissenters wanted much more. They saw in the vast Franciscan crowd so much undiscovered potential for goodness and growth. Without certain changes, the randomness—that was, for Francis, a way of being Spirit-led—would continue to limit what they might accomplish.

This conflict, which was taking place between friars but also inside of Francis, boiled over one evening. Cardinal Ugolino was with the friars at St. Mary of the Angels, overseeing a chapter meeting, as Rome wanted him to do, when some of the friars approached him for a private word. The vicar general, Elias, was surely at Ugolino's side.

"Lord Cardinal, will you please persuade our father, Francis, to listen to the learned brothers and allow our life to be more closely modeled after the Rules of Sts. Benedict, Augustine, or Bernard?"

Francis overheard this and then shocked the large gathering of friars by taking Ugolino's hand and leading him to the platform where together they stood before the assembly. Everyone quickly hushed.

"My brothers," Francis began in his normal voice—he didn't need to shout; if a brother had dropped a fork it would have disturbed the total silence with a clatter—"God called me to walk in the way of humility and showed me the way of simplicity. I do not want to hear any talk of the Rules of St. Augustine or St. Bernard or St. Benedict." He continued: "The Lord has told me that he wants to make a new fool of me in the world, and God does not want to lead us by any other knowledge than that!" All were staring at the two men, taking in every word.

Ugolino kept silent, dumbfounded, and then after a few moments sat down. That large gathering of friars heard Francis's words and were afraid.[6]

A few months later, on Christmas Eve 1222, a violent earthquake centered in Brescia shook much of northern Italy. It would have measured approximately 6.5 on the Richter scale. Thousands of homes were crushed, along with thousands of people inside them, from Milan to Venice, from the western Alps to the Adriatic Sea. For two weeks, aftershocks rumbled throughout Lombardy and the plain of the Po River, and hundreds of churches crumbled. People were forced to live in open fields and tents—a situation that would go on for months and then years. Many of the friars believed the quake to be a message from God.

At twenty-eight, Anthony of Padua was already showing signs of the brilliance in biblical preaching that would later bring Pope Gregory IX to call him a "jewel case" for the holy scriptures and ask him to publish a collection of his sermons. Many of the young friars were drawn to Anthony's spirit for exploring and expounding upon the biblical text. He brought the desire to study to the friars, inadvertently causing a separation between some of the older men drawn to Francis by his anti-intellectual stance (he was deliberately *not* a monk in a scriptorium), and some of the younger men—equally thirsty for living the Gospel—who wanted to know better what it said.

Francis loved Anthony, in whom he recognized true faith, and he knew that there was no contradiction in him between learning and their evangelical way of life. The same couldn't be said of some of the young friars who, inspired by Anthony's passion for learning, rather suddenly wanted to keep their noses in books. Francis, after all, taught that "those who are illiterate should not be eager to learn." "Instead," he said to the friars at this time, "let them pursue what they most desire above all things: to have the Spirit of the Lord and his holy manner of working, to pray always to him with a pure heart and to have humility, patience in persecution and weakness, and to love those who persecute us, find fault with us, or rebuke us."[7]

And yet, that wasn't what many of the friars desired most of all. Many of them increasingly wanted to study theology, sing in choir, refrain from physical work, and live without so much traveling around. There was a monasticizing trend among the friars. This sent Francis once again back to his Rule. In October 1223, he gathered together the trusted Leo, Caesar of Speyer, and Bonizo of Bologna to retreat near the city of Rieti in order to draft what he knew would be the final version. The *Regula non bullata* needed to be simplified in order to retain the focus on what mattered most. The *Regula bullata*, or last Rule, was the result.

The setting for its composition was a place enjoyed by many popes and cardinals over the centuries who desired to escape the heat of Rome in the summertime. To the more temperate Rieti, easily accessible by traveling up the ancient Via Salaria, they escaped. Francis knew this region from the summer of 1209 when, en route to see Innocent III, he took refuge in the valley of Poggio Bustone and was, according to legend, warmly received by the locals in a way that surprised the friars, who were still being mostly scorned in their native Umbria. Fourteen years later, the friars stayed in Fonte Colombo, three miles south of Rieti, while Francis composed this last Rule. To this day, the place is referred to as the Franciscan Sinai.

Caesar of Speyer was the one who took up the pen this time. Bonizo kept track of their meager physical needs. All four of them argued and sweated over what was being lost in their order and how to regain it. This last Rule was—in contrast to the one of two years earlier—confirmed by Pope Honorius III later that year on November 29, 1223. It was shorter and stricter, and better organized and conceived, than the earlier version. But it was also more gracious. For instance, no longer was a friar told that he could not provide spiritual counsel to a woman. And a friar's asceticism was no longer supposed to extend to hating his physical body.

During the summer months, many of the friars were aware that Francis was working yet again on their Rule. Some were worried about being able to keep its principles. How times had changed since 1210 when the first eleven with him before Innocent III were eager to embrace the simplicity and poverty that was early Franciscanism! Now the movement had entered its institutional stage—thrust on the group by the sheer size and the international character of their fraternity. Many believed that what the movement needed going forward was less severity and more flexibility.

A large group gathered around Elias, saying "We have heard that Francis is making a new Rule. We are afraid that he will make it too harsh, in ways that we cannot observe. We want you to go and tell him that we will not be bound to this Rule. Ask him to please make it for himself and not for us."

"I won't go up the mountain to tell him without you beside me," Elias responded. So a group of them went up to where Francis was.

Elias called to his friend. When Francis heard Elias and saw the others, he replied, "What do you all need from me?"

Elias said, "They have heard that you are making a new Rule, and being afraid that it may be too harsh, they've protested to me that they will not be bound by it. Make it for yourself and not for them."

"Didn't I say that they would not believe me?" Francis said, looking up to the sky. He stood there for an uncomfortably long time. He appeared to be listening intently to something unseen. The friars murmured among themselves.

Francis then turned back. "Did you hear him?" he implored. "Did you hear?!" At this, Elias and the others went away, confused and terrified.[8]

Additions and interpretations—what Francis called "glosses"—were attached to the Rule almost from the moment it was promulgated. The majority of the friars wanted to know, in a way that no one seems to have asked in 1209 or 1211, how literally they were supposed to interpret its instructions. It became common to see in the Rule statutes or *institutiones sanctas*, "holy regulations," and then to separate the spirit of a principle from its specific application or law. Some of these glosses were aimed at making more specific a principle that Francis intended to stand as a generality. For instance, Francis taught that, when eating, a friar should be satisfied to consume whatever was put before him; the friars who set about writing new regulations let it be further stipulated that when meat was offered, one was to eat three bites only. Whether these were oral teachings at least congenial to Francis or strictures of certain idealist enthusiasts, it is difficult to say. One can imagine, for example, that the custom of not wearing beards was a simple, corporate understanding of modesty among the early friars (it goes unmentioned in the Rule) that was later turned into a statute of obedience. What we know for certain is that Francis never wanted his men to become like monks or his friaries to become like monasteries, where nearly every moment and action, holy or not, is regulated.

Neither Francis nor the first minister general, John Parenti, who would be elected over Elias after Francis's death, created such statutes or laws. And Elias himself seemed to understand the spirit of Francis in these matters, so much so that Salimbene, who always wrote without any affection for Elias whatsoever, remembered that in this, at least, he was like his friend Francis: "Every friar did what seemed right to himself in those days. Some lived in cities, near the churches of Waldensian brethren, and others lived in hermit cells with windows through which they still chatted with women. Others lived, against custom, serving the sick and wandering the world, alone, without another friar by his side. Some had beards; some not. Some didn't even have the common cord on their tunic, but wove together colorful, strange threads, clearly happy that they stood out from the rest."[9]

Finished with their work, Francis and the others traveled the short distance from Fonte Colombo to the small town of Greccio, also in the Rieti valley. They were there by the third week of Advent and Francis felt inspired to reenact the Incarnation in a new way.

He had already become legendary for the ways he interacted with creatures that others disregarded. There were the worms he helped across the road and the fish that was caught and presented to him as a gift only to be blessed and thrown back in the lake; and then of course there was the uncanny way he seemed able to communicate with birds on the road, "preaching" and exhorting them to sing to their Creator, not to mention that wolf in Gubbio that he seemed to tame. There was also his unusual affection for bees, rocks, wood, water, and flowers. All of these stories mark him as the gentlest of men. A fantastic, unbelievable quality is attached to some of these tales, but they hold a kernel of extraordinary truth—of one who learned and practiced a gentle approach to the world.

Nowhere in the hundreds of legends and stories, however, is there mention of what one might expect foremost from such a man of the Bible—a fulfillment of the often forgotten injunction to the people of Israel to help working animals with their burdens. Chapter 23 of Exodus includes the instruction, "When you see the donkey of one who hates you lying under its burden and you would hold back from setting it free, you must help to set it free." The injunction is phrased like a Talmudic argument that offers the most extreme example; one might safely replace "one who hates you" (some translations read "your enemy") with "your neighbor." In other words, help the animal in the field that is crushed by its burden. But we have no stories of Francis doing that sort of thing; we don't see him walking alongside oxen or carrying an ass's load. Francis seems to have been drawn mostly to wild animals, ones that exhibit some of the carefreeness that seems childlike, innocent, or pure.

His imagination was abuzz with the nativity narrative from Matthew and Luke when he entered Greccio that late December. As he thought of the holy days to come, he could see in his imagination what happened that first starry night in Bethlehem. This fancy was likely sparked by his seeing a mother and her newborn as he walked around town on Christmas Eve morning. Bonaventure sets the scene and tells the story: Francis arranged for a live crèche, the first of its kind. He put on a nativity play, placing the woman and child in the center, gathering some working barn-yard animals, including an ox and a donkey, around them. He knew little of animal husbandry; his own upbringing had been far from that life, but the smells and feel of animal creatures were like home to him.

Including an animal in a liturgical celebration had precedents. In northern France, the celebration of the Feast of the Ass during the week of Christmas had become common a generation or two before Francis's birth. On the Feast of the Circumcision in January, a donkey was often led into the church as "*Orientis partibus*" was sung, recalling how at least that one animal may have witnessed the birth of the Christ Child back in Bethlehem.

Francis then began to sing, as a rabbi sings the Torah, the gospel story of the birth of Christ in Bethlehem—"with full voice," Celano says. And he didn't simply sing; he sang beautifully. When he came to the word *Bethlehem*, it was as if he filled "his whole mouth with sound but even more with sweet affection."[10] The Incarnation took on a new meaning that day.

CHAPTER 27

THAT HOLY, INEXPLICABLE MOMENT

September 1224, La Verna

"Sometimes she heard with her bodily ears such sounds and melodies that she might not have heard from a man less he spoke to her in a loud voice," explained fifteenth-century Englishwoman Margery Kempe about herself in a bizarre, third-person way, claiming audible, divine companionship.[1] Christian mystics in the centuries after Francis spoke and wrote in ways that he would never have even contemplated.

That people experience divine revelation cannot be denied. Human history is replete with instances of men and women undergoing periods of being "outside themselves" (what Erik Erikson calls "ego-loss"),[2] experiencing sudden realizations (or "enlightenments"), hearing voices when no one else is around, and suddenly changing the course of their lives due to what they can name as nothing other than a revelation from beyond. Francis took a more introspective approach to his mystical experiences. He didn't speak of their content, only of his approach and intentions. On one occasion, Francis said to Leo, "When I cannot hear mass, then I adore the Body of Christ with the eyes of my mind in prayer, just as I adore [that Body] when I see it during mass." On another, Francis said to some other companions, "When you are visited by God with some new consolation during prayer, before you finish praying raise your eyes to heaven and join your hands together and say to him, 'You have sent this sweetness, O Lord, to a real sinner. I now send it back to you, so that you can reserve it for me.'"[3]

Such comments put Elias's trumpeting of Francis's stigmata experience, which was quiet and inexplicable to Francis, into larger perspective. The world's first manifestation of stigmata came down to us as history only as a result of the letter Elias wrote the day after Francis died (first mentioned at the end of chapter 2). For this reason, any biographer must only hesitantly tell of this as a historical event. To place this moment within a narrative is to risk ignoring its essential mystery.

"I announce to you a great joy and the news of a miracle," Elias wrote to the pope and all of the friars in his letter announcing the death of their spiritual teacher. "Such a sign that has never been heard of from the dawn of time except in the Son of God, who is Christ the Lord."[4]

What happened precisely to Francis, in and on his body, no one will ever know. We only know what Elias told the world: "Our brother and father appeared crucified, bearing in his body the five wounds which are truly the marks of Christ. His hands and feet had, as it were, the openings of the nails and were pierced front and back revealing the scars and showing the nails' blackness. His side, moreover, seemed opened by a lance and often emitted blood." That "as it were" in Elias's second- or thirdhand account would prove enormous.

How interesting that Francis, a humble man who nevertheless always measured himself against the standards set by Christ for everyone, never said to Elias, or anyone else for that matter, what Jesus said to Thomas in the Upper Room after the resurrection: "Put your finger here and see my hands. Reach out your hand and put it in my side. Do not doubt but believe" (Jn 20:27). Francis never told others about what happened to him upon Mount La Verna. He seems to have understood, in the recent words of Pope Francis, how "more difficult than loving God is letting ourselves be loved by him."[5]

The Italian Renaissance painter Giovanni Bellini portrays Francis looking like Virgil, well-built and tall, a commanding presence, at the moment he receives the stigmata. That isn't how it happened. To Francis and to the brothers who were nearby, it didn't exactly *happen* because it couldn't be spoken of. "Mysteries are called mysteries because we recognize in them a truth which we can barely face, or articulate," James Baldwin once wrote.[6] The account that appears in Celano's biography[7] is told at least at thirdhand, and the distance between Francis's firsthand experience and any secondhand account was already an enormous gulf, for Francis talked in detail about the event with no one. We mostly have accounts of what the others heard: Francis's suffering, which seemed to continue from that day until his death two years later.

The mystical occurrence took place a year after he created the live nativity at Greccio, in the harvest month of September. Leo, Caesar, Bonizo, and Rufino accompanied Francis to Mount La Verna to pray. It was a familiar place to them all, and they were there to spend a penitential period of prayer and fasting. Elias wasn't with them—and his absence becomes conspicuous later on when it is he who announces what happened.

Afternoons burned hot in the September sun at that elevation. The raven that fed Elijah in the wilderness seemed to be present, too—at least according to the legend of those days that was passed down generations after the events took place. Francis asked to be left alone most of the time. He wanted to see only Leo, and then only for necessary provisions, which were always made available from a distance. Had it been anyone else, this behavior might have seemed unkind, but Leo and the handful of others knew how Francis craved quiet. Other medieval prophets and reforming men were more extreme in their desires for solitude. A century before, Bernard of Tiron, for example, had rowed himself to an island several miles off the coast of France and remained there for years—until one of his followers finally convinced him to return.

Then there came a moment for Francis that mirrors a line from *Paradise Lost*: "What call'st thou solitude, is not the Earth."[8] Francis was alone that late afternoon on his knees in prayer.

One of the spiritual practices he shared with Clare was a way of praying with intense and imaginative concentration upon the Passion of Christ. They would meditate on what the gospels say of the Passion events, imagine being present there with the Son of God, "stand" as witnesses to the atrocity of the Crucifixion itself, and then mourn his death anew each time. "She learned the divine offices of the cross as she had been taught by Francis," Celano said.[9] This sort of practice was not unique to these two friends and mystics but is a feature in the lives of many mystics throughout the history of the Church. Celano even described Clare as becoming, as it were, "drunk on tears for the Passion of Christ," so completely taken over did she become at those moments. But she would only become so taken after concentrating upon the five wounds of Jesus, and after cinching a painfully knotted cord against her skin, more and more tightly "as a secret reminder of the Savior's wounds." Celano also provided the important and often neglected detail that Clare tended to reserve the canonical hours of Sext and None for these particular meditations. Sext was prayed at noon, and None in the midafternoon—when the sun was high and hot.

Suddenly, Francis was faced with the figure of Christ in the form of a six-winged seraph above him—not a man standing before him but a transfigured image of Christ in the sunny sky on a hot afternoon. Francis faced the seraph, dumbfounded, in the same kneeling posture of years earlier, when he had heard the icon crucifix speaking to him in San Damiano.

This holy, inexplicable moment occurred sometime between the Feast of the Exaltation of the Holy Cross (September 14) and the Feast of St. Michael the Archangel (September 29). No one bothered to make note of the exact day, perhaps because what happened took place over a period of time.

In the immediate moments after Francis's intense experience, he probably resembled Adam in *Paradise Lost*, who after conversing with God in the Garden said "He ended, or I heard no more, for now / My earthly by his Heavenly overpowered, / . . . Dazzled and spent, sunk down, and sought repair / Of sleep, which instantly fell on me, called / By Nature as in aide, and closed mine eyes."[10] Perhaps it was when he awoke, shaken by his friends, that Francis tried to make sense of what had happened.

His silence regarding that day is similar to that of other mystics in the Middle Ages who kept the intensity of the love of God private and to themselves. The Cistercian William of Saint-Thierry, for example, said in his *Golden Epistle* that God's love was something that made its possessor want to proclaim it, and yet the lover is supposed "to conceal it in one's cell and to store it away in one's innermost being."[11]

Francis said nothing about the experience, but Leo tells us that just afterward was when Francis wrote his "Praises to God" on a tiny piece of vellum that Leo then carried around on his person for thirty years. "You are holy, Lord, the only God. You do wondrous things. You are strong. You are great. You are the Most High . . ."

Then, a few days later, "My lord, I am so very sorry!" is probably what Rufino said when he reached out to touch Francis's chest, to feel what it was that seemed to be paining his friend, and accidentally touched the scar of a serious wound. Rufino said as much because at that moment, Francis called out—startled, suffering, maybe embarrassed—"Save me, God!"

CHAPTER 28

BIRTH OF A POET

March–April, 1225, Assisi

It can be difficult to see Francis clearly because of the legacy and hold that Protestant Calvinism (and its child, Puritanism) has on our understanding of human nature. Children enter the world "odious and abominable to God," wrote John Calvin in his *Institutes* in the sixteenth century, "as they bring their condemnation into the world with them." This is not how one typically imagines a child in the crib. The American Puritan of the Salem witch trials, Cotton Mather, added in a little book written for parents: "Your children are by your means born under the dreadful wrath of God, and if they are not new-born before they die it would have been very good for them if they hadn't ever been born at all."[1] Given such writings in more recent centuries, it is ironic that we often refer to the Middle Ages as barbaric.

These ideas of human nature are not and have never been Catholic. So in his upholding the value and inherent beauty of every human life in the sight of God, Francis was not a radical. Where he *was* radical was in the language he used, the symbols he embraced, and the way that his teachings mingled the created, nonhuman world with the heavenly and the sacramental.

Turning to poetry made perfect sense for Francis, even though religious leaders didn't write in verse. He was walking a road familiar since childhood. He knew Horace and Virgil— songs to mountains, to seas, to meadows, to creatures. In the tenth *Eclogue*, Virgil wrote of carving his love into the bark of young saplings so that the love would grow along with the trees. He also wrote that the shade of those grown junipers can sometimes block the light that fruit need to grow.[2]

Francis became the sort of poet who doesn't so much intend to set down something meaningful as finds meaning strangely revealed to him. All his writings are easy to understand except for this poem he wrote early in 1225—the most important. The "Canticle of the Creatures" stands at the beginning of Italian vernacular poetry and marks Francis as more than a saint. None of its content is explained by what was taught to monks or by priests and theologians. None of the symbolism used in it comes from the pages of the Bible, even though Francis inherited the poet's identification with the natural world from the psalms. His primary insight is in fact more Jewish than Christian. "The soul of every living thing shall bless your name, Adonai, our God," the ancient rabbis wrote for the close of the verses of praise in the morning liturgy.

It was the late winter of 1225 and his health was deteriorating rapidly. Elias took Francis to the hermitage in Cortona that the two enjoyed, but their stay was brief. Then, Elias began to insist on medical treatments for Francis's eyes, which were constantly swollen and full of fluids, but Francis insisted on being near Clare. So like an anchoress in a cell attached to a church, he spent some fifty days and nights beside San Damiano. It was then that he wrote the "Canticle of the Creatures."

With this canticle, he invented the nonliturgical, vernacular, spiritual song. Starting with poems or *laude* (praises), he composed tunes for them. Celano's description of this process reveals the biographer to also be something of a poet: "When the sweetest melody of spirit would bubble up in him, he would give exterior expression to it in French, and the breath of the divine whisper which his ear perceived in secret would burst forth in French in a song of joy." Celano goes on to describe what often happened next: "He would pick up a stick from the ground and putting it over his left arm, would draw across it, as across a violin, a little bow bent by means of a string; and going through the motions of playing, he would sing in French about his Lord."[3]

In his cold cell beside San Damiano, Francis was rapidly going blind and was suffering from other ailments. To his imagination, these troubles were not medical but spiritual. God had graced him, Christ had pierced him, and now the devil was hounding him, like the devil that stands in the background while St. John composes the book of Revelation on the island of Patmos in medieval manuscript illuminations. Francis even saw the tiny mice coming in and out of his cell as having evil portent. How strange for the "nature saint"—and how interesting, then, what he wrote.

"Most high, almighty, Good Lord God, / to you belong all praise, glory, honor, and blessing!" he begins. Then he especially praises as blessed what he can no longer see: "Praised be you . . . with all your creatures, especially our Brother Sun." The sun stood for the Divine Light, and as such it was masculine. Praising and thanking Brother Sun would later become more obvious in the Copernican worldview, as we came to understand the sun as the center of the solar system. What Francis drew from was the first day of Creation according to Genesis chapter 1: "God said, 'Let there be light.'" But his was also the ancient Roman perspective; once again, he was reaching back and beyond his usual biblical understanding of things for a more universal perspective.

After noting Brother Sun's "beauty, radiance, and splendor," Francis praises Sister Moon and the stars for being "bright and fair." This was a nearly blind man expressing the beauty of light even in darkness. Only with the help of Brother Sun could Francis see anything in front of him. He could no longer see stars, but he knew them: they are fixed and they shine. The psalmist said what was essentially echoed by the Greek philosophers, "Praise him, sun and moon; praise him, all you shining stars!" (Ps 148:3). Sun, moon, and stars were heavenly creatures in steady praise of God.

Francis took inspiration from the most unlikely things. Why did he view created things as his siblings? What inspired him to feel an intimate connection with nonhuman things? It is difficult to find precedents, but not later occurrences. Not long ago, the Polish poet Czeslaw Milosz wrote, "My Catholic upbringing implanted in me a respect for all things visible, connected by the property of being, or *esse*, that calls for unceasing admiration."[4] Further back, Bonaventure, the seventh Franciscan minister general, ascended Mount La Verna in order to contemplate the spirituality of his master. On that mountain, Bonaventure concluded, "With respect to the mirror of [God in] sensible things, it is possible that God might be contemplated not only *through* them, but also *in* them in as far as God is present in them by essence, power, and presence."[5] The Church taught the revelation of God in scripture and sacrament, and Francis would never have denied those holy realities, but he also looked into the eyes of creatures and the radiance of the cosmos and saw the Divine.

When he praises created things, as when he preaches to them, Francis seems to be what a philosopher would call a *nominalist*. While not denying the existence of universals, he denies their relevance to life in the real world. He's interested in individual birds, not "birdness." Thus far in the "Canticle," he praises, in the Irish poet Patrick Kavanagh's memorable line, "The placeless Heaven that's under all our noses." And as he goes on to praise God in wind, water, fire, and earth, it is his experience of the specifics of these that he wants to convey.

But Francis shares his experiences with only four of the senses. He communicates sights and sounds. He acknowledges smell when he insists that the friars always use some small portion of their garden for flowers. He uses touch—always—demonstrating its importance when embracing a leper and knowing its necessity when he is near death and wants to feel the ground under his naked body. But he always leaves out taste because, in his theological understanding, Francis follows the position of St. Jerome, who believed that Adam and Eve did not eat of the forbidden fruit in the garden simply or primarily from pride or desire for knowledge but due to gluttony. Taste, the basest of the senses, is what led them to sin of other kinds, including lust, for they immediately noticed their nakedness.

There is an alienness to the language of the "Canticle" that would have been upsetting to the average religious person of Francis's day. Imagine for a moment the double presumption: a subject matter other than heavenly praises in a language suited only for the coarse and secular. In fact, the "Canticle" was the first instance of a religious man using nonreligious language, trope, and imagery to answer religious questions. In that alone it was a challenge to authority. Since Francis's time—in fact, since about 1800—we've come to accept and expect religious questions and answers from outside of organized religion. And we've turned to calling them "spiritual," rather than "religious." Metaphysical otherness has become metaphysical loneliness. The "Canticle" prefigured this shift.

The "Canticle" is also sensuous in a way that must have concerned his contemporaries. Francis wrote of clouds and grass and fruit. After all, he came from the land of oranges, not apples. He was also a singer and composer, and this poem was meant from its creation to be sung. Its author was no prude when it came to using music to express emotion and appeal to the senses. On one occasion, while he was feeling depressed due to the disease in his eyes, Francis asked an unnamed friar who he knew had come to the order with a proficiency in lute playing to offer up something on the instrument to God for the sake of praise. He said, "The children of this world do not understand the divine sacraments. Human lust has turned musical instruments, once assigned to divine praises, into enjoyment for their ears. But I would like you, brother, to borrow a lute secretly and bring it here and to play some decent song to give some wholesome comfort to Brother Body, which is filled with pain."[6] The friar was somehow unable to acquiesce to this simple request.

This revelry, however, soon came to an end. After Cardinal Ugolino began adding his powerful insistence to Elias's previous requests, Francis finally allowed himself to be taken away from San Damiano when spring arrived—to Rieti for treatment of his eyes.

CHAPTER 29

FRANCIS'S CONFESSION

Spring 1225–May 1226, in and around Assisi

If 1225 began as an introspective year for Francis, it ended as a time of increasing intimacy with the triumvirate of those he trusted most: Leo, Giles, and Rufino. The year 1225 saw the continuation of that circle of friendship to the exclusion of other friars who were increasingly busy in ways of less interest to these four. Francis, Leo, Giles, and Rufino spent thousands of hours together in the penultimate year of Francis's life, as Francis lived out Jesus's words from John 15:15: "I do not call you servants any longer, because the servant does not know what the master is doing; but I have called you friends, because I have made known to you everything that I have heard from my Father."

As the brothers' friendship deepened, their order continued to be taken over by the Holy See and curia. Late in 1225, Honorius III promulgated a bull giving his full support for what Francis had already begun to accomplish years earlier during his time in Egypt. "Since no sacrifice is ever more pleasing to God than seeking to gain souls, we confer upon you who are going into the Kingdom of the Miramamolin [the Muslim Kingdom], the authority of the Apostolic See," it partially read. Francis of course hadn't asked for this. And he certainly wasn't pleased that the bull went on to say that only ordained friars could go on these missions or that in a later bull Honorius asked the archbishop of Toledo to make a bishop of one of the friars for the region.[1]

Meanwhile, Elias vanished from the scene. He was almost never at Francis's side. Never did Francis speak ill of his oldest friend and vicar, but one senses that their friendship was passing.

Then, one winter evening just before dark, with a frown of concern, Giles came to Francis and said, "Father, someday soon you will die, and the family of the rest of us will be left behind in this vale of tears."[2] It was a bit melodramatic, but Giles was quoting a metaphor used by the psalmists. "Choose someone in the order, will you, on whom your spirit may rest, and to whom the mantle of your ministry may be passed?"

What happened next, according to the tradition, was that Francis sighed, and not a sigh like any other; he drew "a sigh with every word." In other words, he had trouble saying what he honestly felt to this close friend. Perhaps he was choking on tears as he spoke.

"I don't see anyone who can lead this group of varied men, who can shepherd such a diverse flock. But . . . I can say what sort of person this family needs," Francis replied. And he went on to describe the ideal vicar general, knowing full well that Elias currently held that position. Listing the qualities as one would compose a list of ingredients, Francis continued, "We need someone of great reputation, above reproach. He must show discernment. He must be committed to prayer, both for the sake of his own soul and for the sake of everyone else. We need him to be meek and simple, without being lazy or indulgent, and to never show favorites, taking care of every brother, whether simple or great.

"He should hate money, comfort the afflicted, and never turn his back on anyone, even a brother who runs away from the order who asks for forgiveness. He should understand that he stands in Christ's place as leader of this family and, like our Lord, should delight in insults.

"Finally, I see a shepherd for this order who is a figure of justice, who is surrounded by friends who are honest and receive every person who comes to us with a holy cheerfulness. That is the sort of person we need!"

Often during his last year, Francis spent time alone. It was the mystic who met God on Mount La Verna who also wrote a final confession, a spiritual "Testament," in the first half of 1226.

There is a worrisome tone to this document, as no other writing of his quite possesses. It was carefully dictated to one of his good friends, Caesar of Speyer, in the late spring at Portiuncula. The "Testament" is a short autobiography that is at times sincere and at others more manifest. In it Francis reveals himself as more complex than the joyful friar he was before his experiences in the Nile delta, before Cardinal Ugolino's subtle but serious betrayals, and before Elias had veered so far from what they once loved together.

"The Lord gave me, your Brother Francis, the ability to do penance in the following way," he begins. There is no question who is writing or what he is writing about. And then he tells the story of how lepers once repulsed (were "like acid to") him—until "the Lord himself" led him among them. God, Francis says, turned his heart around, which is the essence of what *conversion* means—being turned around. "And shortly afterward," he concludes his first paragraph with a flourish, "I got up and left the world." What a perfect example of his almost cinematic understanding of a life.

"The Lord gave me a faith in churches," begins the next paragraph, and the one following: "Then God gave me brothers." He is a simple man who is not simply humble: he sees his life humbly. "I worked with my hands, then, and I still desire to do so," opens the fourth paragraph. Then he reminds his brothers to maintain absolute poverty, never to lose sight of the teachings in their shared Rule, to pray the Divine Office, and always to obey their vicar general.

"Whoever observes all of these things will be blessed in heaven with the blessing of the Most High Father and on earth he will be filled with the blessing of his Beloved Son, with the Holy Ghost the Comforter and all the powers of heaven and all the saints. And, I Brother Francis, your servant both in soul and body, confirm this for you with a holy blessing."

CHAPTER 30

OCTOBER 3–4, 1226, REVISITED

June–October 1226, in and around Assisi

"God delivered Francis in His mercy from the perils of this present life," wrote Bonaventure in the opening sentence of his biography. But that is not how Francis saw it. His life was precious to him—and yet he was also a complicated man who loved both the terra firma he walked upon and the heavenly future that filled his God-soaked imagination.

"You should never possess anything worth possessing in the eyes of the world," Francis once said. "All things should end in poverty, should sing to the world of your pilgrimage and your exile."[1]

He faced death not so much as a courageous martyr but as a man who, having tasted a delicious life, knew that in death things would only get better. On the opening page of Plutarch's *Lives*, the world's first biographer noted how geographers "crowd into the edges of their maps parts of the world which they do not know about, adding notes in the margin to the effect, that beyond this lies nothing but the sandy deserts full of wild beasts, unapproachable bogs, Scythian ice, or a frozen sea."[2] There was widespread fear and uncertainty about "the unknown," and in Francis's century, over a millennium after Plutarch wrote those lines, there were still plenty of unknowns. Francis demonstrated none of this sort of fear. He seems to have habitually run into the dangerous unknown without thinking much of it—whether it was in the form of leprous men and women, foreign lands, or what some of his contemporaries considered the personification of evil, the sultan, with whom he dined.

In the year leading up to his death, Francis spoke less than ever before. The cataphatic mystic became an apophatic one, and his experiences were mostly of an interior sort. The final months were quieter still, and his last week was almost silent. These beautiful lines from an early poem of the nineteenth-century Englishman John Clare may capture Francis's emotions during this time: "He turns to heaven to witness what he feels / And silent shows what want of words conceals."[3]

He knew his body was precious because every human body was. Witness the attention he paid to lepers' sores or the way he confessed, in those final days, the unkind attention he had too often paid to Brother Ass, who surely could have served him longer had he been more generous with himself. Even while embracing death, Francis was wise enough to realize that his body was failing him.

A medical-historical approach to the language used by contemporaries to describe his ailments would probably reveal that Francis had battled depression for years, and now his body was not only burdened with glaucoma but leprous. It is likely, in fact, that he suffered throughout the last years of his life from the non-lepromatous (not disfiguring) form of the disease, which was unknown to medieval medicine. Most human beings have a natural immunity to leprosy, or Hansen's disease, but that immunity is compromised most of all when people drink polluted water and eat a poor diet. Leprosy would explain the problems with Francis's eyes and would make more logical sense, given his lifestyle and choices, than a diagnosis of malaria or tuberculosis. It might even explain the nature of the stigmatic wounds on his hands and feet, as two Franciscan physicians have recently attempted to do.[4] If this is so, the miracle of the stigmata is no less than it otherwise might be, for "Francis can be seen as one who became profoundly Christlike in his transformation into the very outcast and suffering Christ he embraced in the leper. His stigmata can be understood as the wounds of a man who became a leper precisely because of his love for the Crucified Leper."[5]

Francis's physical health had deteriorated so much that he knew his life would end. Some said that it seemed as if he were "insensible . . . living within himself. . . . The noise outside did not seize his ears, nor did his eyes wander around on things outside."[6] His vitality had been slipping away for two or three years, and as he declined, it would have been natural, given his other desires and experiences, for his mind to turn toward the afterlife. But according to what we know, he doesn't seem to have spent time pondering heaven or what the mystics call the beatific vision. That would have been too cerebral. Instead, he was drawn to the presence of God that he had known intimately for twenty years, like a son still wanting to know the caress of his mother. The later Franciscan Spiritual Jacopone of Todi expresses this in a poem entitled "How the Soul Complains to God of the Over-ardent Love Infused in Her":

> For Thee, O Love, my heart consumes away,
> I cry, I call, I yearn for Thy caress;
> Living, I perish when Thou does not stay,
> Sighing and mourning for my Blessedness.[7]

In a verse of the "Canticle of the Creatures" added in these final months of his life, Francis goes on to praise "Sister Death," welcoming her as kin. This was not a man afraid to die, but one who seemed to look forward to the experience. Again—as with the other verses of that poem—he asked his brothers to sing the verse. Every human being "lives between two eternities," said Thomas Carlyle, meaning that what is in the middle—called human life and history—is brief. Francis seemed to grasp this and understand that life, as well as the eternities that are separated by it, is important.

Celano tells us how, in the last days before he died, Francis called his favorite friars to him. They were all in the palace of the bishop of Assisi, looking out on the piazza where Francis had stripped naked before his father twenty years earlier. Francis blessed each friar individually, surely with the priestly blessing from Leviticus. He was like Jacob and his brood of twelve—that's who Celano compared him to, and then to Moses, "about to ascend the mountain that the Lord had shown him."[8]

Francis turned to Elias, who was kneeling to his left, and placed his right hand on Elias's head. Like Isaac, blind and not wanting to be wrong, he asked the others present, "Whose head is this?"

"Elias," a few of them confirmed. Elias himself remained silent.

"I want to especially bless you, my son," Francis began, and then he quoted a verse from the New Testament Letter to the Ephesians, in which St. Paul calls for his congregation to live according to "one body and one Spirit" in holy service; Paul concludes that verse by reminding them that they live under "one God and Father of all"—and this is the part that Francis quoted in reference to Elias—"who is above all and through all and in all" (Eph 4:6). In other words, no friar was more important to the community of friars than Elias.

> The Most High has increased my brothers and sons through your guidance. So, too, in you and upon you, I bless them all. May the King bless you in heaven and on earth. I bless you as I am able, and wish I could all the more. What I can't do may the One who can do all things do in you! May God remember your labor and may you find a place of reservation upon all of the just who are to be rewarded. May you receive every blessing you desire and may every request of yours be heard.[9]

At this point, an unnamed friar asked Francis why he had abdicated his leadership of their order back in 1220. He said that he had felt abandoned. "I can't help it if the brothers wouldn't follow in my footsteps. And there were certain prelates who lured them toward other things," Francis replied.[10]

Then he was done. He asked them to carry him out of town, down to Portiuncula.

———————— ✍ ————————

There is no questioning Elias's grief in the moments immediately after Francis's death. "God is the father of orphans," he groaned in his letter to Cardinal Ugolino and the friars. His feeling of abandonment was palpable.

Bartholomew of Pisa wrote toward the end of the fourteenth century that the heart of the saint was removed and buried at Portiuncula.[11] This struck an immediate chord with many who knew Francis's affection for the place—it made a certain kind of sense—but Bartholomew was probably allowing his romantic tendencies to get away with him. No one before him ever mentioned that anything less than the whole Francis lay in state at San Giorgio. As Francis's vicar general and personal vicar, Elias had more control over what happened in those moments than anyone else.

When Elias wrote the letter about Francis to the order, he made no mention of the special blessing he received from Francis's hand. The haughtiness that was to come was absent in those sad moments. However, it is possible to see the separation between the two men in Elias's strange choice of language. On the last page he begins with words that make perfect sense, but then goes on to allude to an obscure passage of the Bible that in the original context represents the words of a prostitute asking for an affair: "It is in keeping with our love for him that we rejoice with Francis. Still, it is right to mourn him! It belongs to us to rejoice with Francis, for he has not died but gone to the fair in heaven, taking with him a bag of money and will not return until the full moon." "For my husband is not at home; he has gone on a long journey. He took a bag of money with him; he will not come home until full moon," reads chapter 7 of the book of Proverbs. It must not have made much sense to the friars, either. "Now we are like orphans without a father," resonated more clearly.[12]

Not long after, Elias was there the day the Pope Gregory IX (the former Cardinal Ugolino) formally canonized his friend. "The solemn day arrives," began Celano in his account, published a year later and written by one who was there, "with ecstatic rejoicing. Bishops gather, abbots arrive, prelates from the most remote areas appear; a king's presence is noticed, with a noble crowd of counts and dukes. All accompany the lord of the whole earth [the pope], and with him enter the city of Assisi in happy procession."[13] What pride Elias must have felt on that July 16, 1228, standing beside Bishop Guido, just behind the pope. He was counted as one of the greatest men of Christendom. Even more, when Guido died an old man two weeks later, it seemed that no one but Elias remained who knew Francis as well from the early days.

As for the hasty, paranoid way in which Elias buried his friend's body, one only has to consider what happened eighteen months later during the burial of Elizabeth of Hungary to see that his actions may have prevented something catastrophic. Elizabeth, the child queen of Hungary who became a Franciscan tertiary and founder of hospitals, was already famous for sanctity and quickly on her way to being sainted when she died at twenty-four in November 1231. This is why, while the body was being buried in Marburg later that day, "the faithful tore at the clothes, hair, ears and nails of the cadaver."[14] The same thing happened earlier that year to the body of Anthony of Padua, the Franciscan friar who, despite his love for theology, was always faithful to the spirit and intentions of Francis. The order lost parts of him, too, before they decided, the following year, to begin construction of a basilica in Padua to safeguard what remained of Anthony's corpse.

PART FOUR

It is God who executes judgment,
putting down one and lifting up another.
                                    —**Psalm 75:7**

CHAPTER 31

GREATER THAN GOTHIC

1227–1228, Assisi

Francis and Elias were walking together one afternoon between Foligno and Assisi when they came upon a poor man stopped in the road. Having been given half a loaf of bread by a farmer outside Foligno, they were carrying it back to Portiuncula to share with their brothers for the evening meal. But when they met the man on the road, Francis said they should stop and break the bread.

The man said nothing to them while he ate. His face was deformed in such a way that he probably hadn't spoken in years. No matter. A quarter hour later, Francis and Elias were back on their way and Francis began to talk.

"His poverty is our shame," he said to Elias.

"Why?" replied Elias. "We fed him."

"Poverty for him is total. It is irreversible."

"You wed yourself to poverty, Francis."

"Yes. Poverty is my Lady. But poverty is his misery. In the future, I should never be richer than another man."[1]

Elias recalled that moment as he stood in one of the great new churches of Christendom, recently constructed in France. Names such as Chartres, Saint-Denis, and Salisbury were on the tongues of prelates and pilgrims, since such towns had recently begun to take towering shape with the emergence of their new Gothic cathedrals. Friars in France had seen and reported back from Chartres, where the remarkable south and north porches were completed before Francis went to Damietta, and the soaring high vaults in the nave were in place before he died. This new architecture was designed to honor height and light, and it drew people who sought God or Beauty.

Under our altar will lie the body of the greatest saint the world has ever seen. Upon his foundation, we also will build a great church, Elias thought to himself.

The Church of the Holy Sepulchre in Jerusalem was also an inspiration to him. This legendary church was often discussed and desired by the leaders of Christendom over the course of Francis and Elias's lifetimes—from the battle in 1187 when Jerusalem was lost to Christians until the end of 1228 when Frederick II negotiated for Christian pilgrims once again to have access to it. Elias had never seen it with his own eyes—he and Francis never made it all the way to Jerusalem—but he knew of its glory, as well as its two-storied structure.[2]

Elias set about making plans to construct the Basilica of San Francesco, as well as a convent to house the friars, within weeks of Francis's death. This is when Elias, most of all, showed himself possessed of the qualities of a true enthusiast. Before there were any signs of his corruption, he was, at least in his own mind, the greatest of Francis's followers. Having seen the ability of reforming religion to effect positive change in the lives of people, society, and the Church itself, Elias wanted still more. Those were things accomplished during Francis's lifetime. Elias would be exceptional among the exceptional friars who remained after Francis's death. He would expect even more of himself and his order. And Elias would not only guard Francis's body but build around his reputation a tower of honor greater than anyone else could imagine.

Francis had expressed his own architectural-spiritual vision years earlier, in his renovations of San Damiano, which was still the motherhouse for the Sisters of Clare. One scholar wrote "Francis was already expressing his own clear idea of what a church should be for the people of his time: a church with a single hall, where clergy and people could come together in communion of prayer and word—a word popular rather than scholastic, moral rather than doctrinal, exhortative rather than exegetical, directed towards 'announcing to the faithful vices and virtues, punishment and glory.'"[3] These simple principles can still be seen in San Damiano today: in the thick wooden planks in the refectory and the close, intimate spaces of the dormitory and the choir.

But Elias—who turned out, not unlike Abbot Suger at Saint-Denis, to have a supreme gift for architectural design and vision—dreamed up what became a double basilica, with a mostly Romanesque Lower Church and an Italian Gothic Upper Church. There were actually many similarities between the two men. Suger was born precisely a century before Elias and became abbot of his monastery at the age of forty-one, very nearly Elias's age at the time of Francis's death. More importantly, Suger was a novice in religious life from the age of nine. Elias and Suger were both men who, from boyhood, probably showed an unusual commitment to a religious life of intensity and passion.

It was into this master project of building the basilica in Assisi that Elias poured himself, especially after the Pentecost general chapter meeting of 1227. There, John of Parenti, the minister provincial for Spain, was elected to replace Elias, whom Francis had named vicar general, as minister general of the entire order.

They do not understand. Elias was deeply disappointed, probably severely wounded. How could the friars who knew how close his relationship had been with Francis—surely the closest of any other man over so long a time—not see fit to look to him for leadership in the aftermath of the saint's death? *How could they be so blind?* The newly elected pope Gregory IX probably had a hand in the friars' decision. Gregory needed Elias to build the basilica, and Elias dedicated himself to the work.

Supervising every detail and sparing no expense, he became almost as excessive in these matters as Abbot Suger had been a century earlier at Saint-Denis, justifying his use of gold and precious gems to adorn God's house. Suger had said, "The charm and beauty of this house of God, the splendor of the multicolor gems, lifts me beyond my everyday concerns, and in meditation I reflect on the diversity of the virtues, transposing what is material into what is immaterial. I feel as if I am living in some strange part of the universe which lies somewhere between the slime of earth and the purity of heaven."[4] The outer wall of the basilica in Assisi is all that portrays any degree of Franciscan simplicity, but it is quickly betrayed when one walks inside.

———————

We've already seen how uncomfortable Francis would have been, to say the least, in the lavish temple being prepared to honor him. He surely would have put a stop to it, had he had the chance. After all, this was the "little poor man" who used found and begged stones to repair his first church. But it wasn't only the basilica that would have concerned the Poverello.[5]

The Sacro Convento, a permanent residence for the friars, was also under construction. Francis had always desired that he and the friars would live like foxes without dens, but Elias's convent, mostly complete by 1230, included a refectory, dormitory, chapter hall, and scriptorium. With the massive Convento came even some of the trappings of monastic seclusion, such as a marble choir screen to shield the friars from the nonreligious at Mass in the nave of the Lower Church, powerful arches, and buttresses. The book collection in the library and scriptorium rivaled that of Avignon a century later. The band of carefree Christ-followers was transforming into a massive religious order. Lines of George Herbert from four centuries later communicate what many friars were thinking: "All Solomon's sea of brass and world of stone

/ Is not so dear to thee as one good groan. / And truly brass and stones are heavy things, / Tombs for the dead, not temples fit for thee."[6]

Some of the brothers who had been closest to Francis rejected Elias's project, naming it for what it was: an insult to the memory of their father. Leo, Rufino, and Angelo reminded their fellow friars what he had said about the sort of church and home that should be built, if and when necessary, for those who call themselves Franciscan: "Let them have poor hovels prepared, made of loam and wood, and some other small cells where the brothers can sometimes pray and may be free to work both for their own greater credit and as a precaution against idle words. . . . It is better that the friars have small and poor friaries and buildings made for them, observing their profession and giving a good example to their neighbors, than if they go against their profession, and show a bad example to others."[7]

They remembered how, several years before his death, when he heard that a house had been constructed for the friars living in Bologna, he had ordered everyone out of it, even those who were ill. Later that year, when the people of Assisi built a house to help accommodate the hundreds of friars due to visit for the Pentecost chapter meeting, Francis climbed on the roof and began tearing off the tiles, one by one. "Only when knights from the commune shouted up that the house was the property of the city and that Francis was destroying public property, did Francis stop and come down."[8]

Mysterious things began to happen. One day during the early stages of construction, Brother Leo snatched and then quickly shattered a large marble vase that Elias had set up as a collection receptacle for financial contributions to fund the new church. Pilgrims' coins spilled to the floor. When Elias found out who had done it—probably when Leo walked up to him and proudly confessed it—he ordered him flogged. Other obstructions were placed in Elias's way, as well.

The complaints of some friars turned into the formation of an order within the order, the "Spirituals," who stood in opposition to the leadership and decisions of any minister general, cardinal, or pope who would turn their fraternity away from its focus on the principles in the Rule. Brother Giles became a prominent member of these Spirituals. Living near Perugia, he had, since Francis's death, gained a reputation for holiness that was approaching the founder's. It was likely Giles who encouraged the more timid Leo to go to the basilica in Assisi and break that vase. When Giles first saw the nearly completed Sacro Convento he said, as if to emphasize that he was a member of a different order from the majority of friars, "Now you have need of nothing except wives!"[9]

His bitterness was matched by other Spirituals' extreme dedication to the original ideal of personal poverty. Leo once refused the offer of a newer tunic to replace the one he was wearing, which was unfit for keeping out the cold of the coming winter months. "I know that I'm soon to die," he is reputed to have said, "so I don't want another tunic now. I want death to find me a poor man."[10] Even the idea of building from the ground up was anathema to Franciscan values. A friar was supposed to adapt to his surroundings and accommodate himself in previously existing structures, inasmuch as dwellings with roofs were important at all. Men like Giles usually constructed their huts out of found materials. Ownership was of course frowned upon, and commissioning new foundations or considering architectural matters important a radical departure. Back in Bologna, Francis had refused to even enter the city when he heard there was a "House of Friars" there.

"The house belongs to me, my son. The house belongs to me!" Cardinal Ugolino sent an urgent message to Francis when he heard that even those who were sick were sent into the street and ordered never to return to any dwelling owned by a Franciscan. Only then did Francis relent and allow the house to be used, lived in by friars who could be turned out at any moment, as strangers and pilgrims who are never quite at home in this world. The same scenario then played itself out later that year when Francis climbed on the roof of the new chapter hall near St. Mary of the Angels, ripping off tiles.[11]

Years earlier, Francis had argued with Elias, who was overseeing the building of a fine house at Portiuncula so that the friars could say the Divine Office as a large assembly. The friars who took Elias's side began to talk about how, in provinces distant from Assisi, beams of wood were actually harder to come by than stones, and so houses were being built for friars out of materials that were contrary to the founder's teachings. Francis had no way of keeping up with all of this.

After his death, a tract of land on Assisi's southwest corner was soon identified, and gifted to the Franciscans and Elias. There, on what had once been known as the Hill of Hell, construction began. On July 18, 1228, the basilica's first stone was laid—two days after Pope Gregory IX officially made Francis a saint. He concluded the papal bull he preached that day in Assisi by saying, "Since the wondrous events of his glorious life are quite well known to us because of the great familiarity he had with us while we still occupied a lower rank, and since we are fully convinced by reliable witnesses of the many brilliant miracles, we and the flock entrusted to us, by the mercy of God, are confident of being assisted at his intercession and of having in heaven a patron whose friendship we enjoyed on earth. With the consultation and approval of our Brothers, we have decreed that he be enrolled in the catalogue of saints worthy of veneration."

CHAPTER 32

HONOR LOST AND REGAINED

1230–1232, Assisi, Rome, Jerusalem

There was Elias, carried on the shoulders of a handful of friars, who burst into the Pentecost general chapter meeting of 1230 shouting "Elias! Elias!" A few days earlier, he had buried Francis's body deep in the rock. Those few friends were attempting to assist him in retaking the minister generalship by coup. But the larger group rejected them out of hand, roundly booing the obnoxious effort, forcing them from the gathering, treating them like the dangerous gang they had become.

Elias retreated to a place of hermitage founded by him and Francis nineteen years earlier in Cortona in the Arezzo of Tuscany, now a Ghibellinian city-state friendlier to the emperor than the pope.

Meanwhile, John Parenti was reelected minister general, and the friars sent a delegation, led by Brother John himself, to Rome on September 1 to meet with Gregory IX, seeking clarity of interpretation around the finer points of the Rule and "Testament" of Francis. With John were Anthony of Padua; Haymo of Faversham, who became minister general several years later; Leo of Milan, who would later become the archbishop of Milan; and a handful of others. Was Francis's commitment to absolute poverty to be maintained? Was his "Testament" a commentary on the Rule, and was it binding on the friars? Gregory promulgated a bull on these subjects, *Quo elongati*, quickly, on September 28.

"I know his mind more fully than you do," the pope wrote to the leaders of the order, putting them on notice from the start. "Although I hold a lower rank than he does [since Gregory himself had just made Francis a saint], I stood by him while he composed the Rule and I obtained its approval from the Holy See."

Francis's "Testament" was a personal document and wasn't binding on others, Gregory explained, "because an equal has no command over another equal." He instructed that "spiritual friends" were permitted to help provide for a friar's daily needs, while those friars were still to keep to the principle of personally owning nothing. This interpretation was similar to how a *Shabbos*-observing Jew might ask a non-Jew to work and handle the money on the holy day: a Franciscan friar, the pope said, could instruct one of those well-meaning "friends" to obtain something for him on his behalf, all the while never personally "receiving coins of money."

"*Sine proprio*" was the phrase for how every friar was to live in poverty, according to the last version of Francis's Rule. What did that mean, exactly, the friars wanted to know—literally "without property," "in poverty," or "without anything of one's own"? More than any other single document or statement, *Quo elongati* shaped the future of the discussion. Gregory's interpretation of "*sine proprio*" paved the way for an understanding of poverty that was less absolute. Simplicity and humility are not necessarily tied to owning nothing in common, he argued, opening the doors wider to the acquisition of all manner of things, pursuits, and buildings. This ruling was essential to rationalizing the ongoing work of the basilica, and although he wasn't there in Rome to see the pope himself, "Elias felt that the opportunity had been given him to take things now into his own hands."[1]

Back in Cortona, like a prophet who takes to the wilderness for a time, Elias was letting his hair grow and pulling on his beard. Was this a deep penance, or was the commune of Cortona a place to cultivate his private anger? "We incorporate anger by hiding it," wrote Montaigne, and he quotes Virgil with lines that might easily apply to Elias in exile:

> So, when with crackling flames a caldron fries,
> The bubbling waters from the bottom rise;
> Above the brim they force their fiery way;
> Black vapors climb aloft, and cloud the day.

Over the next two years some of the friars came and went, reporting back to John Parenti that Elias's sorrow seemed to be genuine. Then, like a member of the College of Cardinals who had made years of backroom dealings in order to maneuver himself into position to be elected pope, Elias returned to Umbria with confidence in the spring of 1232. Work on the basilica continued immediately, which pleased many of the friars, and Elias shored up support among others for a return to the top post. At the next election, a few months later, he was elected minister general; John Parenti was forced to step down. As in 1227, the outcome likely owed much to Gregory IX's doing. *Never mind,* Elias rationalized. He had done his penance and now he would do for Francis what no one else was as capable of doing.

───────※───────

In Rome, Gregory IX was fuming over the actions of Frederick II. As one Italian historian of the last century put it, "The Papacy and the Empire are the two great back-drops to medieval European history. . . . Every movement is conditioned by their looming presence."[2] The emperor had refused to go on the Fifth Crusade back in 1217, leading Honorius III to publicly blame him for the devastating ultimate defeat at Damietta in 1221. In the middle decades of the century, the crusades were often used cynically by the Holy See, which promulgated them. Popes were both reminding the kings of their superiority and keeping imperial armies busy with supposedly holy activity. Reminiscent of Rome in the age of the Antonines, the popes were adept at "preserving peace by a constant preparation for war," to quote Gibbon's *Decline and Fall of the Roman Empire.*

When the Sixth Crusade came, Frederick again waffled on his commitment to lead the West in recapturing Jerusalem. After beginning a journey to the East in 1227, Frederick had turned back, naming illness as the reason. Gregory would hear no excuses and excommunicated him on September 29.

Nevertheless, Frederick still wanted to at least give the appearance of attempting to please the Holy See. In June of the following year, he sailed from Brindisi to Cyprus, then on to Acre, where everyone seemed to know of his falling out with the pope. What was he doing there? Attempting to hold onto his power, perhaps even redeem himself. To the surprise of all Christendom, after a year of negotiations, the excommunicated emperor took back Jerusalem from the Saracens.

More than a century's worth of crusades—atrocities committed, armies lost, and treasuries spent—had done nothing to win back the land of Christ and Calvary; popes and kings had invested a tremendous amount of financial and human resources to do what, on the surface, was understood to be attempting to reclaim the Holy Land for Christendom. Under the surface, there was scapegoating, as popes and kings, as well as the knights and soldiers who accepted the call to go, made the evil of the Muslim "other" paramount; eradicating it became unconsciously synonymous with making (the evil in) one's own life somehow better.

Then, despite living under the official condemnation of the papacy, Frederick performed a bloodless coup. No one knows precisely how, but he regained Jerusalem in 1229 without a single battle. It was a cynic's negotiated truce with Sultan al-Kamil—an agreement that split up Jerusalem and the surrounding holy places—achieved because the two sides had a common foe in Gregory IX. It failed to satisfy either Frederick's or the sultan's constituencies, but it was enough to lead Gregory IX to reverse the excommunication he'd put upon Frederick, and on August 28, 1230, the two men dined together at the papal palace in Anagni.

Meanwhile, back in Assisi, the floor of the Lower Church was now settled into the rock of the mountain on which the entire basilica would soon rest. Francis's body remained a comfortable, quiet, fifteen feet below that marble and cement. And Anthony of Padua died on June 13, 1231.

CHAPTER 33

GRAVY DRIPPING FROM HIS CHIN

1232–1238, in and around Assisi

"I'm shivering, Francis," Elias said one afternoon while they walked down from the caves of Mount Subasio.

"Cold?"

"Freezing!"

"You're already wearing two tunics, Elias."

"It is not enough. And the sky is clear. We'll have frost tonight."

"Sew one of the old sacks into the lining when we get back," Francis told him. "If we can't bear these small hardships of the flesh then we become like the Hebrews wanting to go back to Egypt."[1]

Elias recalled this exchange with a mix of fondness and bitterness.

Toward the end of 1232, Elias built papal apartments for Pope Gregory IX at the Sacro Convento, making Gregory's already frequent appearances in Assisi much simpler and more comfortable. Members of the papal curia, too, began spending more time among the friars.[2] Within weeks, rumors began to circulate that Elias had turned the friars into "tax collectors," so passionate was he about finishing the basilica in Assisi. And he was receiving any patron with whom he might trade spiritual promises for cash.

Elias seemed a different person from what he had been before his exile. He had come back from Cortona a repentant sinner, but his visage changed quickly after he regained power. The friars witnessed seemingly routine exercises of pride and ambition, as well as a consolidation of decision-making power, as if he wanted to be more a king than a minister. It was rumored that he was even spending time in the papal apartments, when Gregory wasn't there, and with alchemists.

Elias remembered what Francis had once taught about how to respond to ministers who refuse to perform the holy office as they have been taught to do. Like Beatrice in Dante's *Paradiso*, who on the verge of the beatific vision is still able to pronounce a curse upon Pope Clement V (the one who moved the Holy See from Rome to Avignon), Francis added this in his "Testament" amid a beautiful teaching on the Franciscan life: "The brothers are bound by obedience to the Rule to turn over to a just custodian anyone who refuses to perform the divine offices as they should. That custodian must then guard the offender day and night, as a man in chains, so as to make escape impossible. Guard him day and night—until you are able to turn him over personally to the Bishop of Ostia, who is our lord and protector." Elias was shirking these responsibilities, now, and many of the friars under him wanted to do just that—turn him over to somebody.[3]

Yet Elias often said that, like a pope, he was going to hold onto his position for life. Throughout this second generalship, he never convened a general chapter meeting, as the Rule requires annually, and he sent far from him any friar objecting to his policies, which were often self-aggrandizing or contrary to the spirit of the Rule. He often had beside him a certain lay brother named John who was known for brutal bullying on behalf of his minister. Elias would regularly empower John, by obedience and for the good of the order, to inflict physical punishments on disobedient brothers. The minister general had few real friends and only a dozen or so friars who remained loyal to him.

Clare, strangely, remained in his corner. On June 11, 1234, Agnes of Prague, a cousin of Elizabeth of Hungary, had entered the Franciscan monastery in Prague that her own dowry had built two years earlier. Encouraged by what Franciscanism offered, Agnes followed the path of giving away all that she possessed for the sake of the needy in her native city. This was her response to the conniving of her father, King Ottokar I, who pressured her to accept a strategic marriage to the son of none other than Emperor Frederick II. Agnes refused, and when her father died in 1233, she was finally able to wiggle free of the political scheme. She immediately began receiving congratulatory letters of spiritual counsel from Clare in Assisi, who knew a kindred sister when she heard what Agnes had done.

Agnes's rejection of Frederick's son reached well beyond Franciscan circles, as evidenced by what Clare wrote in her first letter to her less than a month after she entered the Prague monastery as a postulant: "Hearing the news, which brings you the highest honor, of your holy conversion and manner of life—news that has been reputably disseminated not only to me but to nearly every region of the world—I rejoice and exalt exceedingly in the Lord. Concerning this news, I am not the only one who rejoices, but I am joined by all those who serve and desire to serve Jesus Christ."[4] The joy in heaven was not simply because a life was turned to the way of salvation but because that life was so noteworthy, the path she took so perfectly in line with what Francis had taught, and what she turned away from so repugnant.

Simultaneously, throughout the summer of 1234, Frederick II and hundreds of mercenaries were holding the valley of Spoleto under siege, trying to gain a strategic military foothold in Umbria. Assisi itself was targeted, and San Damiano, vulnerable outside the city walls, was used to gain access to the city. Frederick's men scaled its cloistered walls one night only to meet Clare face-to-face. In one of the most iconic moments in the first century of Franciscan history, she took the monstrance from the chapel and held it in front of her, chasing the men away.

There was much that Clare couldn't have known from her place in San Damiano, but her dealings with the pope had taught her to be about as wary of papal "protection" and advice as she was of imperial protection. She warned Agnes in a second letter: "If someone tells you something else or suggests anything to you that may hinder your perfection and that seems contrary to your divine vocation, even though you must respect him, still, do not follow his advice; instead, poor virgin, embrace the Poor Christ."[5] Subversion from a quiet but powerful corner.

The change in Elias slowly became obvious to all, and it was a shock to the spiritual friends who knew him well to see what he did and didn't do. Friars were increasingly appalled and disbelieving that this could be the brother whom they had long known—and whom Francis had lovingly called "mother." Elias had been a real friar—not a pretender who casually walks into the life and then wanders just as easily away from it. He had been, after all, the vicar of St. Francis himself.

The puzzling figure was Clare. By 1238, San Damiano had some fifty vowed women, and the Second Order had spread to houses throughout central Italy—in Perugia, Spello, Arezzo, and Tuscany. Clare remained loyal to Elias, stayed mute on the subject of the grand basilica, and found fault rather with Gregory IX. Praising Elias in that letter to Agnes of Prague, Clare wished that Elias would somehow convince the pope to allow her and the sisters at San Damiano to follow the true rule of poverty as Francis intended and to be governed as the men were, without monastic principles of strict enclosure, silence, and governance by an abbess or abbot. She may have even threatened hunger strikes to the pope, while putting her trust in Elias to do what was right.

"Don't listen to that person who has more zeal than reason," Gregory IX wrote back to her.[6] *That person* was Elias. Gregory knew him well. But Clare was blinded to Elias's true character, so closely did she still associate him with their friend, Francis.

Soon, the dissenting majority appealed directly to Gregory IX. Jordan of Giano was their leader. He pleaded with the pope to do something.

"Write down your charges against him," Gregory replied.

When Elias got wind of what was happening, he went to see Gregory personally. "What they say about me is untrue, Holy Father," he offered. "Besides, they are in obedience to me. They shouldn't be coming to you. I am their minister general."

Gregory was unmoved. He could see where this was headed. "Any appeal to me, Christ's vicar, is above all other appeals," he told Elias, who then quietly left.[7]

Meanwhile, after the death of Anthony of Padua, Caesar of Speyer was gradually seen, along with other friars such as Giles and Leo and Jordan, as the true inheritor of the spiritual leadership and authority left vacant by Francis. A contemplative, evangelical, and determined man, as well as one of the best preachers of his generation, Caesar was by force of character perceived throughout the provinces as Elias's silent, sworn opposition. The two had been together with Francis in Egypt during the time when Francis met with the sultan; both had been exposed to the teaching of their master, a distinctively Franciscan approach to human conflict: "That approach consisted in the belief that God did not want his creatures to resolve the difficult problems of human existence through further bloodshed but rather through more peaceful means and dialogue in the manner of the nonviolent Jesus, respectful of their common and sacred creaturehood."[8] Early in 1238, Elias had Caesar of Speyer put under house arrest, and within months, one day when Caesar would not be quiet, his jailer beat him mercilessly to death.

We hear of Elias wearing an Armenian cap on his head, recreating the lush Assisi apartments wherever he traveled, sitting on piles of cushions in front of roaring fires, eating like a king, satisfied to have others serving him. On one occasion in 1239, he was in Parma on his way to see Frederick II at the request of Gregory IX, sent to mediate between emperor and pope. The *podestà* of Parma, knowing Elias's reputation, came with some knights to pay his respects to the man. When they were shown into the room, Elias remained sitting by his fireplace, uninterested in greeting his guests.

"What brings you to Parma," asked Gerard of Corigia, the *podestà*.

"I am being both drawn and pushed," Elias replied, as in a riddle.[9] This was part of his arrogance: fostering the reputation that he had the ear of powerful men and yet was accountable only to God. Brother Illuminato, Elias's secretary, who had been with Francis before the sultan and had traveled with him back from the Holy Land two decades earlier, was instructed to keep an ornate book preserving every letter and written communication that Elias received from foreign governments and secular princes and kings; they were so precious to him.

The building of the basilica was rapidly coming to a conclusion. The enthusiasm Elias possessed for the work even led him to ask Friar William of England, a Franciscan who was already dead, to refrain from miracle working. Of course this sounds odd, but it took place in a time when the veil between life and death was perceived as thin. This Friar William is not to be confused with Friar William of Rubruck (born in 1220), the Flemish missionary explorer, or with Friar William of Ockham (born in 1287), the later English scholastic theologian. One of the original followers of Francis, this William replaced John of Capella, who had left the order, as the second twelfth man. But William was renowned for sanctity more in death than in life. He died before Easter 1232 and was buried, as were eleven other friends of the Poverello, near Francis's crypt. A few years later, when the basilica was completed enough to be opened to pilgrims, William's burial marker began to witness an extraordinary amount of miracle activity—so much that Elias, around 1238, was seen kneeling at William's tomb, ordering the minor friar to cease working miracles so that the saint's tomb might better be praised. Elias wanted nothing to stand in the way of recognition of the sanctity of Francis, without whom William would be nothing.[10]

Despite the changes in him, Elias remained faithful to some principles of Francis's teaching, such as the appointment of lay brothers to key positions in the order. But the result was too many illiterate and uncultivated friars in leadership, easily susceptible to conduct unbecoming of religious life. Priests, meanwhile, were required to do manual labor, almost, it seemed, as recompense for imagining that they might be favored by God. "If a lay brother were to overhear a young friar speaking in Latin, he would scold him, saying, 'Stop! You are abandoning holy simplicity for book learning!'" Salimbene, the historian and friar who had once been protected by Elias, remembered later.[11]

Then Elias decided that Psalm 80 referred to the Friars Minor, decreeing that it must be said daily at chapter. "We therefore recited that psalm before the General Chapter for a full month," Salimbene later remembered, "which I have never seen done before or since."[12]

> Restore us, O God of hosts; let your face shine, that we may be saved. You brought a vine out of Egypt; you drove out the nations and planted it. You cleared the ground for it; it took deep root and filled the land. The mountains were covered with its shade, the mighty cedars with its branches; it sent out its branches to the sea, and its shoots to the River. Why then have you broken down its walls, so that all who pass along the way pluck its fruit? The boar from the forest ravages it, and all that move in the field feed on it. Turn again, O God of hosts; look down from heaven, and see; have regard for this vine, the stock that your right hand planted. They have burned it with fire, they have cut it down; may they perish at the rebuke of

your countenance. But let your hand be upon the one at your right hand, the one whom you made strong for yourself. Then we will never turn back from you; give us life, and we will call on your name. Restore us, O Lord God of hosts; let your face shine, that we may be saved. (Ps 80: 7–19)

Elias saw himself—as well as his blessed order—as righteous, a persecuted minority on the run.

CHAPTER 34

AT WAR WITH THE POPE

1240–1244

"I prefer the friars to wander, not to build," Elias remembered Francis saying one day, "not to take part in city and university life, but to feel satisfied in the warmth of the Holy Spirit."[1]

The trouble, Elias pondered, is that we don't all feel that warmth. Elias's idealism slowly rotted away and become almost unrecognizable to anyone but him.

His mind probably wandered back to a Christmas he'd spent with Francis in Rieti. The brothers had known they were coming and prepared a fine feast on a white tablecloth, with glass vessels borrowed from someone in town. Elias was already at the table when Francis came downstairs and spied what had been prepared. Without being noticed, he picked up the staff and pouch of a beggar who had stopped that day, and went outside. There he stood for a few minutes; then he knocked upon the door. One of the friars opened it.

"For the love of God, do you have any alms to give to a poor beggar?" asked Francis of him.

Of course they knew, despite the staff and pouch, that this was Francis. "We are also poor, brother," said Elias, playing along. "These are alms gathered for all of us. Come in and have some." Francis did come in; he sat down, but he sat on the floor by the fire. Then he explained, "When I saw the table sumptuously laid out, I thought, *This isn't the table of poor men who beg for their bread.* I think that elegance and abundance, in the lives of men who want to be poor as Christ was poor, distances us from the heaven we seek."

A few of the friars in Rieti that Christmas cried when Francis sat at their feet, saying these things. They were ashamed.[2]

Like a hawk poised to snatch a smaller bird out of the air—this is one metaphor used by Salimbene to describe how the friars felt under Elias's leadership by 1239.[3] Fear, an emotion nearly unexperienced and unexpressed by Francis, had become a prime motivator. Hot-tempered and paranoid, Elias disciplined freely by taking away precious possessions such as breviaries; demoting brothers to novices, a clear humiliation; and sending disagreeable friars on long, unnecessary journeys, exposing them—like King David sending the husband of Bathsheba off to the front lines—to mortal danger.

Meanwhile, tributes and gifts, whether fancy foods, gold, or ornaments for the basilica in Assisi, were always arriving at Elias's office as indulgences. Fine foods, imported from all over the world, were added to his table. Cherries, crabs, eel, almond milk, and cinnamon became common, and not only when he was entertaining.[4] It was these compromises with the "real world" that ultimately made the Franciscan friar an object of ridicule. He was soon called the fat and drunken friar.

Elias lived in splendor like a king, waited on by boys dressed in colorful shirts, usually eating alone, away from the convent, food prepared by one of the brothers who was made his private chef. He couldn't have been any less Franciscan if he had tried. His arrogance knew no bounds. When he needed to travel from one town or friary to another, he was most often unaccompanied by brothers and riding a horse—both violations of the Rule. Even when going half a mile, he rode that beast.

Elias replaced the spontaneity and wildness that his friend had celebrated—being willing to follow the Spirit into the unknown—with functionality, order, and planning. The friars even kept pets, like puppies, now.[5] Not only did the friars have little connection to the natural world of cicadas, worms, and swallows, but they had brought creation inside and domesticated it.

Throughout his rule of the order, Elias had shown strong preference to lay brothers over priestly ones when selecting lieutenants—even provincial ministers—and friends. He was himself proudly nonordained, a self-styled "simple" friar, just as Francis had been. Elias knew that Francis had valued laymen, wanted all friars to be equally valued, and himself refused priestly ordination. This distant from Francis's witness and after so many clerics had joined the order, there were many who viewed laymen as less important, even "useless for hearing confessions or for giving counsel."[6] There was even the memorable occasion when Francis begged a young postulant not to obtain his own breviary because of the sense of entitlement it would likely breed inside of him—just like a prelate. Elias would ensure that the order remained faithful to this.

But the opposite was really the truth about Elias: his lack of ordination hadn't led to a deep humility. Elias was elaborately complicated; his bee's nest of complex and unaddressed emotions, insecurity chief among them, best begins to explain why he distanced himself from and kept out of leadership positions those to whom it seemed God had granted spiritual authority. And his lay preferences would have a disastrous effect on the order after he was deposed.[7]

Elias's secretary, Brother Illuminato, asked to be relieved of his duties and was sent to the friary in Siena. Brother Bernard of Quintavalle was forced to flee for his life and go into hiding in the March of Ancona. Giles of Assisi and Angelo Tancredi were there in the Marches, as well. Everyone who had known Francis since the early days of his conversion knew that what Elias had done was nearly unforgivable. Giles and Angelo both lived until about 1260 and would later tell their stories to Friar Angelo Clareno, who recorded them in a scathing and sometimes unreliable tale that reads as a martyrology and an apocalypse.[8] Sadly, before long, these differences turned into fights, and brother was quite literally fighting against brother.

Even the mild-mannered poet and historian Thomas of Celano began to worry apocalyptically, seeing in contemporary events a foreshadowing of the end of the world. Celano was likely the composer of the Latin trochaic hymn *"Dies Irae,"* or "Day of Wrath," which was set down at this time, inspired by the opening words of Zephaniah 1:15–16: "That day is a day of wrath, a day of tribulation and distress, a day of calamity and misery, a day of darkness and obscurity, a day of clouds and whirlwinds" (Douay-Rheims). How ominous it was. "How much tremor there will be, when the Judge will come, investigating everything strictly! The trumpet, scattering a wondrous sound through the sepulchres of the regions, will summon all before the Throne," went two of the stanzas. *"Dies Irae"* was sung in the Roman liturgy for centuries, until the reform of the Latin rite at the Second Vatican Council.

As Elias and Gregory IX were transforming the landscape of Assisi and reorganizing the order, Clare continued to play a leadership role, but from a distance and from her cloister. Her stable, monastic, communal religious life was different from the mendicancy of her brothers. Her Rule, approved by the Holy See just before her death but drafted years earlier, outlines how she and the sisters lived differently from the men. For example, leadership was shared; when a woman arrived at San Damiano seeking entrance, Clare instructed that a majority of the sisters were to approve her joining. Similarly, the abbess, in Clare's Rule, was to spiritually accompany and at times admonish the sisters but never to command them "anything that is against their soul." She loved the severity of Francis's ideals, but she also maintained a warmth of personal relationships that Francis never seemed to feel necessary. She had not just a woman's touch but an emotional intelligence that her good friend occasionally seems to have lacked—or simply deemed less important.

At the same time, Clare was very much a mother and guardian to the other women at San Damiano. She took it upon herself to walk about and add blankets to those she felt might be cold after the others had gone to sleep. She was the one to comfort sisters who were sad or depressed and to give permission to lessen the rigor of common observance when a lighter touch might be better suited to the needs of a young novice.[9]

Some brothers saw themselves forming a direct line from Francis's earliest spiritual intentions to the present day and went often to visit Clare and the sisters, hearing confessions and administering the Eucharist but also listening to her counsel. While he was still alive, Francis had actually warned the friars against visiting the sisters too often, but after his death they needed to reconnect with what united them.

These friars were the ones who were increasingly identifying as Spirituals because they felt a strong connection to the last Rule of Francis and its emphasis on living strictly according to the Gospel. They would later fight bitterly, sometimes with deadly consequences, with the leaders of the order and with the papacy in ways that would have saddened Francis and Clare. Leo, Angelo, Rufino, Giles, Juniper, Bernard, and Masseo all lived to grieve not only Francis's death but also what they perceived to be the loss of their integrity and way of life. Meanwhile, Elias and Pope Gregory IX, along with others within the order, were replacing dancing with processions. They were turning simplicity and humility into grandeur for the newly canonized. In their hands, the wildness of evangelical poverty and preaching was becoming tame and organized.

Some of the friars, grieved and confused by the direction of the order and angered by Elias's open wantonness, finally appealed once more to Pope Gregory for help. "Elias had upset the whole order by his worldly living and his cruelty," remembered Thomas of Eccleston, a contemporary chronicler.[10] So a certain Friar Haymo of Faversham moved to formally rebuke Elias before a tribunal in Paris; Elias refused to attend. Nevertheless, Haymo was able to involve ministers provincial "and many of the best brothers" to convene a general chapter meeting—which Elias had refused to do during his tenure as minister general— attended by Brother Arnulph, a member of the papal curia and the emissary of Gregory IX, as well as seven cardinals. At that general chapter, in 1239, "brothers were chosen from the whole order to provide for the reformation of the order."

Elias refused to recognize the need for reform, nor the authority of the reforming agents. Nevertheless, he was summoned by the pope to face his accusers at last:

> Immediately Brother Elias, losing patience, said openly that he was lying; and his followers began likewise to make like charges and to raise a tumult; and those of the other party began to do likewise against them. Then the pope, much moved, commanded them to be silent, saying: "This is not the way of religious." Then the pope remained seated for a long time, as though in silence and meditation he would turn them to shame. Meanwhile, the lord Reginald, protector of the order, suggested openly to Brother Elias that he give his resignation into the hands of the pope; he publicly replied that he would not. Then the pope, first commending his person and the friendship he had had with St. Francis, concluded that it seemed to him that his ministry had been acceptable to the

brothers; but since it did not now please them, as was just shown, he decreed that he should be removed from office. And immediately he released him from the office of minister general. There was then such immense and inexpressible joy that those who merited to be present said they had never seen anything like it.[11]

Now deposed by Gregory IX, Elias refused to obey. A petulant Elias turned instead to Emperor Frederick II, deciding to devote himself fully to this powerful ruler whom the pope had once again excommunicated. He traded in his garments of (compromised) poverty for the robes of a consultant at court. He knew that Gregory IX was, in more ways than one, at war with the emperor. One encyclical written by Gregory at this time refers to Frederick as the "beast rising from the sea."[12] Most ignominious of all, the apostate emperor's armies were invading papal lands from all sides, and like the Hindu god Krishna in Arjuna's chariot in the ancient Indian epic, we next see Elias sitting, without his friar's frock, beside Frederick on the battlefield.

So numerous were the Franciscans, beautiful in spirituality and humanism after Francis's death, that their fall from glory in 1239 was noticed by everyone. Children were even singing about Franciscan disgrace in the streets of Italy:

> Friar Elias has gone astray
> For he has taken the evil way.

CHAPTER 35

PENANCE

1240–1253, from Rome to Cortona

Gregory IX and Frederick II never trusted each other. The pope was conniving; the emperor, arrogant.

Gregory had attempted to feed the ego of the beast in 1234 by calling for another crusade, hoping Frederick would finally turn his enormous ambition and threatening attention toward the East. But Frederick remained near home—and kept conquering and controlling every piece of land south of the Brenner Pass, in the realm we today know as Italy. Because they were also the sworn enemies of the pro-Guelf papacy, Frederick recruited Saracens, who at other times he had brutally murdered, and Ghibelline men, even though they were Frederick's natural enemies (he was born Guelf). He marched and paraded, often with prisoners in chains, African elephants on display. By 1238, Frederick's rule encompassed even the city of Rome and Gregory IX was fleeing to Anagni, that frequent papal hideout. Then, in 1239, Gregory excommunicated Frederick once again, with a declaration that was read in churches all over the Christian world. A year later is when we see Elias joining Frederick in open rebellion. He turns on Gregory as a career criminal might witness against his former mates, knowing exactly what he had done because, of course, he had been breaking the law right there beside him.

"The Pope is seething with wrath, covetous for wealth, and extorting by all means at his disposal," Elias said, adding:

"Gregory IX is also fraudulently using money that has been collected in the name of saving the Holy Land!"[1] Coming from the former confidant of Francis—a saint who many knew despised money so much that he once forced a friar, by holy obedience, to pick up coins in his mouth and place them in donkey dung because he'd touched the same with his hands after they were left as an offering in Portiuncula—the accusation carried extra weight.[2]

Gregory's excommunication of Frederick, likewise, accused Frederick of many crimes, mostly financial (taxing clergy and using church revenues for nonchurch purposes). He who wins is often the best at doing wrong.

Like Elias, Frederick too had some of the enthusiast in him. He was a proud humanist, but his devotion to religion was also sincere. He was always a protector of the Catholic faith, if not in step with the papacy, as well as a friend to Jews and Muslims—their livelihoods as well as their faith practices. This openness in itself often earned him the wrath and distrust of the Church. It was this affection for real faith and practice that brought Frederick and Elias together, not simply their shared dislike for Pope Gregory. "Holy devotion" is what Frederick called it in a letter to Elias, and holy devotion is what Frederick said he felt for the newly honored Franciscan saint Elizabeth of Hungary. She was the widow of Frederick's second cousin. He personally saw to it that her body was faithfully translated to its permanent shrine in Marburg.[3]

Elias seemed to think that his presence in Frederick's court was a kind of absolution to the condemned, rather than a commiseration between them. His presence in Frederick's camp propped up the embattled emperor, giving some level of credence to his shooting back at the pope, claiming that he, Frederick, was the divinely appointed ruler who most honored the creed, while Gregory IX was the true antichrist, a false prophet.[4]

In the end, the people of Rome "voted" with the papacy over the empire. Romantically, dramatically, and cynically, on February 22, 1240, Pope Gregory himself walked the streets of Rome, with the most precious saints' relics the city possessed in tow.

"This is *their* city! This is *your* city!" he yelled to the crowds.

Risking his own safety, as well as perhaps the future of the Church and the Papal States, on the religious feelings of the people of Rome, Gregory won. Frederick then fled. He would several times more flirt with challenging a pope or attempting to take Rome, but never with success.

From 1239 to 1241, Elias had lived in the commune of Cortona, the place in Tuscany that he and Francis loved, while undertaking diplomatic missions abroad for the emperor. (It was after the failed spiritual coup of 1230 that Elias, in self-exile, had begun to build another great church to Francis's memory—this time in Cortona.) On at least one occasion after he was deposed, he attempted to pay a pastoral visit to the Poor Clares there and was reprimanded by Albert of Pisa, the new Franciscan minister general.[5]

Albert knew both Francis and Elias well, having been received into the order back in 1211, one of the golden years of the fraternity. A humble, faithful man, he was also the first priest to become minister general. These facts would prove important to Elias's salvation.

Despite chafing at the notion of having to obey another friar, Elias soon found himself desiring a return to the brotherhood that he had spurned and disgraced. He begged for pardon in a letter to Pope Gregory IX, sending the letter by messenger directly to Albert, who showed a tremendous spirit of generosity in his willingness to receive it. Then, in one of those strange accidents of history, Albert died suddenly before he was able to deliver the petition to its final destination. In Rome at the time of his death on January 23, 1240, he may have been there primarily to put that missive into Gregory IX's hands. Instead, another friar discovered Elias's repentant letter in the pocket of Albert's cassock after his death and, in a fit of disgust and revenge that was equally understandable and unbefitting his tonsure, destroyed it.[6]

Gregory IX himself died the following summer, in August 1241, an old man, never having reconciled with Elias, with whom he shared so much life and intrigue for two decades. His successor was elected two months later in one of the more fascinating papal elections in history. Several of the electing cardinals were essentially captives of Frederick II, who surrounded Rome with his forces, keeping the cardinals from reaching the city. The war dragged on between the Hohenstaufen and the Holy See, between pro-imperial and pro-papal forces. Of the seven cardinals who remained in Rome, a few of them sought peace with Frederick at almost any cost, while the others had been Gregory IX's closest allies and sought to continue the hard line Gregory had pursued with the emperor. Between them, they managed to settle on a compromise candidate, the frail cardinal bishop of Sabina. He took the name Pope Celestine IV, but then he died seventeen days later, probably of natural causes.

Thus began a nearly two-year interregnum during which the Holy See sat vacant. Not until June 25, 1243, was Innocent IV elected pope, a choice that initially pleased the emperor, for they shared family connections.

Elias meanwhile remained in a hermitage in Cortona, surrounded by a handful of allies. He could have traveled to Rome under Frederick's protection, but there was no telling who might capture him, known Frederick sympathizer that he was, in the Holy City itself. He would likely have ended up in a papal prison. Meanwhile, the support of the emperor waned, and he and Elias soon ceased all contact. One gets the impression that Elias was increasingly in more than physical exile, and mostly of his own making. Yet he began to make private penance for his misdeeds.

Meanwhile, the construction of his marvelous basilica in Assisi was nearly complete. Bells were raised into the towers and rung. In 1244, then–Minister General Crescentius of Jesi, realizing that many of the stories of the saint's doings and teachings still remained unpublished, requested another effort at telling the story of Francis's life and charism. So friars throughout Europe, many of them now elderly and in poor health, were asked to record their memories of the early days. Using these remembrances, Thomas of Celano wrote again, adding his *Second Life* as a supplement to the first.

In 1247, John of Parma was elected minister general. Born in the year that Francis and Elias first stood before Innocent III, John immediately began to return the order to the principles set out in the last Rule. A sincere man who also knew the history of the order, John quickly sent another friar, Gerard of Modena, to Cortona to meet with Elias. He instructed Gerard to sit and listen for whether Elias wished a return to the true faith in his old age. By this time, Elias was well over sixty. Elias saw Gerard, but only long enough to decline the invitation. His bitterness ran deep, and although he no longer put much trust in Frederick II, he feared the papacy even more.

In his poetic epic *The French Revolution*, Thomas Carlyle writes of King Louis VI, dying of smallpox in 1774: "For his Majesty has religious faith; believes, at least in a Devil." Such a faith does not sustain or satisfy, but it is probably the stickiest sort in the life of a powerful Christian. Frederick II was such a man: royal, presumptuous, arrogant; once fearless, he at the end feared hell and hoped desperately for heaven. His battles with the papacy continued, ravaging much of the Italian peninsula, up until the moment Frederick accepted that his own end was near. By 1249, he'd lost most of his positions and two of his sons. As Advent 1250 approached, sick with dysentery, he removed his imperial signets and received the habit of a Cistercian monk. The excommunicated emperor was then able to arrange to receive last rites from an old ally, Archbishop Berard of Palermo. He died on December 13, 1250. He was nearly fifty-six.

"Let heaven and earth rejoice!" said Pope Innocent IV when he heard the news.

When word of Frederick's end reached Elias in Cortona, he was unmoved.

———— ✥ ————

Three years later, in 1253, Elias had become accustomed to his posture as the rebellious one. Somewhere deep inside, he imagined that he knew best what Francis had accomplished and that he had been thwarted, to the detriment of all Christendom, in his attempts to make Franciscanism truly great. He knew that attaching himself to the emperor's side had probably been a mistake, but he also felt that the disregard for his program for Francis's spiritual movement shown by many of the brothers with whom he'd grown up in it was equally unforgivable. For a while it had seemed that Frederick might pave the way for him to accomplish his intentions better than the pope ever could.

Then during Passiontide, one of the priests in Cortona, Bencius, recognized that Elias was approaching his end. He was at this time a man of seventy-two years, having lived an extraordinarily long life for any man in late medieval Europe. For whatever reason, Bencius believed that reconciliation might be possible. Many of the friars in Cortona still believed in the essential goodness of their former leader.

"Minister General Elias," he addressed him, showing honor that wasn't due, "would you like to confess your sins to a sympathetic ear?"

"I would."

So on April 19, Bencius absolved Elias of all sin, welcoming him back into the arms of Mother Church. It was Holy Saturday, that day of mystery in the Christian calendar when Christ descends into hell, tramples its gates, and tells Satan that his power is once and for all destroyed. Elias then spent Easter in a posture of prayer that reminded his brothers more of the early days than of their old minister general's frailness and age. On Easter Monday, Elias received the Holy Eucharist, and the following day, April 22, 1253, he died. So it was that while Pope Innocent IV was seated upon St. Peter's throne, Elias of Assisi was buried, to his eternal disappointment, in the Church of St. Francis—but in Cortona.

Four months later, on August 11, the last of the original leaders of the Franciscan movement, Clare, died in Assisi. A basilica was soon created for her, like a bookend on the other side of the city she and Francis made famous, and there her body remains.

Two years after Elias's death, a handful of friars made their way to Cortona and, without the cover of darkness, dug up their old minister general's body. As Elias had transferred Francis from San Giorgio to the secret rock in the belly of San Francesco, so they carried Elias's bones reverently from Cortona back to Assisi. There they placed them in the crypt where one finds Leo, Rufino, Masseo, and Angelo still today. There Elias lay for a few weeks, finally in the home he so treasured. But Elias does not lie there today; an anonymous but surely triumphant friar discovered the unauthorized translation of the body of the shamed minister general, dug it back up, and dispersed the bones in such a way that they could never again be found.

CODA

People give the name of zeal to their propensity to mischief and violence, though it is not the cause, but their interest that inflames them.

—**Michel de Montaigne**

CHAPTER 36

DECEMBER 12, 1818

A few weeks after Elias's death in Cortona, on May 25, 1253, Pope Innocent IV was in Assisi for the dedication of the Basilica of San Francesco. It was the twenty-third anniversary of the day on which Francis was supposed to have been buried in the Lower Church.

A generation later, the Franciscans accomplished what Francis never wanted: they produced their first Holy Father. Nicholas IV, born the year after Francis died, was elected by the cardinals on February 22, 1288. In May, he issued a bull calling for an even larger basilica, repaired, modified, and more lavishly decorated. "The friars at Assisi responded by inaugurating two decades of intensive work on their mother church."[1]

Primarily because of Nicholas IV, the basilica one sees in Assisi today is not the same one that Elias built. The difference is akin to Old St. Peter's versus the St. Peter's in Vatican City today. In fact, that comparison is especially apt since St. Peter's rests upon the bones of its saint, just as San Francesco's foundation is the body of St. Francis deep beneath the high altar of the Lower Church.

Nicholas IV's enlargement was mostly to the Lower Church, where the nave and transepts were circled with new side chapels, allowing opportunities for recognition of donors. But the pope and friars also aimed to increase the area around the high altar in the Lower Church—for pilgrims seeking penance, confession, and indulgences. Ironically, Elias's secrecy had left the location of the tomb so mysterious as to confound most attempts to give piety a specific focus. Nicholas IV changed that through the incentives he created and the renovations he commissioned, and the thaumaturgic power of Francis's body (and the ability of the basilica to take in pilgrims' contributions) was restored.

The Franciscan pope granted an indulgence ("a remission before God of the temporal punishment due to sins whose guilt has already been forgiven, which the faithful Christian who is duly disposed gains under certain prescribed conditions through the action of the Church which, as the minister of redemption, dispenses and applies with authority"[CCC, 1471]) of three years plus forty days to anyone visiting the basilica during the octave of St. Francis's feast day. A year later, and then again two years after that, Nicholas offered similar incentives of time off purgatory to encourage pilgrims to patronize Francis's tomb.[2]

Also pivotally, Nicholas IV's bull resulted in changes to the Upper Church—an artistic, evangelistic campaign to cover the walls of the nave with frescoes telling the story of who Francis was, what he did, and how it changed the world. Cimabue, and perhaps Giotto, had already been painting in the transepts and above the high altar in the decade before 1288: images of the Last Judgment, the apostles, and the evangelists that are still appreciated today. Now, scenes from the Old and New Testaments were stacked above a circle of Giotto's twenty-eight images from the life of Francis that make up "the greatest surviving spectacle of medieval mural painting."[3]

One result is that a nearly blond Francis walks about in the Upper Church. A confident, handsome figure stands in those frescoes. Giotto has stripped him of the insecurities that filled the meanderings of his conversion, as well as the doubts that accompanied the young would-be friar to Rome to see Innocent III in 1210. What is left is the saint of Bonaventure's *Life*. The basilica's famous Upper Church fresco cycle makes him into—actually, reinvents him as—a self-assured hero. That was the intention of Bonaventure's retelling of Francis's life: to make the saint more easily visible, removing much of the man.

Cults of saints were big business. With greater numbers of pilgrims come greater numbers of prayers, and with more prayers come more miracles. Other saints of the thirteenth century— like Dominic in Bologna or Anthony in Padua—were the object of visible devotion, their bodies having been placed in raised or elevated tombs, as shrines within easy reach of the faithful. In the case of Francis, hiding the body from view had resulted in a dramatic decrease in miracles credited to the saint. Since the body had been moved in 1230 from San Giorgio, the pilgrims and miracles had, in fact, all but dried up.[4] In his desire to protect and honor Francis, Elias had inadvertently discouraged pilgrims from flocking to Assisi. Nicholas IV would change that.

The pope called for the enlargement and adornment of the double church, and he called for alms from pilgrims to assist the project. The iconographic frescoes made Francis once again larger than life. Could Nicholas have foreseen the power of the as-yet-unseen artistic mode of realism to make Francis's legends immediately powerful again in the human imagination? Regardless, interest in Francis hasn't abated since the late thirteenth century, in large part thanks to a forward-thinking pope and a genius of a painter.

Within three generations of Francis's death, through this cultivation of beauty, attentiveness to storytelling, and manipulation of the cult of saints, Francis became a commodity, as salvation itself was often a commodity in the medieval Church. "By 1300 the vast majority of pilgrims were not coming to Assisi in the hope of physical healing in this world, but in the confident expectation of being spiritually cleansed for the hereafter, through the ritual performance of penance, the sacrament of confession and the receipt of indulgences."[5]

Elias had been successful. He had brought glory to Francis. He had made Assisi one of the primary centers of pilgrimage in the Christian world. His good friend, Elias ensured, would be forever honored, a hero of the faith. But consider the words of Friedrich Nietzsche: "If there is anything essentially unevangelical, it is surely the concept of the hero. What the Gospels make instinctive is precisely the reverse of all heroic struggle, of all taste for conflict."[6]

The concluding scene of our story takes place nearly six hundred years after Elias hid the body of Francis deep in the rock of the Lower Church. Only then was the hidden crypt finally discovered.

Several partial excavations led up to the fateful night in December 1818. In 1607, for instance, a humble workman in the Basilica discovered what seemed to be a small hole several feet beneath the high altar of the Lower Church. He wondered if it might lead to a tunnel that, in turn, would lead to some sort of crypt. Everyone knew that Francis was buried deep in this holy mountain, but only two or three people at any given time had known precisely where, and they weren't telling. It was said that the pope always knew the precise location of the body, and that he would confide this information to one friar in Assisi. Somehow he would communicate the same to his successor, perhaps by sealed letter. This was probably one of a handful of secret bits of knowledge beyond the bounds of recorded history that popes have mysteriously passed one to the next. In the fifteenth century, two popes at different times instructed a few friars in Assisi to add more sealant to the crypt, so worried were they about the fighting going on between Assisi and Perugia; they knew that Perugians would desire nothing more than to steal Assisi's greatest relic.

When the workman told someone what he thought he'd found, that someone told someone else. Within days, an order came directly from the pope that anyone touching that hole or seeking any other of its kind would face certain excommunication.[7]

In 1806, Franciscan Minister General Nicola Papini asked Pope Pius VII for permission to begin seeking the tomb of St. Francis. It was agreed that this should be done, but only in total secrecy, at night, during the dead of winter, with only a handful of the most trusted friars in assistance. Papini oversaw the operation directly. Every morning, he and the others would clean up the evidence of the excavations from the night before, and for three months they made very slow process. Just as they were getting close, Napoleon came. The French despot, who had held Rome, as well as Pope Pius VI, captive in 1798, took control of the Papal States in 1807 and Rome in early 1808. It was therefore deemed to be too risky for the exploratory work to continue. The effort was aborted.

In 1818, later, the papal commissioner for antiquities, Carlo Fea, received permission from another pope to look again. Fea was an archaeologist, scholar, lawyer, translator, explorer, and champion of the archaeological legacy of Rome and the Church. Years before going to Assisi, he'd led excavations and preservations on many important Roman monuments and places, including the Pantheon and the Forum, charged as he was by the exiled Pius VII with the task of rebuilding Rome's store of antiquity treasures in the wake of years of deliberate French plundering.

Fea possessed a determined personality. He also was a thorough scholar and knew what had failed in the past. It is no wonder, then, that he led the first successful excavation of the tomb by digging much deeper in the concealed crypt, lower than the crews who had aborted earlier attempts in 1755 and 1802–1803 had ever thought to go.[8] By December 8, the sixty-five year-old Fea and his team were deep enough to begin to see the sarcophagus. On December 12, 1818, a Saturday morning, four friars and a cardinal walked tremulously into the crypt. There they found Francis's bones, his stone pillow, and the silver coins left behind by Brother Elias.

We have only two extant pieces of writing from Francis's own hand; this indicates that he wasn't a man of letters but also raises a question: How influential would he have been had he merely died quietly in October 1226? Could it be that Elias was right— that without the changes he brought to the order and without his efforts toward making Assisi one of Christendom's most popular pilgrimage destinations, Francis's sanctity would have gone largely unobserved? In the generation after Elias's death, a woman named Margaret joined the Third Order Franciscans in Cortona. She tended to the sick, the mentally ill, orphans, and the homeless. This was St. Margaret of Cortona, patron of the falsely accused. Is Elias falsely accused of nearly destroying what Francis started?

Elias told the world of that most singular miracle, Francis's stigmata, immortalizing his friend beyond what was imaginable for any saint before him. He began to transform his order into one that would easily grow into the largest in the Catholic Church, extending to every corner of the globe. Elias designed and built, at all costs, that temple to Francis's honor and memory, which Giotto immortalized seventy years later.

But Elias also nearly destroyed the movement his friend began. Its work and spirit were transformed into something that Francis would have had trouble recognizing as his own. After Francis's death, Elias seems to have believed that he knew best how to continue the work of a supreme idealist, but his enthusiasm turned more misguided as the years went on. "It was appropriate," one historian has written, "that it should have been the municipality of Assisi which in 1937 put up a memorial to [Elias], because he made a more lasting contribution to the development of the city than ever he did to the evolution of the Franciscan ideal."[9]

Today, four of Francis's close friends—Brothers Leo, Rufino, Masseo, and Angelo—remain interred alongside the rediscovered tomb. The crypt remains spacious by medieval standards, and pilgrims who visit the basilica seeking to connect with the spirit of the Poverello are able to circumambulate the tomb in prayer.

"*Silenzio*," basilica attendants whisper into microphones, reminding pilgrims of the proper decorum in such a holy place. As they file in and out of the spacious crypt below the Lower Church, circling where the Poverello lies, those pilgrims have no idea of the journey those bones took to get there.

ACKNOWLEDGMENTS

Reader, beware: scholars disagree regarding some of the facts and details in this book. For example, there are some who believe that the evidence does not point to Elias's deliberately burying Francis's body alone as a gesture of separation from other leaders of the order and the papal curia. This interpretation goes as follows: "The funerary procession became increasingly chaotic as it approached the Basilica. . . . [Thus] the procession was brought to a hurried conclusion and the burial conducted privately within the Basilica while the crowd was locked outside."[1] Perhaps more importantly, there is no direct evidence that Francis and Elias knew each other before adulthood. I have suggested that they did as the most plausible explanation for Francis's special affection for Elias and for his continued willingness to trust Elias even after others in the order seem to have clearly known, by Elias's actions, that Elias did not share Francis's heart for the Gospel.

As Rosalind Brooke wrote more than a half century ago, "Elias left no autobiography, and found no Boswell to impress an image of his personality."[2] Brooke's 1959 book went a long way toward discovering that personality and its impact upon the early Franciscan movement, but her work had few if any followers. I make no claims to build upon her scholarship in the present work, only to have been inspired by it. For instance, I follow her advice that the most reliable source we have for understanding

Elias's life is the first biography of Francis (the *Vita Prima*, or *First Life*) written by Thomas of Celano. In that book, Elias is mentioned on six occasions; each of these is a scene in *The Enthusiast*.

Many thanks go to the scholars whose work has aided me greatly. These include David Burr, Michael F. Cusato, Rosalind Brooke, and Jacques Dalarun. Their books and articles are mentioned in the notes. I deliberately avoided rereading the recent excellent biographies of Augustine Thompson, O.P., and André Vauchez while writing my first complete draft because, in a real way, to paraphrase Ludwig Wittgenstein, knowing the facts of the world is never the end of the matter. But then I was grateful to turn to them to check many of my details against their research. Obviously, any mistakes that remain are my own.

Scholar of religion Wendy Doniger recently wrote in *The New York Review of Books*, "It's hard to imagine how you could write about any subject as sensitive as religion or history without outraging someone."[3] I honestly hope that I have.

"The Book was what mattered—he had lived with it all these years, fondled it in his waking thoughts, used it as an escape from anxiety, a solace in long journeys, in tedious conversations. Did he find himself in a library, he made straight for the shelves which promised light on one cherished subject; did he hit upon a telling quotation, a just metaphor, an adroit phrase, it was treasured up, in miser's fashion, for the Book. The Book haunted his day-dreams like a guilty romance." So wrote Ronald Knox autobiographically in the opening paragraph of *Enthusiasm: A Chapter in the History of Religion*. I understand the feeling. This has been that book for me. Some of my inspiration came from reading Knox; I have many arguments with Knox's work, but his is a book with a profound ability to provoke and challenge.

The brief chapters of part 1 of this work have the reader imagining with me what happened inside the Basilica of San Francesco in Assisi when Francis was secretly buried there. That great building is also an inspiration to me, as I've often stood and sat there, most recently in June 2015, pondering its stones, frescoes, crevices, and crypts for answers. It is a place of great mystery and history for all who seek to understand Francis. I even feel caught up in the history of the place. On September 26, 1997, the worst earthquake in Assisi's history hit the basilica, knocking a large section of the Vault of the Evangelists, including Cimabue's *St. Matthew* and Giotto's *St. Jerome*, to the floor and tragically killing four people. This delayed my first visit, since the basilica was understandably closed for months. When I did make it inside for the first time, in spring 2001, I was looking at a space recently changed irrevocably by forces of nature. What wouldn't I understand as a result? It makes me think of the German mystic, Friedrich Hölderlin, who once wrote, "Beginning and end / Greatly deceive us."[4]

Thank you to my fine editor at Ave Maria Press, Jonathan Ryan, and to Tom Grady, publisher. Thanks to Professor Thomas Bolin, who reminded me of the Buddha's parable of the man shot by a poisoned arrow at just the right time, and thanks to Professor Sean C. Stidd for discussing details of the book on many occasions over breakfast at Angelo's in Ann Arbor. We probably should have tipped the staff more. Thank you to Ana Hernandez, James Martin, S.J., and, above all, my wife, Michal Woll, for their encouragement. Thank you to the Mount Tabor Ecumenical Centre for Art and Spirituality in Barga, Italy, for the generous invitation to colead a retreat on the subject of Francis with Monsignor Timothy Verdon and Professor Mark Burrows, both of whom I also heartily thank. And thanks to Mark Bosco, S.J., for the enlightening conversation over pasta in Rome!

NOTES

PROLOGUE

1. Richard Viladesau, *The Beauty of the Cross: The Passion of Christ in Theology and the Arts from the Catacombs to the Eve of the Renaissance* (New York: Oxford University Press, 2008), 87.

2. John Keats, "Sleep and Poetry," in *John Keats: The Complete Poems*, ed. John Barnard (New York: Penguin Classics, 1977), lines 116, 124–125.

3. Erik H. Erikson, *Young Man Luther: A Study in Psychoanalysis and History* (New York: W.W. Norton, 1962), 16.

4. Eileen Power, *Medieval People* (London: Methuen, 1950), vii.

5. Herbert Butterfield, *The Whig Interpretation of History* (London: G. Bell and Sons, 1931), 9.

6. Thomas Carlyle, "On History," 1830. Various editions.

2. THE FOLLOWING MORNING

1. See Regis J. Armstrong, J. Wayne Hellmann, and William J. Short, eds., *Francis of Assisi: Early Documents*, vol. 1, *The Saint* (New York: New City Press, 1999), 118, 286.

2. This comes from the account in Jordan of Giano's *Chronicle* 50. See *XIIIth Century Chronicles*, trans. by Placid Herman (Chicago: Franciscan Herald Press, 1961), 57.

3. This is my rendering, but see also Regis J. Armstrong, J. Wayne Hellmann, and William J. Short, eds., *Francis of Assisi: Early Documents*, vol. 2, *The Founder* (New York: New City Press, 2000), 489.

3. THREE-AND-A-HALF YEARS LATER

1. Helpful for my understanding of Francis's tomb in the basilica in Assisi were Janet Robson and Donal Cooper, "Imagery and the Economy of Penance at the Tomb of Saint Francis," *Architecture and Pilgrimage, 1000–1500: Southern Europe and Beyond* (Farnham, England: Ashgate, 2013), 165–186; and Donal Cooper, "*In Loco Tutissimo et Firmissimo*: The Tomb of St. Francis in History,

Legend and Art," in *The Art of the Franciscan Order in Italy*, ed. William R. Cook (Boston: Brill, 2005), 1–37, plates 1–13.

2. Heiko A. Oberman, *Luther: Man between God and the Devil* (New Haven, CT: Yale University Press, 2006), 26.

3. William Shakespeare, *Julius Caesar*, Act 2, scene 1.

4. Robson and Cooper, "Imagery and the Economy of Penance at the Tomb of Saint Francis," 169.

5. Thomas of Celano, *First Life* (London: Society for Promoting Christian Knowledge, 2000), 10. This is my rendering, but see also Armstrong et al., *Francis of Assisi: Early Documents*, 1:290–291.

6. Bonaventure, *Life of Saint Francis* (various editions), chap. 15, para. 8. For thirteenth-century sources, translations are usually my own, unless I reference the page number of a specific, recent translation.

7. Most biographers make no mention of this possible scene or of the burial of Francis's body. Also, some scholars have offered other reasons why coins were discovered in Francis's tomb beside his body. For example, an art historian/expert says, as if conclusively, that the coins, minted between 1181 and 1208, are evidence "indicating that at one point supplicants had been able to cast offerings into the open coffin" (Cooper, "*In Loco Tutissimo*," 13). That hardly seems obvious. My suggestion, that Elias put them there, is just as plausible.

8. Quoted in Cooper, "*In Loco Tutissimo*," 9.

4. THE FOUNDER AND THE ENTHUSIAST

1. On the story of Elias as told by Thomas of Celano, see Rosalind B. Brooke, *Early Franciscan Government: Elias to Bonaventure* (New York: Cambridge University Press, 1959), 8–20. Note: I primarily follow Brooke's interpretation in regarding Thomas's *Vita Prima* as our most reliable source for understanding Elias. I also follow John Moorman's understanding of Elias throughout, as outlined in *A History of the Franciscan Order: From Its Origins to the Year 1517* (New York: Oxford University Press, 1968), 96–104.

2. Thomas of Celano, *First Life*, 98, 109 (these are the sections of the work, as divided by scholars).

3. For both the quotation and the dating of composition of this letter (mentioned in paragraphs that follow), I am following Joan Mueller, *Clare of Assisi: The Letters to Agnes* (Collegeville, MN: Liturgical Press, 2003), 30 and 27, respectively.

4. A canon of Leon who later became a bishop wrote a book during this time in which he referred to "that most holy brother Elias, St. Francis' successor." Quoted in Brooke, *Early Franciscan Government*, 14.

5. Thomas of Celano, *Second Life* (London: Society for Promoting Christian Knowledge, 2000), 182. My own paraphrases.

6. But some commentators have argued the reverse: that Salimbene betrayed Elias by becoming such a critical and one-sided detractor despite all the

good that Elias obviously did for him as a young man. See Brooke, *Early Francis-can Government*, 45–55.

PART TWO

1. Francis would have taken being called a failure as a compliment.

5. WHEN WE FIRST MET

1. For the population of Francis's Assisi, I am following André Vauchez, *Francis of Assisi: The Life and Afterlife of a Medieval Saint*, trans. Michael F. Cusato (New Haven: Yale University Press, 2012), 5.

2. Thomas of Celano, *First Life*, 80; see also Marion A. Habig, ed., *St. Francis of Assisi: Writings and Early Biographies: English Omnibus of the Sources for the Life of St. Francis*, 4th ed. (Chicago: Franciscan Herald Press, 1983), 296—henceforth referred to simply as *Omnibus*.

3. For this detail regarding baptism, as well as the one that follows, I am following Augustine Thompson, *Cities of God: The Religion of the Italian Communes, 1125–1325* (University Park, PA: The Pennsylvania State University Press, 2005), 311–312.

4. Augustine Thompson, *Francis of Assisi: The Life* (Ithaca, NY: Cornell University Press, 2013), 5.

5. For Virgil "seeing" Pan, see his *Eclogue X*, lines 26–27.

6. J. L. Baird, G. Baglivi, and J. R. Kane, eds., *The Chronicle of Salimbene de Adam* (Binghamton, NY: Medieval and Renaissance Texts and Studies, 1986), 75.

7. See F. R. P. Akehurst and Stephanie Cain Van D'Elden, eds., *The Stranger in Medieval Society* (Minneapolis: University of Minnesota Press, 1997), 2.

8. Thompson, *Francis of Assisi: The Life*, 5.

9. This is the summary of Elizabeth W. Mellyn, *Mad Tuscans and Their Families: A History of Mental Disorder in Early Modern Italy* (Philadelphia: University of Pennsylvania Press, 2014), 99.

10. Augustine Thompson, "The Origins of Religious Mendicancy in Medieval Europe," in *The Origin, Development, and Refinement of Medieval Religious Mendicancies*, ed. Donald S. Prudio (Boston: Brill, 2011), 8.

6. WHAT EVERY CHRISTIAN KNOWS

1. This phrase is from Johannes Fried's *The Middle Ages*, trans. Peter Lewis (Cambridge: Harvard University Press, 2015), x. Fried debunks the Burckhardt thesis.

2. Ibid., 2.

3. Charles Taylor, *A Secular Age* (Cambridge: The Belknap/Harvard Press, 2007), 3.

4. J. Shinners and E. A. Lowe, trans. *The Bobbio Missal: A Gallican Mass-Book*, (London: Harrison and Sons, 1920), 56.

5. Thomas of Celano, *Second Life*, 105. This is my translation.

6. Michael Robson, *St. Francis of Assisi: The Legend and the Life* (Herndon, VA: Geoffrey Chapman, 1997), 58–59.

7. Thompson, "Origins of Religious Mendicancy," 11–12.

8. Czeslaw Milosz, *To Begin Where I Am: Selected Essays*, ed. Bogdana Carpenter and Madeline G. Levine (New York: Farrar, Straus and Giroux, 2001), 2.

7. AVOIDING THE DIVINE GRASP

1. Thomas of Celano, *First Life*, 2; Habig, *Omnibus*, 230.

2. Augustine of Hippo, *Confessions*, trans. Henry Chadwick (New York: Oxford University Press, 1992), book X, 187.

3. As quoted by Fulcher of Chartres in *A History of the Expedition to Jerusalem, 1095–1127*, ed. Harold S. Fink, trans. Frances Rita Ryan (New York: W.W. Norton, 1972), 66–67.

8. UNCLEAN LOVE

1. "After the Christians . . ." is from the Enlightenment French writer Louis Jaucourt, quoted in Timothy S. Miller and John W. Nesbitt, *Walking Corpses: Leprosy in Byzantium and the Medieval West* (Ithaca, NY: Cornell University Press, 2014), 119. See the same source for the reference to leprosaria in every large town north of Rome, 120.

2. Jonathan Sumption, *Pilgrimage: An Image of Mediaeval Religion* (Totowa, NJ: Rowman and Littlefield, 1975), 101.

3. Francis of Assisi, "Testament," in Armstrong et al., *Francis of Assisi: Early Documents*, 1:124.

4. Pope Francis, "Angelus," February 8, 2015, https://w2.vatican.va/content/francesco/en/angelus/2015/documents/papa-francesco_angelus_20150208.html. The pope preached these words in anticipation of the "World Day of the Sick" approaching on February 11. The Yves Congar quote comes from its most famous source: Gustavo Gutierrez's *A Theology of Liberation* (Maryknoll, NY: Orbis Books, 1973), 155.

5. Brian Davies's translation, from Brian Davies, *Thomas Aquinas's "Summa Theologiae": A Guide and Commentary* (New York: Oxford University Press, 2014), 241 (2a2ae, 24, 2).

9. HEARING GOD

1. Hans Belting, *The Image and Its Public in the Middle Ages: Form and Function of Early Paintings of the Passion*, trans. Mark Bartusis and Raymond Meyer (New Rochelle, NY: Aristide D. Caratzas, 1990), chap. 6.

2. Reiner Stach, *Kafka: The Decisive Years*, trans. Shelley Frisch (Princeton: Princeton University Press, 2013), 97.

3. Thomas of Celano, *First Life*, 18.

4. Quoted in Todd Hartch, *The Prophet of Cuernavaca: Ivan Illich and the Crisis of the West* (New York: Oxford University Press, 2015), 145.

5. This scene is from Thomas of Celano, *First Life*, 6. Elias is not mentioned by name as the close friend who accompanies Francis to the grotto, but many scholars have assumed Elias to be the one.

6. Thomas of Celano, *First Life*, 6; in Armstrong et al., *Francis of Assisi: Early Documents*, 1:187.

10. A FATHER PROBLEM

1. William Shakespeare, *King Lear*, Act 3, scene 5.

2. *The Legend of the Three Companions*, VIII, 23; in Armstrong et al., *Francis of Assisi: Early Documents*, 2:82.

3. Ibid., 503.

4. Michael de la Bedoyere, *Francis of Assisi: The Man Who Found Perfect Joy* (Manchester, NH: Sophia Institute Press, 1999), 66.

5. Thomas of Celano, *First Life*, chap. 4, para. 9, my translation. See also Armstrong et al., *Francis of Assisi: Early Documents*, 1:189.

6. "I want to shout it . . ." is a slight adaptation from *The Mirror of Perfection*, 17. Unless otherwise noted, quotations and anecdotes from *The Mirror* are my own renderings, and the reference after the title in the notes is to chapter (standard in all editions). The other scenes here come from the anonymous text "The Sacred Exchange between Saint Francis and Lady Poverty," perhaps written by Caesar of Speyer in the year or years just after Francis's death; para. 16; in Armstrong et al., *Francis of Assisi: Early Documents*, 1:534. The two questions immediately above also come from "The Sacred Exchange," which is the primary source for understanding Francis's devotion to poverty as personified in Lady Poverty: para. 5, 9, 530–531.

7. See tale #8 in *The Fabliaux: A New Verse Translation*, trans. Nathaniel E. Dubin, intro. R. Howard Bloch (New York: Liveright, 2013), lines 55–56, p. 57. The quotations that follow from this same tale are lines 90 and 100–101.

11. DON'T TOUCH ME

1. From the opening paragraph of "The Testament." See *Francis of Assisi in His Own Words: The Essential Writings*, trans. Jon M. Sweeney (Brewster, MA: Paraclete Press, 2013), 96.

2. Thomas of Celano, *First Life*, 83; Habig, *Omnibus*, 298.

3. John Keats, "Sleep and Poetry," lines 49–52, from *Poems* (1817).

4. Rainer Maria Rilke, *The Selected Poetry of Rainer Maria Rilke*, ed. and trans. Stephen Mitchell (New York: Vintage International, 1989), 109.

5. Thomas of Celano, *Second Life*, 95; in Habig, *Omnibus*, 440. Thanks to Fr. Richard Rohr for singling out this quote for me.

6. Basil the Great, "*Introduction to the Ascetical Life*," in *Saint Basil: Ascetical Works*, trans. M. Monica Wagner (New York: Fathers of the Church, 1950), 15.

7. Henry James, "Italian Hours," in *Collected Travel Writings: The Continent* (New York: Viking Press, 1993), 503.

8. Giacomo Galeazzi, "'Don't Let Yourselves Be Robbed of Hope, It Is Time for Redemption,'" *Vatican Insider*, March 21, 2015, http://vaticaninsider.lastampa.it/en/the-vatican/detail/articolo/francesco-napoli-39922/.

12. FINDING THE REASON

1. Thomas of Celano, *First Life*, para. 21. In the paragraphs that follow, other references are made to Thomas of Celano in this *First Life*, and these are to para. 21–24.

2. Following here Raphael Brown's suggestion in *The Little Flowers of Saint Francis* (New York: Image Books, 1958), 330.

3. Thomas of Celano, *First Life*, chap. 9.

4. "The Anonymous of Perugia," 11; in Armstrong et al., *Francis of Assisi: Early Documents*, 2:38.

5. Thomas of Spalato, in 1222, according to Cajetan Esser, *Origins of the Franciscan Order* (Chicago: Franciscan Herald Press, 1970), 97.

6. "The Anonymous of Perugia," 15; in Armstrong et al., *Francis of Assisi: Early Documents*, 2:40.

7. Brown, *The Little Flowers*, chap. 62; or "The Assisi Compilation," chap. 60.

8. This anecdote, including the words spoken by Bishop Guido, comes from Thomas of Celano, *Second Life*, chap. 66, para. 100, only very slightly modified from Armstrong et al., *Francis of Assisi: Early Documents*, 2:313.

13. THE SLAUGHTER

1. Peter of Vaux de Cernay, from his *History of the Albigensian Crusade*, as quoted in R. I. Moore, *The War on Heresy* (Cambridge: Harvard University Press, 2012), 241.

2. Eamon Duffy, *Saints and Sinners: A History of the Popes*, 4th ed. (New Haven: Yale University Press, 2014), 151–52.

3. Virgil, *The Eclogues and Georgics*, trans. C. Day Lewis (New York: Oxford World's Classics, 2009), *Eclogue I*, lines 24–25; 4.

14. SKIRTING HERESY

1. Max Weber. "The Nature of Charismatic Authority and Its Routinization," in *Theory of Social and Economic Organization*, trans. A. R. Anderson and Talcott Parsons (New York: Free Press, 1997), 356.

2. See Augustine Thompson's "Origins of Religious Mendicancy," 22. The quote from Benedict's Rule is taken from Patrick J. Geary, ed., *Readings in Medieval History*, vol. 1, *The Early Middle Ages*, 3rd ed. (Orchard Park, NY: Broadview Press, 2003), 170.

3. The full anecdote appears in Rosalind B. Brooke (ed. and trans.), *Scripta Leonis, Rufini et Angeli Sociorum S. Francisci: The Writings of Leo, Rufino and Angelo, Companions of St. Francis* (New York: Oxford/Clarendon Press, 1970), 18.

4. Patience Andrewes, *Frederick II of Hohenstaufen* (New York: Oxford University Press, 1970), 11.

5. See Marjorie Reeves, *The Influence of Prophecy in the Later Middle Ages: A Study in Joachimism* (New York: Oxford University Press, 1969), part 2, particularly pages 135–190.

6. For more on this, see Phyllis Tickle and Jon M. Sweeney, *The Age of the Spirit: How the Ghost of an Ancient Controversy Is Shaping the Church* (Grand Rapids: Baker Books, 2014), particularly chap. 12.

7. See Malcolm Lambert, *The Cathars* (New York: Blackwell, 1998), particularly chap. 8, "The Battle for Souls in Italy," 171–214.

8. The list of Church illuminaries who cannot say this is long, including Thomas Aquinas, accused of heresy by his own bishop two years after his death.

15. SHOWING THE POPE

1. Marjorie Reeves, *The Influence of Prophecy in the Later Middle Ages: A Study in Joachimism* (New York: Oxford University Press, 1969), 142.

2. James M. Powell, ed. and trans., *The Deeds of Pope Innocent III: By an Anonymous Author* (Washington, DC: The Catholic University of America Press, 2004), 56.

3. Georges Duby, *France in the Middle Ages 987–1460: From Hugh Capet to Joan of Arc*, trans. Juliet Vale (Malden, MA: Blackwell, 1991), 164.

4. Innocent III, *Between God and Man: Six Sermons on the Priestly Office*, trans. Corinne J. Vause and Frank C. Gardiner (Washington, DC: The Catholic University of America Press, 2004), 71–72.

6. Powell, *Deeds of Pope Innocent III*, 5.

7. Ibid., 55.

8. "The Testament," *Francis of Assisi in His Own Words*, 97.

16. WHERE TO LAY THEIR HEADS

1. Rosalind B. Brooke, *Scripta Leonis, Rufini et Angeli Sociorum S. Francisci*; 161.

2. "We don't need . . .": *The Mirror of Perfection*, 5. "It is easier. . .": Thomas of Celano, *First Life*, 42; in Armstrong et al., *Francis of Assisi: Early Documents*, 1:220.

3. *The Mirror of Perfection*, 6 in the Leonard Lemmens edition; Armstrong et al., *Francis of Assisi: Early Documents*, 3:219.

4. *The Mirror of Perfection*, 100; in Armstrong et al., *Francis of Assisi: Early Documents*, 3:348.

5. Jyoti Sahi, quoted in Michael Amaladoss, *The Asian Jesus* (Maryknoll, NY: Orbis Books, 2006), 150.

6. Thompson, "Origins of Religious Mendicancy," 6.

7. *The Mirror of Perfection*, 19.

8. Ibid., 5.

9. Virgil, *The Eclogues*, trans. Guy Lee (New York: Penguin Books, 1984), 20.

17. AN ANTITHEOLOGY FLOWERS

1. These details come from the chronicles of Thomas of Eccleston, ca. 1258; see Brooke, *Early Franciscan Government*, 50–51.

2. See chap. 16 of *"The Little Flowers of Saint Francis"* in Jon M. Sweeney, ed. and trans., *The Complete Francis of Assisi: His Life, The Complete Writings, and The Little Flowers* (Brewster, MA: Paraclete Press, 2015), 306.

3. Thomas of Celano, *First Life*, 68–69.

4. *"The Little Flowers of Saint Francis,"* chap. 7; in Sweeney, *The Complete Francis of Assisi*, 288.

5. Rowan Williams, *The Anti-Theology of Julian of Norwich: The 34th Annual Julian Lecture* (Norwich, UK: The Friends of Julian of Norwich, 2014), 1, 4.

6. Étienne Gilson, *The Philosophy of St. Thomas Aquinas*, 3rd ed., trans. Edward Bullough, ed. G. A. Elrington (St. Louis, MO: B. Herder, 1937), 48.

7. This is my summary. See also Thich Nhat Hanh, *Zen Keys: A Guide to Zen Practice* (New York: Harmony Books, 1994), 42.

8. This sermon appears in Michael Goodich, ed., *Other Middle Ages: Witnesses at the Margins of Medieval Society* (Philadelphia: University of Pennsylvania Press, 1998), 146–49.

9. On Peter Lombard's *Sentences*, see Philipp W. Rosemann, *The Story of a Great Medieval Book: Peter Lombard's "Sentences"* (Toronto: Broadview Press, 2007); and *Mediaeval Commentaries on the "Sentences" of Peter Lombard*, 2 vols., ed. G. R. Evans and Philipp W. Rosemann (Boston: Brill, 2002 and 2010).

10. Bonaventure, *Works of St. Bonaventure*, vol. 2, *Itinerarium Mentis in Deum*, rev. ed., ed. Philotheus Boehner and Zachary Hayes (St. Bonaventure, NY: St. Francis Institute Publications, 2002), 9, 148.

18. THE WOMAN

1. Virginia Woolf, quoted in *Virginia Woolf*, by Hermione Lee (New York: Vintage, 1999), 13.

2. Thomas Merton, *The Seven Storey Mountain*, 372. (New York: Mariner Books, 1999), 410.

3. As quoted in Thomas of Celano, *Second Life*, 208.

4. Bert Roest, "Female Preaching in the Late Medieval Franciscan Tradition," *Franciscan Studies* 62 (2004): 132.

19. FINDING HIS EQUILIBRIUM

1. These quotations from Giles are my own translation from a forthcoming collection of his complete sayings.

2. John Berryman, "Dream Song #22," in *The Dream Songs: Poems*, ed. Daniel Swift (New York: Farrar, Straus and Giroux, 2014), 22.

3. "Preaching to the Birds," chap. 13 of *The Little Flowers*, in Sweeney, *Complete Francis of Assisi*, 300–301.

4. W. B. Yeats, "Nineteen Hundred and Nineteen," *The Collected Poems of W. B. Yeats* (New York: Macmillan, 1950), 206.

20. THE FRANCISCAN MOVEMENT IS BORN

1. "Preaching to the Birds," chap. 13 of *"The Little Flowers of Saint Francis,"* in Sweeney, *Complete Francis of Assisi*, 300–301.

2. From Bernard of Besse, "A Book of the Praises of Saint Francis," in Armstrong et al., *Francis of Assisi: Early Documents*, 3:46.

3. Thomas of Celano, *First Life*, 81.

4. Cajetan Esser, *Origins of the Franciscan Order* (Chicago: Franciscan Herald Press, 1970), 93.

5. Thomas of Celano, *Second Life*, 208.

21. BROTHERS SHOULD BE LIKE MOTHERS AND SONS

1. *The Mirror of Perfection*, 10.

2. Ilia Delio, "Clare of Assisi and the Mysticism of Motherhood," in *Franciscans at Prayer*, ed. Timothy J. Johnson (Boston: Brill, 2007), 38.

3. My translation of "A Rule for Hermitages," but see *Francis of Assisi in His Own Words*, 61–62.

4. This dream is recounted, along with other memories of Sister Filippa, in *Other Middle Ages: Witnesses at the Margins of Medieval Society* (Philadelphia: University of Pennsylvania Press, 1998), 234.

5. Thomas of Celano, *First Life*, 98.

22. WHEN IN ROME . . .

1. On Innocent III and the Fourth Lateran Council, see Innocent III, *Between God and Man*, 51–77.

2. *Francis of Assisi in His Own Words*, 46.

3. The first portion of this quote is taken verbatim from Innocent III, *Between God and Man*, 57. The second portion, the verses from Lamentations 1:1, 4–5, are from the JPS translation in Adele Berlin and Marc Zvi Brettler, ed., *The Jewish Study Bible*, 2nd ed., (New York: Oxford University Press, 2014). The third portion, the gloss of Innocent, is again taken verbatim from *Between God and Man*, 57.

4. This is the NRSV translation, except that I have replaced their use of the word "mark" with *"Tau,"* the last letter of the Hebrew Bible, as the word appears in the original and as Innocent III read it aloud that day.

5. From Jessalynn Bird, Edward Peters, and James M. Powell, eds., *Crusade and Christendom: Annotated Documents in Translation from Innocent III to the Fall of Acre, 1187–1291*, (Philadelphia: University of Pennsylvania Press, 2013), 43.

6. Christie Fengler Stephany, "The Meeting of Saints Francis and Dominic," *Franciscan Studies* 47 (1987): 219.

7. Brooke, *Early Franciscan Government*, 62.

8. Joshua J. McElwee, "Pope Francis Warns Religious Orders Not to Accept 'Unbalanced' People," *National Catholic Reporter*, April 13, 2015, http://ncronline.org/news/vatican/pope-francis-warns-religious-orders-not-accept-unbalanced-people#.VSzRd7-X8WE.facebook.

23. BROTHER MUSLIM

1. "The Haughtiness of Brother Elias," chap. 19 of "*The Little Flowers of Saint Francis,*" in Sweeney, *The Complete Francis of Assisi*, 313–316.

2. Klaus Mann, *André Gide and the Crisis of Modern Thought* (London: Dennis Dobson, 1948), 9.

3. Sophia Rose Arjana, *Muslims in the Western Imagination* (New York: Oxford University Press, 2015), 19.

4. André Vauchez, *Francis of Assisi*, 162; and Sophia Rose Arjana, *Muslims in the Western Imagination*, 15.

5. Bird et al., *Crusade and Christendom*, 45.

6. Ibid., 46.

7. Christoph T. Maier, *Preaching the Crusades: Mendicant Friars and the Cross in the Thirteenth Century* (New York: Cambridge University Press, 1994), 10.

8. Mahmood Ibrahim, "Francis Preaching to the Sultan: Art and Literature in the Hagiography of the Saint," in *Finding Saint Francis in Literature and Art*, ed. Cynthia Ho, Beth A. Mulvaney, and John K. Downey (New York: Palgrave Macmillan, 2009), 48–49. On Sultan al-Kamil and the Damietta (Fifth) Crusade see Paul M. Cobb, *The Race for Paradise: An Islamic History of the Crusades* (New York: Oxford University Press, 2014), 207–212.

9. Bird et al., *Crusade and Christendom*, 190 and n. 80.

10. *The Qur'an*, trans. M. A. S. Abdel Haleem (New York: Oxford University Press, 2010), 33.

11. Armstrong et al., *Francis of Assisi: Early Documents*, 3:799.

12. Andre Jansen makes this suggestion; discussed in Edith van den Goorbergh and Theodore Zweerman, *Respectfully Yours, Signed and Sealed Francis of Assisi: Aspects of His Authorship and Focuses of His Spirituality* (St. Bonaventure, NY: The Franciscan Institute Press, 2001), 267.

13. Innocent III, *Between God and Man*, 61.

14. Michael Robson, *The Franciscans in the Middle Ages* (Woodbridge, UK: The Boydell Press, 2006), 3–4.

15. The quote is from Harold E. Goad's "Brother Elias as the Leader of the Assisian Party in the Order," in *Franciscan Essays II* (1932), 68. Goad makes this statement in the context of Francis's full lifetime, as true until the moment of Francis's death; I believe the sources and evidence suggest, instead, that the centrality of Francis in the order ended while Francis was away in the East.

16. Francis may have learned this way of doing first, asking permission later, from the practice of hermits in medieval Europe who were known to "preach

first, request permission later, or, perhaps, not at all," according to Thompson, "Origins of Religious Mendicancy," 10.

17. Christoph T. Maier, *Preaching the Crusades: Mendicant Friars and the Cross in the Thirteenth Century* (New York: Cambridge University Press, 1994), 22.

18. This image is from Alessandro Manzoni's great early-nineteenth-century Italian novel, *The Betrothed*, chap. 1. Various editions and translations.

24. FRANCIS RENOUNCES

1. Brown, *The Little Flowers*, 321. And the details of the account of this legend come from Sweeney, *The Complete Francis of Assisi*, 310.

2. These quotations and the metaphor are my renderings from Thomas of Celano, *Second Life*, 23.

3. *Francis of Assisi in His Own Words*, xx.

4. "The Assisi Compilation," 64; in Armstrong et al., *Francis of Assisi: Early Documents*, 2:166–167.

5. Thomas of Celano, *First Life*, 83; this is taken directly from Habig, *Omnibus*, 298.

6. Patience Andrewes, *Frederick II of Hohenstaufen* (New York: Oxford University Press, 1970), 5.

7. On Frederick II's court, excommunication, and crusade: Ibid., 13–23; Thomas Curtis Van Cleve, *The Emperor Frederick II of Hohenstaufen: Immutator Mundi* (New York: Oxford University Press, 1972), 158–175.

8. "Few acts in Frederick's life are to us today more incomprehensible." John Julius Norwich, *The Middle Sea: A History of the Mediterranean* (New York: Vintage Books, 2007), 156.

9. See Jordan of Giano, in Hermann, *XIIIth Century Chronicles*, 33.

25. THE KNOT UNRAVELS

1. "The Assisi Compilation," 33; in Armstrong et al., *Francis of Assisi: Early Documents*, 2:139–140.

2. "The Legend of Perugia," in Habig, *Omnibus*, 74.

3. Brooke, *Scripta Leonis, Rufini et Angeli Sociorum S. Francisci*, 9.

4. Thomas of Celano, *Second Life*, 82.

26. PURCHASING THE FIELD

1. See "Letter to Those Who Rule over People," in *Francis of Assisi in His Own Words*, 64. Adapted slightly.

2. Thompson, *Francis of Assisi: The Life*, 117.

3. *Francis of Assisi in His Own Words*, 34.

4. Thompson, *Francis of Assisi: The Life*, 122.

5. *Francis of Assisi in His Own Words*, 24.

6. "The Legend of Perugia," 114, in Habig, *Omnibus*, 1088–1089.

7. "The Later Rule," quoted from *Francis and Clare: The Complete Works*, trans. Regis J. Armstrong and Ignatius C. Brady (New York: Paulist Press, 1982), chap. X, 144.

8. This is the first story told in *The Mirror of Perfection*.

9. Salimbene is paraphrased and condensed, here, from *From St. Francis to Dante*, 82. Translations from the Chronicle of the Franciscan Salimbene (1221–1228), 2nd edition (Philadelphia, PA: University of Pennsylvania Press, 1972).

10. Thomas of Celano, *First Life*, 86; in Armstrong et al., *Francis of Assisi: Early Documents*, 1:256.

27. THAT HOLY, INEXPLICABLE MOMENT

1. *The Book of Margery Kempe*, ed. and trans. Lynn Staley (Kalamazoo, MI: Medieval Institute Publications, 1996), 64. I have altered the translation slightly.

2. Erikson, *Young Man Luther*, 39.

3. Brother Leo quote from "The Breviary of Saint Francis," in Gerhart B. Ladner, *Images and Ideas in the Middle Ages: Selected Studies in History and Art* (Roma: Edizioni di Storia e Letteratura, 1983), 232. The second quote, from other companions, is taken from Thomas of Celano, *Second Life*, ch. 65, para. 99, my translation; see also Armstrong et al., *Francis of Assisi: Early Documents*, 2:312.

4. Armstrong et al., *Francis of Assisi: Early Documents*, 2:490. The quotation from Elias's letter immediately after this one is also taken verbatim from this edition.

5. Pope Francis, "Morning Meditation," June 7, 2013, http://w2.vatican.va/content/francesco/en/cotidie/2013/documents/papa-francesco-cotidie_20130607_science-love.html.

6. James Baldwin, "Malcolm and Martin," in *The Portable Malcolm X Reader*, ed. Manning Marable and Garrett Felber (New York: Penguin Books 2013), 508.

7. See Thomas of Celano, *First Life*, 95.

8. John Milton, *Paradise Lost*, VIII, 369.

9. Thomas of Celano, *Life of St. Clare*, chap. 30. Various editions; this is my translation.

10. John Milton, *Paradise Lost*, VIII, 452–453, 457–459.

11. William of Saint-Thierry in van den Goorbergh and Zweermen, *Respectfully Yours, Signed and Sealed Francis of Assisi*, 287–288.

28. BIRTH OF A POET

1. John Calvin, *The Institutes of the Christian Religion* I, 8; Cotton Mather, quoted from the original published in 1699 in Zachary Leader, *Reading Blake's Songs* (New York: Routledge and Kegan Paul, 1981), 6. I have modernized the spelling/grammar of Mather.

2. Virgil, *Eclogue X*, lines 53–54, 76–77.

3. Thomas of Celano, *Second Life*, 127; in Habig, *Omnibus*, 467.

4. Czeslaw Milosz, "A Footnote, Many Years Later," in *Selected and Last Poems, 1931–2004* (London: Penguin Modern Classics, 2006), xvii.

5. Bonaventure, *Works*, 2:63.

6. Thomas of Celano, *Second Life*, 89; in Armstrong et al., *Francis of Assisi: Early Documents*, 2:330.

29. FRANCIS'S CONFESSION

1. Armstrong et al., *Francis of Assisi: Early Documents*, 1:563.

2. This scene is provided by Thomas of Celano, *Second Life*, 184–186. Thomas does not identify which friar asked the question of Francis.

30. OCTOBER 3–4, 1226, REVISITED

1. Francis, as summarized by the anonymous authors of *The Mirror of Perfection*, chap. 5.

2. Plutarch, *Plutarch's Lives*, trans. John Dryden, ed. Arthur Hugh Clough (New York: Modern Library, 2001), 1: 1.

3. From "Rural Evening," in *John Clare*, The Oxford Authors, ed. Eric Robinson and David Powell (New York: Oxford University Press, 1984), 73, lines 89–90. I've fixed one misspelling of Clare.

4. See Joanne Schatzlein and Daniel Sulmasy, "The Diagnosis of St. Francis: Evidence for Leprosy," *Franciscan Studies* 47 (1987): 181–217. This quote comes from p. 193. The authors summarize their findings, even including the stigmata as evidence: "We may summarize the case history of St. Francis as that of a medieval Italian male of probably poor nutritional status with a history of prolonged and intimate exposure to leprosy.... In his last two years he developed ulcerated wounds of both hands and feet, six months of anasarca (total body swelling), inanition, and wasting, punctuated by a single episode of hematemesis (vomiting blood), terminating in the expiration of the patient at the age of 44" (p. 185).

5. Ibid., 216–217.

6. From the account of an anonymous German Benedictine monk, in Armstrong et al., *Francis of Assisi: Early Documents*, 3:847.

7. Jacopone of Todi, in Evelyn Underhill, *Jacopone da Todi, Poet and Mystic—1228–1306: A Spiritual Biography* (New York: E. P. Dutton, 1919), 371 (Lauda XC).

8. Thomas of Celano, *First Life*, 108; in Armstrong et al., *Francis of Assisi: Early Documents*, 1.

9. Thomas of Celano, *First Life*, 108; in Armstrong et al., *Francis of Assisi: Early Documents*, 1:276. I have slightly amended the Armstrong translation.

10. *The Mirror of Perfection*, chap. 41.

11. Cooper, "*In Loco Tutissimo*," 3, n. 4.

12. Armstrong et al., *Francis of Assisi: Early Documents*, 2:491.

13. Thomas of Celano, *First Life*, 124; in Armstrong et al., *Francis of Assisi: Early Documents*, 1:294.

14. Cooper, "*In Loco Tutissimo*," 9.

31. GREATER THAN GOTHIC

1. This scene is from *The Mirror of Perfection*, 17.

2. See Rosalind B. Brooke, *The Image of St Francis: Responses to Sainthood in the Thirteenth Century* (New York: Cambridge University Press, 2006), 68–69.

3. Marino Bigaroni, "San Damiano–Assisi: The First Church of St. Francis," *Franciscan Studies* 47 (1987): 79–80.

4. Abbot Suger, quoted in Anselme Dimier, *Stones Laid before the Lord: Architecture and Monastic Life*, trans. Gilchrist Lavigne (Kalamazoo, MI: Cistercian Publications, 1999), 171.

5. On changes to Franciscan values regarding buildings and architecture: Louise Bourdua, *The Franciscans and Art Patronage in Late Medieval Italy* (New York: Cambridge University Press, 2004), intro. and chap. 1.

6. George Herbert, "Zion," from *The Temple* (1633), lines 17–20.

7. Brooke, *Scripta Leonis, Rufini et Angeli Sociorum S. Francisci*, tale 16.

8. Augustine Thompson, *Francis of Assisi: A New Biography* (Ithaca: Cornell University Press, 2012), 105.

9. The Leo and Giles anecdotes come from Brooke, *The Image of St Francis*, 51.

10. From a late-thirteenth-century collection of stories, in Armstrong et al., *Francis of Assisi: Early Documents*, 3:798.

11. For these two incidents see Thomas of Celano, *Second Life*, 27–28; and *The Mirror of Perfection*, chap. 6–7.

32. HONOR LOST AND REGAINED

1. John R. H. Moorman, *The Sources for the Life of S. Francis of Assisi* (Manchester, England: Manchester University Press, 1940), 85.

2. Giuliano Procacci, *History of the Italian People* (New York: Penguin Books, 1991), 13.

33. GRAVY DRIPPING FROM HIS CHIN

1. *The Mirror of Perfection*, 15.

2. Donal Cooper and Janet Robson, *The Making of Assisi: The Pope, the Franciscans and the Painting of the Basilica* (New Haven: Yale University Press, 2013), 74.

3. Many of these details come directly from Salimbene of Adam. See *The Chronicle of Salimbene de Adam*, 149–150.

4. Clare of Assisi, in Joan Mueller, *The Letters to Agnes* (Collegeville, MN: Liturgical Press, 2003), 3. See 1–2 for historical background on this letter.

5. Ibid., 30.

6. For this quote and a few of the facts related to Clare in this section, see André Vauchez, *Francis of Assisi*, 170 and 166–170.

7. This conversation between Gregory IX and Elias is derived from a medieval account in Hermann, *XIIIth Century Chronicles*, 64–67.

8. Michael F. Cusato, "An Unexplored Influence on the *Epistola ad fideles* of Francis of Assisi: The *Epistola universis Christi fidelibus* of Joachim of Fiore," *Franciscan Studies* 61 (2003): 274. In this article, Cusato comes down strongly on the side of interpreting Francis's actions in the Levant with the sultan as a deliberate attempt to oppose the Fifth Crusade.

9. *The Chronicle of Salimbene de Adam*, 74–77.

10 This story first appeared in the Latin chronicle, written in about 1370, known as *Chronica XXIV Generalium Ordinis Fratrum Minorum*. See A. G. Little, *Franciscan Papers, Lists, and Documents* (Manchester, England: Manchester University Press, 1943), 22–23.

11. This quotation of Salimbene of Adam is my rendering, adapted from those in G. G. Coulton, *From St. Francis to Dante*, 83.

12. This is a direct quote from Salimbene of Adam, in Brooke, *Early Franciscan Government*, 48. The two quotations immediately preceding it are paraphrased, for space, from the same source.

34. AT WAR WITH THE POPE

1. This teaching of Francis is recorded in a later source, Arnald of Sarrant, *The Kinship of Saint Francis*, in Armstrong et al., *Francis of Assisi: Early Documents* 3:712.

2. *The Mirror of Perfection*, 20.

3. *The Chronicle of Salimbene de Adam*, 85.

4. Salimbene mentions these foods in his chronicle, ibid., xi–xii.

5. Ibid., 135.

6. Salimbene of Adam, in Brooke, *Early Franciscan Government*, 52. See also *The Chronicle of Salimbene de Adam*, 82.

7. At the general chapter meeting in Rome in 1239, Agnello of Pisa was elected as minister general to replace Elias; Agnello was the first priest to hold the office, and the friars decreed that lay brothers would no longer hold offices or leadership positions. Their very admission to the order would receive extra scrutinizing henceforward.

8. See David Burr, "History as Prophecy: Angelo Clareno's *Chronicle* as a Spiritual Franciscan Apocalypse," in *Defenders and Critics of Franciscan Life:*

Essays in Honor of John V. Fleming, ed. Michael F. Cusato and G. Geltner (Boston: Brill, 2009), 119–138.

9. For the details from Clare's "Form of Life," see Regis J. Armstrong, trans., *Clare of Assisi—The Lady: Early Documents*, rev. ed. (New York: New City Press, 2006), chap. 2 and 10, p. 110 and 122. For Clare's ways of caring for the sisters see Thomas of Celano's (although the authorship is contested) *Life of Saint Clare*, chap. 25, or *The Lady: Clare of Assisi, Early Documents*, 312.

10 These accounts from Thomas of Eccleston all come from *XIIIth Century Chronicles*, 154–156.

11. Ibid.

12. André Vauchez, *Francis of Assisi*, 162.

35. PENANCE

1. These are paraphrases from the account of Elias's words left by Matthew Paris, *Chronica majora*, 3, 628.

2. See Thomas of Celano, *Second Life*, 65.

3. David Abulafia, *Frederick II: A Medieval Emperor* (New York: Penguin Press, 1988), 247–248.

4. Ibid., 319.

5. Brooke, *Early Franciscan Government*, 184.

6. See Angelo Clareno, *A Chronicle or History of the Seven Tribulations of the Order of Brothers Minor*, trans. David Burr and E. Randolph Daniel (St. Bonaventure, NY: Franciscan Institute Publications, 2005), 75–76; and Brooke, *Early Franciscan Government*, 166–168.

36. DECEMBER 12, 1818

1. Cooper and Robson, *The Making of Assisi*, 6.

2. Cooper and Robson, "Imagery and the Economy of Penance," 165–170.

3. Cooper and Robson, *The Making of Assisi*, 8.

4. See Cooper, "*In Loco Tutissimo*," 1–37.

5. Cooper and Robson, "Imagery and the Economy of Penance," 169.

6. Friedrich Nietzsche, *The Antichrist*, chap. 29.

7. This and many other details in this chapter come from Brooke, *The Image of St. Francis*, chap. 10, 454–471. For this specific reference, see p. 454.

8. Cooper, "*In Loco Tutissimo*," 12–15.

9. M. D. Lambert, *Franciscan Poverty: The Doctrine of the Absolute Poverty of Christ and the Apostles in the Franciscan Order 1210–1323* (London: SPCK, 1961), 74. Fr. Richard Rohr recently put this cheekily when he wrote, "Francis and Clare, two dropouts who totally spurned the entire success, war, and economic agendas of thirteenth-century Assisi, have now been fully sustaining its economy for eight hundred years through the pilgrims and tourists who pour into this lovely medieval town! For centuries now, the Bernardone and Offreduccio families have been very proud of their children—but they surely were not

when those children were alive." *Eager to Love: The Alternative Way of Francis of Assisi* (Cincinnati: Franciscan Media, 2014), xv.

ACKNOWLEDGMENTS

1. Cooper, "*In Loco Tutissimo*," 8–9.

2. Brooke, *Early Franciscan Government*, 8.

3. Wendy Doniger, "India: Censorship by the Batra Brigade," *New York Review of Books*, May 8, 2014, 36.

4. Friedrich Hölderlin, "At One Time I Questioned the Muse," in *Poems and Fragments*, trans. Michael Hamburger (London: Anvil Press Poetry, 2004), 635.

INDEX

Jon M. Sweeney is an independent scholar and one of religion's most respected writers. His work has been hailed by everyone from PBS and James Martin, S.J., to Fox News and Dan Savage. He's been interviewed on CBS *Saturday Morning*, Fox News, CBS-TV Chicago, *Religion and Ethics Newsweekly*, and on the popular program *Chicago Tonight*. Several of his books have become Book-of-the-Month Club and Quality Paperback Book Club selections. His popular medieval history, *The Pope Who Quit*, was published by Image/Random House and optioned by HBO. It was a selection of the History Book Club and received a starred review in Booklist. His book, *When Saint Francis Saved the Church*, received a 2015 award for excellence in history from the Catholic Press Association. His other words include *Inventing Hell*, *The Complete Francis of Assisi*, and *The St. Francis Prayer Book*. Sweeney writes regularly for *America* and *The Tablet*, and is also the editorial director at Franciscan Media. He is married, the father of three, and lives in Vermont.

AVE

AVE MARIA PRESS

Founded in 1865, Ave Maria Press,
a ministry of the Congregation of
Holy Cross, is a Catholic publishing
company that serves the spiritual and
formative needs of the Church and its
schools, institutions, and ministers;
Christian individuals and families; and
others seeking spiritual nourishment.

For a complete listing of titles from

Ave Maria Press

Sorin Books

Forest of Peace

Christian Classics

visit www.avemariapress.com

AVE | AVE MARIA PRESS
Notre Dame, IN
A Ministry of the United States Province of Holy Cross